NEW PENGUIN SHAKESPEARE

GENERAL EDITOR: T. J. B. SPENCER

ASSOCIATE EDITOR: STANLEY WELLS

WILLIAM SHAKESPEARE

✳

ROMEO AND JULIET

EDITED BY
T. J. B. SPENCER

PENGUIN BOOKS

PENGUIN BOOKS

Published by the Penguin Group
Penguin Books Ltd, 80 Strand, London WC2R 0RL, England
Penguin Putnam Inc., 375 Hudson Street, New York, New York 10014, USA
Penguin Books Australia Ltd, 250 Camberwell Road, Camberwell, Victoria 3124, Australia
Penguin Books Canada Ltd, 10 Alcorn Avenue, Toronto, Ontario, Canada M4V 3B2
Penguin Books India (P) Ltd, 11 Community Centre, Panchsheel Park, New Delhi – 110 017, India
Penguin Books (NZ) Ltd, Cnr Rosedale and Airborne Roads, Albany, Auckland, New Zealand
Penguin Books (South Africa) (Pty) Ltd, 24 Sturdee Avenue, Rosebank 2196, South Africa

Penguin Books Ltd, Registered Offices: 80 Strand, London WC2R 0RL, England

www.penguin.com

This edition first published in Penguin Books 1967
Reprinted with revised Further Reading 1996
48

Printed in England by Clays Ltd, St Ives plc
Set in Monotype Ehrhardt

CONTENTS

INTRODUCTION

MOST discussions of *Romeo and Juliet*, and most stage productions, give a simplified view of the play. It is 'a play of young love', 'a paean of romantic love', 'the great typical love-tragedy of the world', and so on. Such remarks do an injustice to the complexity of *Romeo and Juliet*. It is a work of art which weaves together a large number of related impressions, ideas, images, and moral judgements. It changes from violence to beauty, from bountiful love to malicious hate. There is music and dancing; fantasy and bawdry; the heights of joy and the depths of misery; the lively festivity indoors and the tranquil moonlight outdoors; the unhappy dawn in the bedroom and the desperate suicides in the tomb.

But the effect of the play is not described by a catalogue of the variety of tone and movement in it. The episodes and changes work upon each other to produce something which delights the mind like music. Nothing in European drama had hitherto achieved the organization of so much human experience when Shakespeare, at about the age of thirty, undertook the story of Juliet and Romeo.

Because it is one of the most familiar of Shakespeare's plays – not only in itself but also in operatic and film versions – it is known with preconceptions. It may be that the traditional and popular attitude to Juliet and Romeo, as a pair of the world's most lovable lovers, is derived from the stage tradition rather than from an accurate knowledge of the play. The limelight has inevitably shone upon the star actors and actresses who have taken the parts of the lovers, especially since women took over the female roles which Shakespeare wrote for his boys to perform. This has had some serious consequences.

First, the comments of Mercutio, vigorous and ribald, have become difficult for an audience to understand; and therefore his scoffing treatment of love as what we should now call 'sex' is to some extent softened in performance. Secondly, the moralizings of Friar Laurence are often rendered weaker than Shakespeare's text authorizes. The Friar is the restraining voice of prudence, but also of good sense. He is well-meaning, kindly, good-humoured. He is ineffectual, certainly. He fails to avert the disaster which befalls the lovers. But that is only to say that the worldly wisdom of others cannot always avert the ill consequences of violent passion. It is probable that Shakespeare's audience would have taken the observations of the Friar more seriously than we do, and that their sympathy with the lovers would not have prevented them from accepting the Friar as the voice of wisdom.

In love stories of the kind to which *Romeo and Juliet* belongs the audience is on the side of the lovers and against the 'old folks' who wish to control them. This is the usual convention in Shakespeare's plays; one has only to think of Fenton and Anne Page in *The Merry Wives of Windsor*, of Posthumus and Imogen in *Cymbeline*, and of Florizel and Perdita in *The Winter's Tale*. We condone the impetuosity of Romeo and Juliet because our hearts plead for them. We accept and applaud the petty deceits by which a young woman truly in love outwits the tyrannies of parents who make the distressing blunder of trying to marry her off to the wrong man. But what Shakespeare does here is to make the whole situation more subtle and tantalizing. The unwelcome suitor, the Count Paris, is not old and unpleasant but an agreeable and romantic young man. The heroine's confidante (the Nurse) is not a friend nor an ordinary servant, but one with whom she has close emotional ties, yet who does not really understand the kind of love the heroine feels. The lover's friend (the Friar), while supporting him, restrains him and warns him of the consequences of his conduct. The lovers, moreover, are married and consummate their passion during the course of the play instead of being eventually dismissed to happiness, as at the end of a comedy.

This situation enables Shakespeare to present a great variety of moral assumptions and explorations in his dramatic entertainment. What is the value of love? And whose valuation of it are we inclined to accept? Or (more precisely) what are our relative estimations of passion and prudence? Too much prudence we despise. Too much passion we deplore. In vivid theatrical terms and with surpassing agility of intelligence, Shakespeare seems to enjoy giving us, in this play, the possible views of love, represented by different characters. There is Juliet's – both before and after she has fallen in love; Romeo's – both while he thinks he is in love with Rosaline, and after his passion has been truly aroused by Juliet; Mercutio's – his brilliant intelligence seems to make ridiculous an all-absorbing and exclusive passion based upon sex; Friar Laurence's – for him love is an accompaniment of life, reprehensible if violent or unsanctified by religion; Father Capulet's – for him it is something to be decided by a prudent father for his heiress-daughter; Lady Capulet's – for her it is a matter of worldly wisdom (she herself is not yet thirty and has a husband who gave up dancing thirty years ago); and the Nurse's – for her, love is something natural and sometimes lasting, connected with pleasure and pregnancy, part of the round of interests of a woman's life.

The opening scene is a curious, and certainly successful,

experiment. In a few minutes Shakespeare has set the
quarrel new abroach and established the passionate an-
tagonism between the two families and their dependants.
But the frivolities of the servants with which the play
begins devalue the importance of the quarrel; and, with
equal audacity, Shakespeare puts into their mouths mere
mockery of the relations between the sexes. Sampson and
Gregory make their ribald jests about women being the
weaker vessels, and so forth. Was this the appropriate way
to begin the world's greatest love-tragedy? It is one way
of thinking about love. Another extreme attitude is next
offered to us in the delicate description of Romeo's
melancholy behaviour as the slighted lover of Rosaline, in
the conversation between his father Montague and his
friend Benvolio (I.1.105–55). The fantasies of Sampson in
desiring the women of the Montagues – he will be 'civil
with the maids' of the opposing house and 'cut off their
heads . . . the heads of the maids, or their maidenheads' –
have a parallel in Romeo's wish for the girls of the Capulet
family. For Rosaline, his first love, is also a Capulet, and
Juliet's cousin. (She is described as 'My fair niece Rosaline'
in Father Capulet's letter of invitation to the party, I.2.68,
and as 'the fair Rosaline whom [Romeo] so loves' at line
82. It is to have a chance of rejoicing in the 'splendour'
of his Rosaline that Romeo consents to go as an uninvited
guest to the 'ancient feast of Capulet's'.) But Rosaline does
not wish to have *her* head cut off.

BENVOLIO
Then she hath sworn that she will still live chaste?
ROMEO
She hath; and in that sparing makes huge waste.
For beauty, starved with her severity,
Cuts beauty off from all posterity.   I.1.217–20

Throughout the first half of the play there are constant and deliberate collisions between romantic and unromantic views of love. On the one hand Mercutio, and on the other hand the Nurse, make their comments on the highfalutin notions of love which they hear. Lady Capulet talks about marriage to her daughter in an exaggerated strain; her praise of the Count Paris is in striking contrast to the Nurse's:

LADY CAPULET
The valiant Paris seeks you for his love.

NURSE
A man, young lady! Lady, such a man
As all the world – why, he's a man of wax.

LADY CAPULET
Verona's summer hath not such a flower.   I.3.75–8

In the first few scenes Romeo is the Petrarchan lover in the Petrarchan situation, creating poetical and pitiful phrases in honour of the chaste and unattainable Rosaline. Mercutio impresses this upon us when he sees Romeo entering: 'Now is he for the numbers that Petrarch flowed in. Laura, to his lady, was a kitchen wench – marry, she had a better love to berhyme her' (II.4.38–40). But the joke here is, of course, that it is a transformed Romeo who is approaching, in high spirits because he is accepted by his new un-Laura-like love, Juliet. Rosaline is a very appropriate first love of the youthful Romeo. She is coldly chaste. Her rejection of his suit is due not to her dislike or despising of the lover, but to her rejection of love. This all emphasizes Romeo's purity and inexperience. If Rosaline had been made a fickle beauty or a wanton, the effect would have been distressing to us and derogatory to Romeo. Moreover, Shakespeare does not actually introduce Rosaline. That would involve us too strongly in Romeo's emotions, and possibly

Rosaline's, too. With appropriate artistic tact the whole affair is reported to us at second hand. We are only told enough about her for the dramatic purpose of a contrast with Juliet. She is, according to Mercutio, a 'pale hard-hearted wench'; she is a 'white wench' with a 'black eye' (II.4.4, 14). This means that she is of the physical type (pale, with dark eyes and dark hair) that is mentioned elsewhere by Shakespeare with an interesting strength of feeling – not only the 'dark lady' in the *Sonnets*, but also the Rosaline in *Love's Labour's Lost* whom the enamoured Berowne describes as

> *A whitely wanton with a velvet brow,*
> *With two pitch balls stuck in her face for eyes. . . .*
> III.1.186–7

But the Rosaline of *Romeo and Juliet* 'hath Dian's wit' (I.1.209) and 'hath forsworn to love'. Romeo hyperbolically declares that

> *The all-seeing sun*
> *Ne'er saw her match since first the world begun.* I.2.91–2

But the curt dismissal of his enthusiasm by Benvolio does not allow us to have the usual sympathy for a lover's estimate of his beloved:

> *Tut, you saw her fair, none else being by.*

There is indeed a kind of defiance, or presumption, on the part of Romeo. In the way he talks about his love for his lady Rosaline he courts disaster. Benvolio does not treat this love of his seriously, and makes a perfectly reasonable proposal – let him try honestly to see his Rosaline alongside other beautiful ladies.

> *Compare her face with some that I shall show,*
> *And I will make thee think thy swan a crow.* I.2.85–6

Romeo rejects this suggestion, using over-emphatic language.

> *When the devout religion of mine eye*
> *Maintains such falsehood, then turn tears to fires;*
> *And these, who, often drowned, could never die,*
> *Transparent heretics, be burnt for liars!*

But precisely what Benvolio foresees takes place. Romeo's sight of Juliet obliterates Rosaline from his mind. He admits as much to Friar Laurence the following morning. 'Wast thou with Rosaline?' asks the Friar. And Romeo replies as if amazed:

> *With Rosaline, my ghostly father? No.*
> *I have forgot that name and that name's woe.*   II.3.41–2

So much for 'the devout religion' of his eye! And Shakespeare does not let us forget this estimate of Romeo, the 'young waverer', as the Friar calls him:

> *Holy Saint Francis! What a change is here!*
> *Is Rosaline, that thou didst love so dear,*
> *So soon forsaken? Young men's love then lies*
> *Not truly in their hearts, but in their eyes.*   II.3.61–4

Juliet's attitude to love, before its arrival, is shown as quite different from the presumption of Romeo – it is one of modesty and lack of comprehension. Her mother's suggestions about marriage only receive the reply:

> *It is an honour that I dream not of.*   I.3.67

But within twenty-four hours she is married. Even more ironical, in the context of the play, is her reply to her mother's proposal on behalf of Paris, whom she expects to meet at the party that evening:

> *I'll look to like, if looking liking move.*
> *But no more deep will I endart mine eye*
> *Than your consent gives strength to make it fly.* I.3.98–100

With equal skill, and equally to the delight of the perceptive listener, Shakespeare subtly differentiates between
Juliet and Romeo in the effects of their passion upon them.
In spite of her self-abandonment to love, Juliet is strong
and practical, and becomes increasingly so. Even in the
conversation by moonlight this trait of character is ex-
quisitely brought out. Juliet's questions are directly to the
point. Romeo's replies are poetically phrased compliments.

JULIET
> *Art thou not Romeo, and a Montague?*

ROMEO
> *Neither, fair maid, if either thee dislike.*

JULIET
> *How camest thou hither, tell me, and wherefore?*
> *The orchard walls are high and hard to climb,*
> *And the place death, considering who thou art,*
> *If any of my kinsmen find thee here.*

ROMEO
> *With love's light wings did I o'erperch these walls.*
> *For stony limits cannot hold love out,*
> *And what love can do, that dares love attempt.*
> *Therefore thy kinsmen are no stop to me.* II.2.60–69

They continue in this vein for some time. Romeo produces
elaborately evasive eloquence in response to Juliet's direct-
ness: 'If they do see thee, they will murder thee . . . I
would not for the world they saw thee here . . . By whose
direction foundest thou out this place?' Romeo indulges
in beautifully perceptive descriptions of the situation. But
Juliet's language is unambiguous.

> *If that thy bent of love be honourable,*
> *Thy purpose marriage, send me word tomorrow,*
> *By one that I'll procure to come to thee,*
> *Where and what time thou wilt perform the rite. . . .*
>
> II.2.143–6

The mutual passion of Juliet and Romeo is surrounded by the mature bawdry of the other characters. Somehow, it is not impaired by it. Sampson and Gregory begin the play with their fantasies of exploits with the Montague women. The Nurse tells her naughty husband's comment on Juliet's fall forward ('Thou wilt fall backward when thou hast more wit'; and the little girl 'stinted and said "Ay"', I.3.43, 49). She anticipates the bride's experience shortly to come:

> *I am the drudge, and toil in your delight.*
> *But you shall bear the burden soon at night.* II.5.75–6

And when she thinks that Juliet is about to marry Paris, she has the same lewd jokes as before:

> *Sleep for a week. For the next night, I warrant,*
> *The County Paris hath set up his rest*
> *That you shall rest but little.* IV.5.5–7

She invents double meanings in what Juliet's mother says when trying to interest Juliet in the Count Paris:

LADY CAPULET
> *So shall you share all that he doth possess,*
> *By having him making yourself no less.*
NURSE
> *No less? Nay, bigger! Women grow by men.* I.3.94–6

And she bids farewell to Juliet:

> *Go, girl, seek happy nights to happy days.* I.3.106

15

Likewise, Mercutio's ribald tongue is rarely inactive. His conjuring of Romeo by Rosaline's demesnes, and his chatter about raising 'a spirit in his mistress' circle' (II.1.24), about medlars and poppering pears (lines 36-8), take place just before Juliet appears on her balcony in the moonlight. Mercutio cannot even say that it is twelve o'clock without an astonishingly ribald jest (II.4.109-10). And among the dreams induced by Queen Mab he describes young women's erotic ones:

> This is the hag, when maids lie on their backs,
> That presses them and learns them first to bear,
> Making them women of good carriage.   I.4.92-4

Even the Friar, hearing that Romeo has not been to sleep that night, exclaims: 'God pardon sin! Wast thou with Rosaline?' (II.3.40).

Nothing in this highly-sexed world seems to damage the intense purity of Juliet's anticipation of the 'amorous rites' that are to be 'Played for a pair of stainless maidenhoods' (III.2.13). Again and again the innocence of the lovers is emphasized. They have youthful exuberance and also youthful moodiness. Their reactions to the disappointments of love are extreme. Juliet lies, says her nurse, 'Blubbering and weeping, weeping and blubbering' (III.3.88); and Romeo falls to the ground tearful and broken. The emphasis on Juliet's age – she has not yet reached her fourteenth birthday – is especially remarkable. (We are not told Romeo's age, and it obviously does not matter.) Capulet explains to her suitor Paris:

> My child is yet a stranger in the world;
> She hath not seen the change of fourteen years.
> Let two more summers wither in their pride
> Ere we may think her ripe to be a bride.   I.2.8-11

And lest the audience forget this, an emphatic repetition
of the fact is given in the next scene:

LADY CAPULET
Thou knowest my daughter's of a pretty age.
NURSE
Faith, I can tell her age unto an hour.
LADY CAPULET
She's not fourteen.
NURSE
. . . Come Lammas Eve at night shall she be fourteen.
Susan and she – God rest all Christian souls! –
Were of an age. Well, Susan is with God.
She was too good for me. But, as I said,
On Lammas Eve at night shall she be fourteen.
That shall she, marry. I remember it well.

I.3.11–13, 18–23

Shakespeare is here deliberately altering the Juliet of his
sources. She is sixteen in Arthur Brooke's poem and eighteen in Bandello and Painter. In Shakespeare's time the
permissible age of females for marriage was twelve, but
such early marriages were rare. It is not easy to see why
Shakespeare's Juliet should be as young as he indicates.
The effect would hardly have been different if she had been
sixteen as she is in Brooke. Perhaps he was partly influenced
by the Italian background of the story, for the belief that
Italian girls matured early was widespread. The Nurse
swears by her virginity at twelve years old (I.3.2), and that
can only have one meaning. Juliet is, moreover, consistent
with some of Shakespeare's other young heroines. We
remember that Marina in *Pericles* was also fourteen and
Miranda in *The Tempest* fifteen.

*

By the middle of the 1590s, when Shakespeare wrote
Romeo and Juliet, he had already experimented with
tragedy in the grand manner with *Titus Andronicus*; and
he had explored other tragic material in the plays he had
been writing on English history – the four-part dramatiza-
tion of the reigns of Henry VI, Edward IV, and Richard
III. Yet we feel that it was with *Romeo and Juliet* that he
began to learn the art of tragedy-writing. It is unfair to
press a comparison between this unhappy love-story and
the great tragedies of Shakespeare's maturity; even (as a
tragedy based upon love) with *Antony and Cleopatra*. Yet
already in *Romeo and Juliet* there are most of the charac-
teristics of that form of 'Shakespearian tragedy' which we
try to extract from *Hamlet*, *Macbeth*, *Lear*, and *Othello*,
with their subtle interplay of chance and choice, fate and
character.

These four things may not be adequately united in
Romeo and Juliet. Consider, first, chance. It may be said
that the catastrophe of the action depends upon a mere
accident which has no connexion with any other character
or event within the play – that Friar John was unable to
deliver Friar Laurence's letter to Romeo at Mantua because before setting out he happened to enter a house
suspected of the plague. This chance action directly produces the tragic conclusion.

Secondly, the decisions made by the persons in the play
– decisions which in the light of subsequent events can be
seen to have been badly calculated – are only partly, not
fully, related to their characters. We do not feel that they
are always inevitable choices. They do not always, within
the world of the drama, carry absolute conviction. The
challenging of Tybalt by Mercutio, the deadly vengeance
that Romeo takes, the Nurse's advice to Juliet to abandon
Romeo and to marry Paris – any *one* element in the plot

might have been different and led to a comfortable conclusion. Mostly, however, it is the pervasive irony of the decisions which helps to bind the plot together. The characters are frequently saying things which, in the context of the play but unknown to themselves, have a deeper and more cruel meaning. The well-meaning Friar, who tries to manipulate the situation for the benefit of all concerned, is prepared to encourage the lovers as a means of reconciling the two hostile families:

> *In one respect I'll thy assistant be.*
> *For this alliance may so happy prove*
> *To turn your households' rancour to pure love.* II.3.86–8

The audience apprehends that the event will indeed reconcile the two families, but only at the cost of the destruction of the lovers.

Thirdly, fate is strongly emphasized as a force which drives the story forwards. The Chorus-prologue announces a 'pair of star-crossed lovers', and a note of fateful premonition is struck with great intensity several times in the play; first, and splendidly, in the words which Romeo suddenly speaks before he enters the home of the Capulets to join the party:

> *my mind misgives*
> *Some consequence, yet hanging in the stars,*
> *Shall bitterly begin his fearful date*
> *With this night's revels and expire the term*
> *Of a despisèd life, closed in my breast,*
> *By some vile forfeit of untimely death.* I.4.106–11

The forebodings of Juliet – as if she had some intuition of the consequences of her passionate abandon to her love for Romeo – come later. As she leans from the balcony in the moonlight, in the midst of her delighted absorption in her lover, she acknowledges her fears:

> *Although I joy in thee,*
> *I have no joy of this contract tonight.*
> *It is too rash, too unadvised, too sudden;*
> *Too like the lightning, which doth cease to be*
> *Ere one can say 'It lightens'.*   II.2.116–20

After their bridal night, when dawn has come and Romeo must away to banishment in Mantua, Juliet looks from the balcony, after her lover has climbed down, and exclaims:

> *O, thinkest thou we shall ever meet again?*   III.5.51

Romeo tries to reply reassuringly, with comforting phrases which the audience feels to be meaningless:

> *I doubt it not; and all these woes shall serve*
> *For sweet discourses in our times to come.*

But Juliet is not comforted or reassured:

> *O God, I have an ill-divining soul!*
> *Methinks I see thee, now thou art so low,*
> *As one dead in the bottom of a tomb.*

The next time Juliet sees Romeo will, indeed, be as he lies dead beside her in the tomb of the Capulets.

A similar foreboding, intended to make more fateful the course of events, is expressed by Romeo at Mantua, just before he hears the false news of the death of Juliet. He has again had a dream, and – though he had long ago (I.4.53 ff.) been warned of the activities of Queen Mab – he takes undue note of it:

> *If I may trust the flattering truth of sleep,*
> *My dreams presage some joyful news at hand.*
> *My bosom's lord sits lightly in his throne,*
> *And all this day an unaccustomed spirit*
> *Lifts me above the ground with cheerful thoughts.*

I dreamt my lady came and found me dead –
Strange dream that gives a dead man leave to think! –
And breathed such life with kisses in my lips
That I revived and was an emperor.   V.1.1–9

They were a 'pair of star-crossed lovers' and their fate was hanging in the stars. When Romeo hears the false news of Juliet's death, his first words are:

    Is it e'en so? Then I defy you, stars!   V.1.24

And before he drinks off the poison, in the tomb with Juliet, he exclaims:

            O here
Will I set up my everlasting rest
And shake the yoke of inauspicious stars
From this world-wearied flesh.   V.3.109–12

The Friar finally acknowledges that both chance and fate have overcome his good intentions:

          Ah, what an unkind hour
Is guilty of this lamentable chance! . . .
A greater power than we can contradict
Hath thwarted our intents.   V.3.145–6, 153–4

And he tries to persuade Juliet to leave the tomb where Romeo now lies dead.

The verbal emphasis is frequently on fate; but the logic of the play seems to be, rather more than we should like, on chance. This makes the play less satisfying artistically. But we need to remember that the weakness, in comparison with Shakespeare's later tragedies, is more noticeable to us than it would have been to Shakespeare's contemporaries. For astrology is now a discredited study. What Shakespeare himself thought of it, we cannot certainly say (but the fact that some of his characters in other plays ridicule it shows at any rate that he, like many intelligent persons in his time, was capable of taking a sceptical attitude). Whatever his opinions may have been as a private individual, the belief in the fateful *influence* of the stars upon human life was a convenient one for dramatic purposes. There can be no doubt that Shakespeare's audience would have responded much more intensely than we do to such phrases as Romeo's misgivings about 'some consequence, yet hanging in the stars', his proud 'I defy you, stars', and his final decision to shake off 'the yoke of inauspicious stars'.

Perhaps (since we cannot live ourselves back into a belief in the stars) we understand the play better if we think of it as a tragedy of 'bad luck'. Romeo is consistently 'unlucky', though he as consistently means well. His own rather futile words, when his interference has cost Mercutio his life, are, 'I thought all for the best' (III.1.104). But he is fortune's fool. Everybody is favourable to him (with the single exception of the absurd fire-eating Tybalt). His friends and parents are devoted to him. Friar Laurence does all he can for him. Even Capulet, the head of the rival family, when he finds that Romeo has come to his party, speaks well of him and will not allow him to be molested.

> '*A bears him like a portly gentleman.*
> *And, to say truth, Verona brags of him*
> *To be a virtuous and well-governed youth.*
> *I would not for the wealth of all this town*
> *Here in my house do him disparagement.* I.5.66–70

But Romeo courts his bad luck. He is a man of (to put it mildly) uncertain responsibility. What guides him? He scarcely knows. At one moment, before entering the Capulets' house and meeting his fate in the person of Juliet, he seems to trust Providence:

> *He that hath the steerage of my course*
> *Direct my sail!*   I.4.112-13

It is difficult, however, to take this seriously. Leaving his
fate to the steerage of heaven means not much more than
following the course of his own feelings. On one occasion,
at least, prudence or discretion guides him: after his marriage to Juliet, he well-meaningly declines the duel with
Tybalt and tries to pacify both him and the equally fiery
Mercutio. But once Mercutio has been slain, he exclaims:

> *Away to heaven respective lenity,*
> *And fire-eyed fury be my conduct now!*   III.1.123-4

The 'fire-eyed fury' is a remarkable change from his pious
trust in Providence as a pilot which guided the human soul.
He had made his magniloquent boast to Juliet in the
moonlight:

> *I am no pilot; yet, wert thou as far*
> *As that vast shore washed with the farthest sea,*
> *I should adventure for such merchandise.*   II.2.82-4

But eventually the pilot trusted by Romeo proves to be
a desperate one indeed – merely the poison which is to
deprive him of his life. In the last scene it is to the vial of
poison that he speaks:

> *Come, bitter conduct, come, unsavoury guide!*
> *Thou desperate pilot, now at once run on*
> *The dashing rocks thy seasick weary bark!* V.3.116-18

Romeo's impetuosity ('I stand on sudden haste') is impressed upon the audience even by the way he talks about
the poison he is to buy. He demands from the Apothecary:

> *A dram of poison, such soon-speeding gear*
> *As will disperse itself through all the veins,*

> *That the life-weary taker may fall dead*
> *And that the trunk may be discharged of breath*
> *As violently as hasty powder fired*
> *Doth hurry from the fatal cannon's womb.*   V.1.60–65

He gets what he asks for. The Apothecary gives him the poison with the commendation:

> *if you had the strength*
> *Of twenty men it would dispatch you straight.*
>
> V.1.78–9

This is borne out by the event. Romeo drinks the poison, and exclaims, 'O true Apothecary! | Thy drugs are quick' (V.3.119–20).

But there is something to be said on the other side in considering Shakespeare's characterization of Romeo. Our impression of his rashness is to some extent diminished by contrast both with Tybalt and with Mercutio, neither of whom shows any restraint in the murderous pursuit of his 'honour'. Moreover, though his impetuosity remains, there are many small indications of Romeo's maturing in the fifth Act. Notably he has a new concern for others: he feels for the Apothecary as a human being ('Buy food and get thyself in flesh', V.1.84); he arranges for a letter to his parents (1.25, 3.23–4); he takes thought for his servant Balthasar ('Live, and be prosperous; and farewell, good fellow', 3.42); and he feels for the plight of young Paris, one writ with him 'in sour misfortune's book' (3.59–67, 74–87).

*

Shakespeare spends a great deal of drama-time in building up the environment in which we can understand and assess the two lovers. The opening scene of the play

presents the state of the feud between the two families, just
as the close of the play presents the reconciliation. Romeo
is not mentioned by any of the characters until line 116
and does not appear until line 155. Juliet does not appear
until the third scene. In the second scene Capulet talks of
his daughter, but she is not named and, for all the audience
knows, she might be the Rosaline who has already been
spoken about. (It is when Romeo reads aloud the list of
those invited by Capulet to his party, including 'My fair
niece Rosaline', that we know that Capulet's daughter is
not this Rosaline.) Only after 342 lines, nearly one-eighth
of the play, does the Nurse call out '– Where's this girl?
What, Juliet!' (I.3.4) and Juliet make her entry, so that the
actress (in the modern theatre) has a chance of imposing
her presence upon the audience. Shakespeare clearly wants
us to feel the state of affairs in Verona and in the two
Veronese households before we are captivated by the
charms of youthful love.

We are given no account of the origins of the feud between the Capulets and the Montagues. It is simply *there*,
unexplained, apparently of long standing. It is introduced
into the play in no dignified way – merely the occasion of
some absurd scuffling among the servants of the two
houses, giving an opportunity to the quarrel-loving Tybalt
to show himself off. It is not only the Prince and the Friar
who are anxious to put an end to the feud; the older
generation of Capulets and Montagues feel responsible and
uneasy. In the opening scene Capulet expresses his bitter
feelings against Montague; but when he calls for his long
sword, his wife retorts 'A crutch, a crutch! Why call you
for a sword?' (I.1.76). And Lady Montague is equally, but
differently, firm with her husband: 'Thou shalt not stir
one foot to seek a foe' (line 80). Montague is himself
obviously inclined to peace; and Capulet admits:

> 'tis not hard, I think,
> For men so old as we to keep the peace.   I.2.2–3

The Prologue says that the story is one of 'death-marked love', but this is true only after the Tybalt–Mercutio–Romeo duels. By the code of honour in drama Romeo was bound to avenge the treacherous slaying of his friend, but he is thereafter a murderer and so 'death-marked'. The audience can now watch the inevitable movement towards the tragic conclusion which the Prologue had announced. The happiness of the lovers had been at every moment precarious, but it is now doomed. Their first meeting had taken place under the eyes of Tybalt, who thereupon vowed to strike Romeo dead. But now Juliet expresses her longings for her marriage-bed while we know that Romeo has slain Tybalt and is banished from Verona. That night when the lovers are together we hear Capulet planning to marry his daughter to Paris within the next few days. And after we exult in Juliet's courage in taking the potion which could bring them out of the difficulties, we watch in agony while Romeo without news from the Friar misunderstands the situation and prepares for suicide.

The family circle in which Juliet is shown consists of three: her father, her mother, and her nurse. Shakespeare carefully represents Capulet as a self-willed, obstinate man; quite capable of keeping the fiery Tybalt in order, and equally prompt with a denunciation of his only daughter when she shows any resistance to his will. In the second scene of the play, while talking courteously to Paris, he is a kindly father, regardful of his daughter's affections:

> But woo her, gentle Paris, get her heart.
> My will to her consent is but a part,
> And, she agreed, within her scope of choice
> Lies my consent and fair according voice.   I.2.16–19

Yet his language to his daughter when she shows herself
unwilling to marry Paris is vituperative – similar to that he
had used to Tybalt at the party (I.5.77–88):

> *How, how, how, how, chopped logic? What is this?*
> *'Proud' – and 'I thank you' – and 'I thank you not' –*
> *And yet 'not proud'? Mistress minion you,*
> *Thank me no thankings, nor proud me no prouds,*
> *But fettle your fine joints 'gainst Thursday next*
> *To go with Paris to Saint Peter's Church,*
> *Or I will drag thee on a hurdle thither.*
> *Out, you green-sickness carrion! Out, you baggage!*
> *You tallow-face!*   III.5.149–57

Lady Capulet is never shown in sympathetic relationship
with her daughter; nor indeed with her husband, for there
is more than a touch of ill-suppressed female tartness in
her replies.

CAPULET

> *I have watched ere now*
> *All night for lesser cause, and ne'er been sick.*

LADY CAPULET

> *Ay, you have been a mouse-hunt in your time.*
> *But I will watch you from such watching now.* IV.4.9–12

It is Lady Capulet who promises Juliet that she will send
someone to Mantua with poison to finish off Romeo. And
when Juliet, in abject misery, appeals to her (III.5.197–9):

> *Is there no pity sitting in the clouds*
> *That sees into the bottom of my grief?*
> *O sweet my mother, cast me not away!*

all that Lady Capulet can reply is:

> *Talk not to me, for I'll not speak a word.*
> *Do as thou wilt, for I have done with thee.*

In her agony Juliet turns to her nurse:

27

> *What sayest thou? Hast thou not a word of joy?*
> *Some comfort, Nurse.*

But that easy-going indulgence which had allowed the Nurse to encourage the affair with Romeo, now prompts her to recommend the easy way out – to marry Paris. When the Nurse has gone Juliet looks after her: 'Ancient damnation!' she cries scornfully. It is one of the great moments of the play; for the audience should feel the change that has taken place in Juliet, from that inexperienced girl of near fourteen who walked on the stage in Act I to the married woman who has been caught up into a train of passionate events and now stands alone, in dire extremity and prepared to face death (or the simulation of death) for the sake of her love. For the rest of the play Juliet conducts herself with the dignity and noble fortitude of womanhood. She is self-reliant; she is courteous to Paris, candid with the Friar, detached with her mother and father; and she keeps her own counsel with her nurse. Romeo never achieves this level of responsibility.

We observe, indeed, the progressive isolation both of Juliet and of Romeo in their environments. Their love gradually separates them from their friends and families. Neither of her parents knows of her love, and her nurse has little awareness of its strength. The Friar has the confidence of each of them. But, recommending sanity, sobriety, and prudence, he does not enter the lovers' world of feeling, and he in general terms disapproves of their passion. Juliet and Romeo understand each other's love. But the poignancy of Juliet's situation becomes keener when they have been separated by Romeo's banishment from Verona. She addresses the retreating figure of her nurse: 'Go, counsellor! | Thou and my bosom henceforth shall be twain' (III.5.240–41); and her mother: 'Farewell!

28

God knows when we shall meet again.' Neither can help her. 'My dismal scene I needs must act alone' (IV.3.14, 19).

Romeo is gradually isolated from his group, as is Juliet from hers. Benvolio and Mercutio, who had mocked at his adolescent infatuation with Rosaline and smothered it with smut, do not have the chance of understanding the new Romeo. And just as Shakespeare did not scruple to set the easy-going moral indulgence of the Nurse alongside the purity of Juliet, so he lets us feel the passion of Romeo alongside the intelligence of Mercutio. He developed Mercutio's character (there was only a hint of it in his sources), and made him one of the most *sympathetic* of Shakespeare's parts for actors. Mercutio is gay and brave and mocking. He is not really involved in the family feuds. He is a kinsman of the Prince. He is invited to the party of the Capulets. At the same time he 'consorts' with the Montagues, Romeo and Benvolio. He despises Tybalt, the 'king of cats', apparently principally for his method of fencing: 'A duellist, a duellist. A gentleman of the very first house, of the first and second cause. Ah, the immortal *passado*! the *punto reverso*! the *hay*!' (II.4.23–6). And when he has received a death-wound due to Romeo's ineptitude, his vivacity and exuberance of wit still shine through. We respond most keenly and appreciatively to Mercutio as he makes his exit with that wonderful mocking speech, deeply felt, grimly comic. 'Ask for me tomorrow, and you shall find me a grave man. I am peppered, I warrant, for this world. A plague a'both your houses! Zounds, a dog, a rat, a mouse, a cat, to scratch a man to death! A braggart, a rogue, a villain, that fights by the book of arithmetic!' (III.1.97–102). Mercutio is most attractive in his dying speech, and most deeply regretted by the audience, for, expert in his stagecraft, Shakespeare has given Mercutio such engaging lines that he makes us excuse Romeo in his rash avenging of Mercutio – we *want* him to show himself a man against the detestable Tybalt, in spite of our terror at the consequences since he has just come from his marriage with Juliet. But Mercutio has given his final curse: 'A plague a'both your houses!' And it is a dying man's curse, which for the Elizabethans was ominous and certain to be fulfilled. His departure immediately darkens the scene and the situation. This is the first death; half a dozen will follow in the second part of the play.

For the comic element in the first two Acts has been strong. Apart from the foreboding note that is sometimes struck, the first part of the play is, in tone and temper, not unlike *Much Ado About Nothing*. It is the death of Mercutio which reminds us that this is a tragedy. In the theatre everyone has the experience of the audience's sudden change of feeling when Benvolio enters and says that 'brave Mercutio is dead' (III.1.116). And Romeo, by his rhyming couplet, conveys the turn of fortune's wheel:

> *This day's black fate on more days doth depend.*
> *This but begins the woe others must end.*

Mercutio had been a foil to Romeo. After he disappears his place is taken by Paris. Mercutio's sense of reality had provided a contrast to Romeo's artificiality of sentiment. In the last three Acts Paris is built up as a lover whose conventionality and inexperience reinforce our impression of Romeo's new range and depth of feeling.

＊

Character statements and plot situations are not the only means by which Shakespeare controls in his audience their varying emotional attitudes to the events. There are poetical methods by which a conflict of values in the play is represented, a series of contradictions in the valuing of love in life.

Juliet's explicit statement is:

> My bounty is as boundless as the sea,
> My love as deep. The more I give to thee,
> The more I have, for both are infinite.   II.2.133–5

But against that, the notes of brevity are constantly impli-
cit as judgements. 'Too sudden' is Juliet's comment on her
avowal of love to Romeo:

> Too like the lightning, which doth cease to be
> Ere one can say 'It lightens'.   II.2.119–20

And the significant word is echoed by Romeo when he
comes to the tomb to join Juliet in death.

> How oft when men are at the point of death
> Have they been merry! which their keepers call
> A lightning before death. O how may I
> Call this a lightning? O my love, my wife!   V.3.88–91

In a terrible sense their love is 'A lightning before death'.
It is not only the flash of lightning; it is also the flash of
gunpowder. The Friar gives the headstrong Romeo a brief
marriage-sermon, with the advice, 'love moderately. Long
love doth so.'

> These violent delights have violent ends
> And in their triumph die, like fire and powder,
> Which as they kiss consume.   II.6.9–11

The theme is taken up again by the Friar, later in the play,
when he is trying to arouse Romeo from despair over his
banishment. By his folly, he says, he is misusing his abilities:

> Thy wit . . .
> Like powder in a skilless soldier's flask
> Is set afire by thine own ignorance,
> And thou dismembered with thine own defence.   III.3.130–34

31

Once more we are reminded of this. For when Romeo buys his poison from the Apothecary, he asks for one that will kill him

> *As violently as hasty powder fired*
> *Doth hurry from the fatal cannon's womb.*   V.1.64–5

What the Friar had prophesied as the consequence of his impetuous love, and his equally impetuous despair, Romeo himself now asks for the poison to bring about. Once more it is the gunpowder flash that is destructive.

The poetical symbol of the brevity of the love is, then, the flash of lightning or the destructive flash of gunpowder. This impression is reflected in the dramatic construction. Shakespeare gives very precise indications, within the play, of the headlong speed with which the events proceed. The story opens on Sunday morning and ends on the following Thursday at dawn; and the month is July when nights are short (for we are told, I.3.15–18, that it is a little more than a fortnight before Juliet's fourteenth birthday, which is on 31 July, the eve of Lammastide). It is about nine o'clock on Sunday morning when Romeo enters, after the quarrel in the streets. Capulet's letter of invitation is sent out that afternoon, and at the party in the evening the lovers first meet. The moonlit night of their conversation is Sunday–Monday and they say good-bye just before morning. Friar Laurence is up at dawn and to him comes Romeo to arrange the marriage. Juliet had promised to send to Romeo at nine o'clock and she does so precisely. But the Nurse is away three hours and meets Romeo about noon. The lovers are married at Friar Laurence's cell that afternoon. Romeo fights the duel with Tybalt and kills him, one hour after the marriage; and when Juliet receives the news and laments this turn of events she says she has been married for three hours. That night (Monday–Tuesday)

is their bridal-night; and they part at dawn, when Romeo
leaves for Mantua. It is now Tuesday morning. Capulet
arranges the marriage of his daughter to the Count
Paris for Thursday morning, but later brings it forward
to Wednesday. That same Tuesday Juliet goes to Friar
Laurence's cell, receives the potion, and drinks it off
that night. Meanwhile Capulet has been up all night
making arrangements for the marriage festivities. In the
morning (Wednesday) Juliet is found as if dead and is
carried to the Capulet tomb instead of being married to
Paris. Romeo's servant sees her entombed and then rides
to Mantua to inform Romeo, who thereupon returns to
Verona, enters the tomb by night, there kills Paris, and
takes his poison. Juliet revives from her drugged sleep at
the appointed time, refuses to leave with the Friar, and
kills herself. The Watch, the citizens, the two families, and
the Prince assemble, and it is a glooming dawn on Thursday morning when the play ends.

It is surprising with what care and accuracy Shakespeare has conveyed all this in the play. (There is only one
serious discrepancy. He makes the Friar say that Juliet's
sleeping potion will last forty-two hours, which is rather
too long a period for the time-sequence of the play. Probably Shakespeare is giving a length of time for the duration
of the effect of the drug which *seems* precise; that is what
the dramatic context requires.) In the story of the lovers
as he found it, the affair lasted for many months. When he
dramatized it he deliberately compressed it all into less
than four days. 'I stand on sudden haste', says Romeo
(II.3.89). The pace of the play thus builds up the dramatic
impression of love as the flash of lightning or the explosion
of gunpowder.

But these momentous and breathtaking four days are
given a context in the passage of time much larger and

longer. This love was a matter of a few days. But in the larger time to which it belongs, in the world in which the play is set, people have grown old, had their frolics and miseries over many years – not within the story as told in the play, but in the world in which this story is but one brief episode. The four days are framed, as it were, by many years. Memories of auld lang syne are constantly referred to. The older characters are all reminiscent in their conversation. This is an engaging device of Shakespeare's, which he was later to use most effectively in the creation of the character of Falstaff. Old Capulet and the Nurse, in particular, carry the mind outside the framework of the play to events and emotions which nevertheless put Juliet and her Romeo in perspective. Brilliantly effective, from this point of view, is the conversation of the Nurse, as she rambles on about the past; her own child Susan, now dead; her husband, also now dead, who was a merry man.
I remember it well.

> *'Tis since the earthquake now eleven years;*
> *And she was weaned – I never shall forget it –*
> *Of all the days of the year, upon that day . . .*
> *For even the day before she broke her brow.*
> *And then my husband – God be with his soul!*
> *'A was a merry man – took up the child.*
> *'Yea,' quoth he, 'dost thou fall upon thy face?*
> *Thou wilt fall backward when thou hast more wit. . . .'*
>
> I.3.23–6, 39–43

Capulet also gives us a sense of time in which to frame the four days of the lovers. Shakespeare certainly makes it plain that Capulet is an old man, in spite of the fact that he has a daughter just out of childhood and a wife twenty-eight or so. It is between twenty-five and thirty years since he was dancing.

I have seen the day
That I have worn a visor and could tell
A whispering tale in a fair lady's ear,
Such as would please. 'Tis gone, 'tis gone, 'tis gone!
                                                    I.5.22–5

The contrast between age and youth, not merely in persons, but in time, is deliberately conveyed. Old Capulet
and his cousin have their reminiscences of the past rather
like Justice Shallow and Justice Silence in the second part
of *Henry IV*. "'Tis gone, 'tis gone, 'tis gone', is also a theme
of *Romeo and Juliet*; the fleeting beauty and fading energy
of youth. The passion of love is, therefore, set very carefully
in a time-scheme so that we can be conscious both of the
incandescent moment and of the life-span of human beings.

*

Romeo and Juliet is, then, more than a love story. Or
perhaps it is the greatest of love stories because it is so
much more. It is about hate as well as about many kinds
of love. It tells of a family and its home as well as a feud
and a marriage. The public life of Verona, as well as the
family life of the Veronese, environs the loves of Romeo
and Juliet. The Prince, the guardian of law and order in
the state, makes his appearance three times, speaking in
the voice of authority. It is not the deaths of the lovers
that conclude the play, but the public revelation of what
had happened. We hear the admonitions of the Prince,
and watch the reconciliation of the families (V.3.171–310);
all this lasts for 140 lines after Romeo and Juliet are dead.

   In the story as told by Luigi da Porto about 1530 and
by Bandello in 1554 (see 'Further Reading', page 46),
Juliet awakes from her trance before the poison has taken
effect upon Romeo. The lovers are thus able to talk together, to lament their unlucky fate, and to take an eternal

farewell. This way of dealing with the episode was incorporated in Shakespeare's play in the eighteenth century; extra dialogue was written for the lovers (adapted from a version by Thomas Otway of 1680), and this 'improvement' was the usual theatrical version of *Romeo and Juliet* from Garrick's time until far into the nineteenth century; and it was retained in the musical version by Gounod. Many of the critics complained about this perversion of Shakespeare's artistry. But the famous actors and actresses who took the roles of Romeo and Juliet doubtless preferred it, for it gave them the stage; and it must indeed have been a moving theatrical experience to watch and hear the lovers as Romeo died by inches in the arms of his grieving Juliet.

Shakespeare, however, was not writing a sentimental drama, but a grand and rich tragedy of human passion and responsibility. By bringing on their families and the Prince, he seems to be deliberately playing down the lovers in this final scene. The long explanatory account by the Friar of their love (V.3.229 ff.) has often been felt to be theatrically unnecessary, and is generally cut in stage performance on the grounds that the Friar communicates to the Prince and the others nothing that the audience does not already know.

But the Friar's speech can be defended on dramatic grounds. The love of Romeo and Juliet is now a public event. It has therefore to be narrated in some detail so that the audience feels it to be such an event, and so that public recognition is given to what has, in fact, been the audience's experience of the play. After the passion and the fighting and the deaths, we need this quiet narrative speech which helps us to put the sequence of events into true proportion, while we watch the heads of the two families realize what has happened and achieve their reconciliation. It is the testy Capulet – a character with whom we have not felt particularly sympathetic – who speaks first:

> *O brother Montague, give me thy hand.*   V.3.296

And the formal concluding speech of the Prince moves back into the tone (and metre) of the Chorus-sonnet with which the play had opened.

> *For never was a story of more woe*
> *Than this of Juliet and her Romeo.*

*

As the play delights by the structural variations in mood and movements of the mind, so does the language, accommodating itself to these variations or supporting them. There is no attempt to make the manner of writing in the play consistent. Partly, it is poetical drama, written in a stylized way, in which the listener or reader is expected consciously to appreciate the beauty or vivacity of the language, rather than to respond to it as natural human expression. Shakespeare eventually united both these qualities of style. In his mature writing one does not admire separately the imaginative language and its appropriateness to character and situation. In *Twelfth Night*, for example, the disguised Viola expresses herself to Count Orsino:

> *She never told her love,*
> *But let concealment, like a worm i'the bud,*
> *Feed on her damask cheek. She pined in thought,*
> *And with a green and yellow melancholy,*
> *She sat like Patience on a monument,*
> *Smiling at grief. Was not this love indeed?*   II.4.109–13

This is admirable writing, but primarily it is expressive of Viola's mood and situation. It is not only poetry; it is dramatic poetry.

There is in *Romeo and Juliet* some writing of an imaginative power comparable to this. But there are also passages in the play which offer difficulties to actor and producer; where the lyrical quality may seem excessively artificial, or where the verbal juggling, usually complicated and rather pointless punning, may seem distasteful.

There are, however, explanations of the 'artificiality' of the love-language in *Romeo and Juliet*. The sonnet was the most popular form of love-poetry at about the time that Shakespeare was writing the play. It is probable, indeed, that he was writing some of his own series of *Sonnets* about that time. Certainly many of the major poets were engaged in imitating Sir Philip Sidney's *Astrophel and Stella*, which had been published in 1591. A dramatist devising an up-to-date play on passionate love would be likely to take account of the contemporary fashion. There was an agreeable topicality, therefore, in writing several speeches of the play actually in sonnet or half-sonnet form: Benvolio's suggested remedy for love (I.2.45–50); Romeo's analysis of his love for Rosaline (I.2.87–92); the first conversation of Juliet and Romeo (I.5.93–106); the address of Paris at the Capulet tomb (V.3.12–17). The two choruses and the final speech of the Prince (V.3.305–10) are also in this familiar tune of love-poetry. And even when the verse is unrhymed or in rhymed couplets and so not reminiscent of the *form* of the sonnet, the images, paradoxes, and lyrical fantasies are those which were being made familiar by the Elizabethan sonneteers. *Romeo and Juliet* was, in this respect, linguistically and poetically a highly 'contemporary' play; and, it must be admitted, it is this topical element which may at first be difficult for the modern reader.

At times, certainly, this conventionality of style is well adjusted to the dramatic situation. The most striking

instance is the first conversation of Romeo and Juliet
(I.5.93–106). This is in form a complete sonnet; and after
their kiss they even begin the first quatrain of another sonnet (lines 107–10), but it is interrupted The meeting is a
moment the audience has been waiting for, and it is doubt-
ful whether, as we watch the experience of love at first sight,
it is possible for us to pay much attention to the words which
are being spoken. The sonnet-duet becomes a piece of
accompanying music. The lines have, indeed, meaning and
subtlety, but it is primarily the movement of the words,
the expectancy of the rhymes, the merging of the final
couplet of the sonnet into their kiss –

JULIET
Saints do not move, though grant for prayers' sake.
ROMEO
Then move not while my prayer's effect I take.

– that give dramatic effectiveness.

The language of love varies somewhat from generation
to generation, and even those words that persist can lose
their brightness. There is a good deal about the religion
of love in *Romeo and Juliet*. Romeo boasts of 'the devout
religion of mine eye' (I.2.87). Juliet calls 'My Romeo!' and
he comments: 'It is my soul that calls upon my name'
(II.2.163–4). Juliet is, indeed, for him 'my soul' (III.5.25).
Hearts are exchanged and so chain the body:

> *Can I go forward when my heart is here?*
> *Turn back, dull earth, and find thy centre out.* II.1.1–2

The Friar upbraids Romeo for contemplating suicide: this
would 'slay thy lady that in thy life lives' (III.3.117). And
when Romeo leaves her at dawn, she exclaims: 'Then,
window, let day in, and let life out' (III.5.41). We must
accept that the neo-Platonic love-language was rather more

meaningful than, when the words have been enfeebled by over-use, it nowadays seems to be.

Rather more troublesome is the frequent verbal quibbling in which the characters indulge, even at moments of deep feeling. We do not have much respect for the pun nowadays; even as a kind of humour the pun is not much admired unless the witty associations are extraordinarily apt, and in a serious context it is felt to be out of place. By Shakespeare and in Shakespeare's time, playing upon words, in serious as well as in comic situations, seems to have been an admired kind of cleverness. And Shakespeare indulges himself freely in *Romeo and Juliet*. The prose dialogue sparkles with linguistic jests. Some of the silly banter between the young men almost defies paraphrase, so full is it (as the Commentary tries to show) of puns, subtle verbal indecencies, and illogical but witty associations, which will often not be apparent to the modern reader without explanation.

Such comic frivolity is well enough, and we can soon enter into the fun. But for Shakespeare puns were by no means beneath the dignity of a tragic situation. There are, in his greatest plays, many examples of his allowing words to acquire a terrible ambiguity at moments of intense emotion. Lady Macbeth takes the daggers back into the room where King Duncan lies murdered:

> *I'll gild the faces of the grooms withal,*
> *For it must seem their guilt.*   *Macbeth*, II.2.56–7

Mark Antony gazes upon the body of the fallen Caesar:

> *O world, thou wast the forest to this hart;*
> *And this, indeed, O world, the heart of thee.*
>   *Julius Caesar*, III.1.207–8

For a long time this kind of ingenuity was considered to be a grave fault of Shakespeare's style. Dr Johnson, who

despised puns, thought that a verbal quibble had 'some
malignant power' over Shakespeare's mind:

> *Whatever be the dignity or profundity of his disquisition,*
> *whether he be enlarging knowledge or exalting affection,*
> *whether he be amusing attention with incidents, or enchant-*
> *ing it in suspense, let but a quibble spring up before him,*
> *and he leaves his work unfinished. A quibble is the golden*
> *apple for which he will always turn aside from his career,*
> *or stoop from his elevation. A quibble, poor and barren as*
> *it is, gave him such delight, that he was content to purchase*
> *it, by the sacrifice of reason, propriety, and truth. A quibble*
> *was to him the fatal Cleopatra for which he lost the world,*
> *and was content to lose it.*

Preface to his edition of Shakespeare, 1765

But nowadays taste has changed and we have learned to
accept Shakespeare's word-play as a serious artistic tech-
nique. He seems to make use of the inevitable ambiguity of
words, rather than to labour (like most good writers) to
resist it. His punning may produce an intense compression
of language, as when the Prince of Verona exclaims:

> *Throw your mistempered weapons to the ground.* . . . I.1.87

Or it may express a frenetic dislocation of apprehension;
and it is in this spirit that we must take, for example,
Juliet's passionate inquiry from her nurse when she fears
the news of Romeo's death. She begins a series of elaborate
puns on the first-person pronoun (I), the vowel (i), the
organ of sight (eye), and the old word for yes (ay).

> *Hath Romeo slain himself? Say thou but 'Ay',*
> *And that bare vowel 'I' shall poison more*
> *Than the death-darting eye of cockatrice.*
> *I am not I, if there be such an 'I'*
> *Or those eyes shut that makes thee answer 'Ay'.*
> *If he be slain, say 'Ay'; or if not, 'No'.*   III.2.45–50

41

Equally disconcerting is Romeo's manner of receiving the news that he is banished. In the midst of his passionate tears he has time to pun on the word 'fly':

> ... *more courtship lives*
> *In carrion flies than Romeo. They may seize*
> *On the white wonder of dear Juliet's hand. ...*
> *This may flies do, when I from this must fly.*
>
> III.3.34-6, 40

Some of the quibbling may not accord with modern taste because it seems to emphasize trivial associations in words; it is not easy to see any appropriate relationship between the insect (fly) and the act of escaping into exile (to fly). An explanation of such apparent infelicities may, of course, be given on psychological grounds. Indignation, it is often observed, can make a man witty, and despair provoke him to laughter. Powerful feelings may find a vent for their energy in verbal acrobatics as well as in an easy unforced manner of expression. But it seems likely that Shakespeare himself, who in his plays usually mentions literary and theatrical matters with a kind of wry irony, was well aware of the follies committed by a 'corrupter of words'. In *The Merchant of Venice*, when reproached for his conduct with the Moorish woman, Lancelot Gobbo can only answer: 'It is much that the Moor should be more than reason; but if she be less than an honest woman, she is indeed more than I took her for.' To this Lorenzo sourly replies: 'How every fool can play upon the word!' (*The Merchant of Venice*, III.5.37-40). Certainly Shakespeare's clowns have a good deal of fun at the expense of their interpreters. Peter in *Romeo and Juliet* (IV.5.125-41) quotes from Richard Edwards's old-fashioned poem on the power of music: 'Then music with her silver sound'. Why 'silver sound', he asks? Why 'music with her silver sound'? He receives from the musicians some possible explanations: 'because silver hath a sweet sound' or 'because musicians sound for silver'. And then Peter gives his own interpretation; the emphasis should be on the word silver; 'music with her *silver* sound', because 'musicians have no gold for sounding'. But alas, there is still an ambiguity: first, the musicians do not receive gold, only silver, for sounding, or playing, their music, and secondly, they are poor and have no gold for sounding, or jingling, in their purses. Peter's exegesis seems almost like a burlesque of the work of a critic preparing a commentary on one of Shakespeare's plays.

Yet too much emphasis must not be put on one aspect of the language of *Romeo and Juliet*. Though the verbal complexity pervades much of the expression it does not determine its quality. It is the images of light, air, sky, and the thronging human passions which possess the mind, rather than the verbal juggling. And at the greatest moment of the play Shakespeare subjects even the ambiguities of words to the sublimity and pathos of the situation. When Romeo hears the false news of Juliet's death, with wonderfully simple words he rises to the dignity of despair (V.1.24–34). But it is a dignity that does not refrain from a pun which emphasizes one of the recurring promises within the play, the final nuptial union of the lovers in the bed of death. Balthasar has reported how he saw Juliet laid low in the family vault and then 'took post to tell it you'.

ROMEO

Is it e'en so? Then I defy you, stars!
Thou knowest my lodging. Get me ink and paper,
And hire posthorses. I will hence tonight. . . .
Hast thou no letters to me from the Friar?

BALTHASAR

No, my good lord.

ROMEO   *No matter. Get thee gone*
   And hire those horses. I'll be with thee straight.

Exit Balthasar

Well, Juliet, I will lie with thee tonight.

It may be admitted that the love represented by Juliet and her Romeo is an immature and incomplete one. Yet it is never undermined in our esteem by the cynicism and disillusion of the other characters, or of ourselves. The intensity of the play lies in its presentation of love rather than death. The last Act is fine, in its way. But in the remembered impression of the play it is the passion of the lovers, their conversation by moonlight, and their parting at dawn, and not their suicides, that remain.

FURTHER READING

Brian Gibbons's Arden edition (1980) and G. Blakemore Evans's New Cambridge edition (1984) provide readers with comprehensively edited texts. Evans has a lengthy, illustrated section on the history of the play in the theatre and a detailed examination of Shakespeare's sources. Gibbons focuses on the play's physicality – what he calls its appetitiveness – both in linguistic and theatrical terms. Evans notes how critical opinion 'has ranged from simple adulation to measured disapproval' and investigates the critical obsession with the play as a failed or experimental tragedy either of fate or character or both. These editions provide material – as do the pages on the play in *William Shakespeare: A Textual Companion* (1987) by Stanley Wells and Gary Taylor – which should be read to supplement the textual discussion in this edition's 'An Account of the Text', especially regarding the influence of the First Quarto (1597) and the Folio (1623) on the shape of any 'final' text. None of these three, however, goes as far as Cedric Watts, in his Harvester New Critical Introduction (1991), who, after arguing that 'the play is textually more protean, variable and flexible than we may at first have supposed', suggests that the only 'honest' edition of *Romeo and Juliet* would be printings of both Q1 and Q2. Shades of *King Lear*.

For many critics, the fault lines of textual instability mesh with those of generic uncertainty and linguistic experimentation. In *Shakespeare's Early Tragedies* (1968) Nicholas Brooke talks dismissively of the play's 'obtrusive poeticalness' in its dramatizing of the world of the love sonnets, comparable, he says, to the way *Titus Andronicus* dramatizes the world of Lucrece. (Gibbons thinks Sidney's sonnet-sequence, *Astrophil and Stella*, is particularly significant for *Romeo and Juliet*.) H. A. Mason's *Shakespeare's Tragedies of Love* (1970) examines and praises the power of this poeticalness and has an interesting discussion of the play's relationship to its major source, Arthur Brooke's poem *The Tragicall Historye of Romeus and Juliet* (1562). A tendency to simple adulation can be discerned in Douglas Cole's collection of essays on the play, *Twentieth-Century Interpretations* (1970). And in *The Osier Cage: Rhetorical Devices in Romeo and Juliet* (1966), Robert O. Evans praises Romeo and Juliet as great rhetoricians whose use of language proclaims 'the transcendence of the intellectual portions of their souls above the others', while in *Passion Lends Them Power: A Study of Shakespeare's Love Tragedies* (1976) Derick Marsh believes that the play succeeds 'in giving new meaning to the typical lovers' cliché of "I cannot live without you"'. Works like these look back to E. E. Stoll's *Shakespeare's Young Lovers* (1935): 'It is poetically, dramatically, not psychologically, that the characters are meant to interest us.'

What interests many critics – especially those closer to measured disapproval in their response to the play than to simple adulation – is the way *Romeo and Juliet* resists or muddles classification. Such a view rejects determinate interpretations, whether they treat the play as a pure tragedy of Fate, as does Bertrand Evans in *Shakespeare's Tragic Practice* (1979), as one of free agency, as in Franklin Dickey's *Not Wisely But Too Well: Shakespeare's Love Tragedies* (1957), as a 'Christian' tragedy, as does James Seward in *Tragic Vision in Romeo and Juliet* (1973), or as a 'medieval' one, as in John Lawlor's essay on the play in *Early Shakespeare* (Stratford-upon-Avon Studies 3, ed. J. R. Brown and B. Harris, 1961). Instead, this line of criticism seizes upon the play's resistance to easy classification as in itself a classifying strategy. Hence Neil Taylor and Bryan Loughrey's assertion in their collection of essays in the Casebook Series, *Shakespeare's Early Tragedies: Richard III, Titus Andronicus, and Romeo and Juliet* (1990), that 'the tragedy is an enactment of painfully contradictory facts', especially the facts of providence and unpredictability. Cedric Watts's fine study also notes the structural paradox whereby 'inelegant' chance and coincidence occur in a context of constant suggestions of divine ordaining in a style combining 'aspiring lyricism and realistic muscularity'. In sentences of measured adulation Watts proclaims the play to be the most thrilling tragedy since Aeschylus, Sophocles and Euripedes; it is 'so memorably enhancive of sexuality as to make the explanations of Marxists and Freudians alike seem descendants of Mercutio's cynical bawdry and the Nurse's mundane practicality'.

A significant muddling agent generically speaking is the amount of comedy in the play. In her classic study, *The Comic Matrix of Shakespeare's Tragedies* (1979), Susan Snyder thinks that *Romeo and Juliet* 'becomes, rather than is, tragic' – because of Mercutio's death 'a well-developed comic movement is diverted into tragedy by mischance'. Maynard Mack in *Everybody's Shakespeare: Reflections Chiefly on the Tragedies* (1993) argues that the play has all 'the attractions of high comedy'. A. C. Hamilton's *The Early Shakespeare* (1967) thinks the play to be a tragic counterpart to the early comedies. In Jill Levenson's book in the Shakespeare in Performance Series (1987) she quotes from George Santayana's 'Carnival' (1922): 'everything in nature is lyrical in its ideal essence, tragic in its fate, and comic in its existence'. She makes much – rightly – of the play's wit, a wit that 'prevents *Romeo and Juliet* from becoming an intense two-hour dirge for young love', from 'settling into melancholy'. At the same time she argues that in the verse that the lovers speak they grow from 'ordinary to archetypal'. Joseph Porter's work, *Shakespeare's Mercutio: His History and Drama* (1988), focuses on the character who (with the Nurse) is a source for so much of the play's astringent humour. Porter perhaps spends too much of the book pursuing the figure of Mercury in history and literature on the somewhat flimsy basis of the mercuriality of Mercutio's combinations: 'an opposition to love, an amiable erotic permissiveness, and a phallocentrism that admits traces of homoeroticism' – none the less his defence of Mercutio is an admirable corrective to a reductive reading of the play.

Michael Taylor, 1996

ROMEO AND JULIET

THE CHARACTERS IN THE PLAY

Dramatis Personae

ESCALUS, Prince of Verona
MERCUTIO, kinsman of the Prince and friend of Romeo
PARIS, a young count, kinsman of the Prince and Mercutio, and suitor of Juliet
Page to Count Paris

MONTAGUE, head of a Veronese family at feud with the Capulets
LADY MONTAGUE *(once on stage)*
ROMEO, son of Montague
BENVOLIO, nephew of Montague and friend of Romeo and Mercutio
ABRAM, servant of Montague
BALTHASAR, servant of Montague attending on Romeo

CAPULET, head of a Veronese family at feud with the Montagues
LADY CAPULET
JULIET, daughter of Capulet
TYBALT, nephew of Lady Capulet
An old man of the Capulet family
Nurse of Juliet, her foster-mother
PETER, servant of Capulet attending on the Nurse

SAMPSON
GREGORY
ANTHONY
POTPAN } of the Capulet household
A Clown
Servingmen

THE CHARACTERS IN THE PLAY

FRIAR LAURENCE, a Franciscan
FRIAR JOHN, a Franciscan
An Apothecary of Mantua
Three Musicians (Simon Catling, Hugh Rebeck, James Soundpost)
Members of the Watch
Citizens of Verona, maskers, torchbearers, pages, servants

Chorus

set the stage.

Enter Chorus

CHORUS

Two households, both alike in dignity
  In fair Verona, where we lay our scene,
From ancient grudge break to new mutiny,
  Where civil blood makes civil hands unclean.
From forth the fatal loins of these two foes
  A pair of star-crossed lovers take their life;   *fated*
Whose misadventured piteous overthrows
  Doth with their death bury their parents' strife.
The fearful passage of their death-marked love
  And the continuance of their parents' rage,   10
Which, but their children's end, naught could remove,
  Is now the two hours' traffic of our stage;
The which if you with patient ears attend,
What here shall miss, our toil shall strive to mend. *Exit*

destiny

53

*Enter Sampson and Gregory, with swords and buck-
lers, of the house of Capulet*

SAMPSON Gregory, on my word, we'll not carry coals.

GREGORY No. For then we should be colliers.

SAMPSON I mean, an we be in choler, we'll draw.

GREGORY Ay, while you live, draw your neck out of collar.

SAMPSON I strike quickly, being moved.

GREGORY But thou art not quickly moved to strike.

SAMPSON A dog of the house of Montague moves me.

GREGORY To move is to stir, and to be valiant is to stand.
Therefore, if thou art moved, thou runnest away.

SAMPSON A dog of that house shall move me to stand. I 10
will take the wall of any man or maid of Montague's.

GREGORY That shows thee a weak slave. For the weakest
goes to the wall.

SAMPSON 'Tis true; and therefore women, being the
weaker vessels, are ever thrust to the wall. Therefore I
will push Montague's men from the wall, and thrust his
maids to the wall.

GREGORY The quarrel is between our masters, and us
their men.

SAMPSON 'Tis all one. I will show myself a tyrant. When 20
I have fought with the men, I will be civil with the
maids – I will cut off their heads.

GREGORY The heads of the maids?

SAMPSON Ay, the heads of the maids, or their maidenheads. Take it in what sense thou wilt.

GREGORY They must take it in sense that feel it.

SAMPSON Me they shall feel while I am able to stand; and 'tis known I am a pretty piece of flesh.

30 GREGORY 'Tis well thou art not fish; if thou hadst, thou hadst been poor-John. Draw thy tool. Here comes of the house of Montagues.

Enter Abram and another Servingman

SAMPSON My naked weapon is out. Quarrel. I will back thee.

GREGORY How? Turn thy back and run?

SAMPSON Fear me not.

GREGORY No, marry. I fear thee!

SAMPSON Let us take the law of our sides. Let them begin.

40 GREGORY I will frown as I pass by, and let them take it as they list.

SAMPSON Nay, as they dare. I will bite my thumb at them; which is disgrace to them if they bear it.

ABRAM Do you bite your thumb at us, sir?

SAMPSON I do bite my thumb, sir.

ABRAM Do you bite your thumb at us, sir?

SAMPSON (*aside to Gregory*) Is the law of our side if I say 'Ay'?

GREGORY (*aside to Sampson*) No.

50 SAMPSON No, sir, I do not bite my thumb at you, sir. But I bite my thumb, sir.

GREGORY Do you quarrel, sir?

ABRAM Quarrel, sir? No, sir.

SAMPSON But if you do, sir, I am for you. I serve as good a man as you.

ABRAM No better.

SAMPSON Well, sir.

Enter Benvolio

GREGORY (*aside to Sampson*) Say 'better'. Here comes one of my master's kinsmen.

SAMPSON Yes, better, sir.

ABRAM You lie. 60

SAMPSON Draw, if you be men. Gregory, remember thy washing blow.

They fight

BENVOLIO Part, fools!

Put up your swords. You know not what you do.

Enter Tybalt

TYBALT

What, art thou drawn among these heartless hinds?
Turn thee, Benvolio, look upon thy death.

BENVOLIO

I do but keep the peace. Put up thy sword,
Or manage it to part these men with me.

TYBALT

What, drawn, and talk of peace? I hate the word
As I hate hell, all Montagues, and thee. 70
Have at thee, coward!

They fight

Enter three or four Citizens with clubs or partisans

CITIZENS Clubs, bills, and partisans! Strike! Beat them down! Down with the Capulets! Down with the Montagues!

Enter old Capulet in his gown, and his wife

CAPULET

What noise is this? Give me my long sword, ho!

LADY CAPULET

A crutch, a crutch! Why call you for a sword?

Enter old Montague and his wife

CAPULET

My sword, I say! Old Montague is come
And flourishes his blade in spite of me.

MONTAGUE

Thou villain Capulet! – Hold me not. Let me go.

LADY MONTAGUE

80   Thou shalt not stir one foot to seek a foe.
              Enter Prince Escalus, with his train

PRINCE
        Rebellious subjects, enemies to peace,
        Profaners of this neighbour-stainèd steel –
        Will they not hear? What, ho – you men, you beasts,
        That quench the fire of your pernicious rage
        With purple fountains issuing from your veins!
        On pain of torture, from those bloody hands
        Throw your mistempered weapons to the ground
        And hear the sentence of your movèd prince.
        Three civil brawls, bred of an airy word
90   By thee, old Capulet, and Montague,
        Have thrice disturbed the quiet of our streets
        And made Verona's ancient citizens
        Cast by their grave-beseeming ornaments
        To wield old partisans, in hands as old,
        Cankered with peace, to part your cankered hate.
        If ever you disturb our streets again,
        Your lives shall pay the forfeit of the peace.
        For this time all the rest depart away.
        You, Capulet, shall go along with me;
100   And, Montague, come you this afternoon,
        To know our farther pleasure in this case,
        To old Free-town, our common judgement-place.
        Once more, on pain of death, all men depart.
              Exeunt all but Montague, his wife, and Benvolio

MONTAGUE
        Who set this ancient quarrel new abroach?
        Speak, nephew, were you by when it began?

BENVOLIO
        Here were the servants of your adversary
        And yours, close fighting ere I did approach.

                        58

I drew to part them. In the instant came
The fiery Tybalt, with his sword prepared;
Which, as he breathed defiance to my ears,   110
He swung about his head and cut the winds,
Who nothing hurt withal, hissed him in scorn.
While we were interchanging thrusts and blows,
Came more and more, and fought on part and part,
Till the Prince came, who parted either part.

LADY MONTAGUE

O where is Romeo? Saw you him today?
Right glad I am he was not at this fray.

BENVOLIO

Madam, an hour before the worshipped sun
Peered forth the golden window of the East,
A troubled mind drive me to walk abroad;   120
Where, underneath the grove of sycamore
That westward rooteth from this city side,
So early walking did I see your son.
Towards him I made. But he was ware of me
And stole into the covert of the wood.
I, measuring his affections by my own,
Which then most sought where most might not be found,
Being one too many by my weary self,
Pursued my humour, not pursuing his,
And gladly shunned who gladly fled from me.   130

MONTAGUE

Many a morning hath he there been seen
With tears augmenting the fresh morning's dew,
Adding to clouds more clouds with his deep sighs.
But all so soon as the all-cheering sun
Should in the farthest East begin to draw
The shady curtains from Aurora's bed,
Away from light steals home my heavy son
And private in his chamber pens himself,

59

Shuts up his windows, locks fair daylight out,
140 And makes himself an artificial night.
Black and portentous must this humour prove
Unless good counsel may the cause remove.

BENVOLIO
My noble uncle, do you know the cause?

MONTAGUE
I neither know it nor can learn of him.

BENVOLIO
Have you importuned him by any means?

MONTAGUE
Both by myself and many other friends.
But he, his own affections' counsellor,
Is to himself – I will not say how true –
But to himself so secret and so close,
150 So far from sounding and discovery,
As is the bud bit with an envious worm
Ere he can spread his sweet leaves to the air
Or dedicate his beauty to the sun.
Could we but learn from whence his sorrows grow,
We would as willingly give cure as know.

Enter Romeo

BENVOLIO
See, where he comes. So please you step aside.
I'll know his grievance, or be much denied.

MONTAGUE
I would thou wert so happy by thy stay
To hear true shrift. Come, madam, let's away.

Exeunt Montague and wife

BENVOLIO
Good morrow, cousin.
160 ROMEO   Is the day so young?
BENVOLIO
But new struck nine.

ROMEO   Ay me! sad hours seem long.
Was that my father that went hence so fast?
BENVOLIO
It was. What sadness lengthens Romeo's hours?
ROMEO
Not having that which having makes them short.
BENVOLIO
In love?
ROMEO
Out –
BENVOLIO
Of love?
ROMEO
Out of her favour where I am in love.
BENVOLIO
Alas that love, so gentle in his view,
Should be so tyrannous and rough in proof!   170
ROMEO
Alas that love, whose view is muffled, still
Should without eyes see pathways to his will!
Where shall we dine? O me, what fray was here?
Yet tell me not, for I have heard it all.
Here's much to-do with hate, but more with love.
Why then, O brawling love, O loving hate,
O anything, of nothing first create!
O heavy lightness, serious vanity,
Misshapen chaos of well-seeming forms,
Feather of lead, bright smoke, cold fire, sick health,   180
Still-waking sleep, that is not what it is!
This love feel I, that feel no love in this.
Dost thou not laugh?
BENVOLIO   No, coz, I rather weep.
ROMEO
Good heart, at what?

BENVOLIO   At thy good heart's oppression.

ROMEO

Why, such is love's transgression.
Griefs of mine own lie heavy in my breast,
Which thou wilt propagate, to have it pressed
With more of thine. This love that thou hast shown
Doth add more grief to too much of mine own.

190 Love is a smoke made with the fume of sighs;
Being purged, a fire sparkling in lovers' eyes;
Being vexed, a sea nourished with lovers' tears.
What is it else? A madness most discreet,
A choking gall and a preserving sweet.
Farewell, my coz.

BENVOLIO   Soft! I will go along.
An if you leave me so, you do me wrong.

ROMEO

Tut, I have left myself. I am not here.
This is not Romeo, he's some other where.

BENVOLIO

Tell me in sadness, who is that you love?

ROMEO

What, shall I groan and tell thee?

200 BENVOLIO   Groan? Why, no.
But sadly tell me who.

ROMEO

Bid a sick man in sadness make his will.
Ah, word ill urged to one that is so ill!
In sadness, cousin, I do love a woman.

BENVOLIO

I aimed so near when I supposed you loved.

ROMEO

A right good markman. And she's fair I love.

BENVOLIO

A right fair mark, fair coz, is soonest hit.

ROMEO

Well, in that hit you miss. She'll not be hit
With Cupid's arrow. She hath Dian's wit,
And, in strong proof of chastity well armed,   210
From love's weak childish bow she lives uncharmed.
She will not stay the siege of loving terms,
Nor bide th'encounter of assailing eyes,
Nor ope her lap to saint-seducing gold.
O, she is rich in beauty; only poor
That, when she dies, with beauty dies her store.

BENVOLIO

Then she hath sworn that she will still live chaste?

ROMEO

She hath; and in that sparing makes huge waste.
For beauty, starved with her severity,
Cuts beauty off from all posterity.   220
She is too fair, too wise, wisely too fair,
To merit bliss by making me despair.
She hath forsworn to love; and in that vow
Do I live dead that live to tell it now.

BENVOLIO

Be ruled by me – forget to think of her.

ROMEO

O, teach me how I should forget to think!

BENVOLIO

By giving liberty unto thine eyes.
Examine other beauties.

ROMEO   'Tis the way
To call hers, exquisite, in question more.
These happy masks that kiss fair ladies' brows,   230
Being black, puts us in mind they hide the fair.
He that is strucken blind cannot forget
The precious treasure of his eyesight lost.

63

I.1–2

Show me a mistress that is passing fair,
What doth her beauty serve but as a note
Where I may read who passed that passing fair?
Farewell. Thou canst not teach me to forget.

BENVOLIO

I'll pay that doctrine, or else die in debt.   *Exeunt*

I.2   *Enter Capulet, County Paris, and the Clown, a*
         Servant

CAPULET

But Montague is bound as well as I,
In penalty alike; and 'tis not hard, I think,
For men so old as we to keep the peace.

PARIS

Of honourable reckoning are you both,
And pity 'tis you lived at odds so long.
But now, my lord, what say you to my suit?

CAPULET

But saying o'er what I have said before:
My child is yet a stranger in the world;
She hath not seen the change of fourteen years.
Let two more summers wither in their pride
Ere we may think her ripe to be a bride.

PARIS

Younger than she are happy mothers made.

CAPULET

And too soon marred are those so early made.
Earth hath swallowed all my hopes but she;
She's the hopeful lady of my earth.
But woo her, gentle Paris, get her heart.
My will to her consent is but a part,
And, she agreed, within her scope of choice
Lies my consent and fair according voice.

64

This night I hold an old accustomed feast,   20
Whereto I have invited many a guest,
Such as I love; and you among the store,
One more, most welcome, makes my number more.
At my poor house look to behold this night
Earth-treading stars that make dark heaven light.
Such comfort as do lusty young men feel
When well-apparelled April on the heel
Of limping winter treads, even such delight
Among fresh female buds shall you this night
Inherit at my house. Hear all; all see;   30
And like her most whose merit most shall be;
Which, on more view of many, mine, being one,
May stand in number, though in reckoning none.
Come, go with me. (*To Servant*) Go, sirrah, trudge about
Through fair Verona; find those persons out
Whose names are written there, and to them say,
My house and welcome on their pleasure stay.

Exeunt Capulet and Paris

SERVANT Find them out whose names are written here! It
is written that the shoemaker should meddle with his
yard and the tailor with his last, the fisher with his pencil   40
and the painter with his nets. But I am sent to find those
persons whose names are here writ, and can never find
what names the writing person hath here writ. I must to
the learned. In good time!

Enter Benvolio and Romeo

BENVOLIO
Tut, man, one fire burns out another's burning.
    One pain is lessened by another's anguish.
Turn giddy, and be holp by backward turning.
    One desperate grief cures with another's languish.
Take thou some new infection to thy eye,
And the rank poison of the old will die.   50

65

ROMEO

Your plantain leaf is excellent for that.

BENVOLIO

For what, I pray thee?

ROMEO   For your broken shin.

BENVOLIO

Why, Romeo, art thou mad?

ROMEO

Not mad, but bound more than a madman is;
Shut up in prison, kept without my food,
Whipped and tormented and – Good-e'en, good fellow.

SERVANT

God gi' good-e'en. I pray, sir, can you read?

ROMEO

Ay, mine own fortune in my misery.

SERVANT Perhaps you have learned it without book. But
60   I pray, can you read anything you see?

ROMEO

Ay, if I know the letters and the language.

SERVANT Ye say honestly. Rest you merry.

ROMEO

Stay, fellow. I can read.

He reads the letter

*Signor Martino and his wife and daughters. County Anselm
and his beauteous sisters. The lady widow of Utruvio.
Signor Placentio and his lovely nieces. Mercutio and his
brother Valentine. Mine uncle Capulet, his wife, and daughters. My fair niece Rosaline and Livia. Signor Valentio and
his cousin Tybalt. Lucio and the lively Helena.*

70   A fair assembly. Whither should they come?

SERVANT Up.

ROMEO Whither? To supper?

SERVANT To our house.

ROMEO Whose house?

SERVANT My master's.

ROMEO Indeed I should have asked thee that before.

SERVANT Now I'll tell you without asking. My master is
the great rich Capulet; and if you be not of the house of
Montagues, I pray come and crush a cup of wine. Rest
you merry.   *Exit Servant* 80

BENVOLIO

At this same ancient feast of Capulet's
Sups the fair Rosaline whom thou so loves,
With all the admirèd beauties of Verona.
Go thither, and with unattainted eye
Compare her face with some that I shall show,   mark
And I will make thee think thy swan a crow.

ROMEO

When the devout religion of mine eye
    Maintains such falsehood, then turn tears to fires;
And these, who, often drowned, could never die,
    Transparent heretics, be burnt for liars!   90
One fairer than my love? The all-seeing sun
Ne'er saw her match since first the world begun.

BENVOLIO

Tut, you saw her fair, none else being by,
Herself poised with herself in either eye.
But in that crystal scales let there be weighed
Your lady's love against some other maid
That I will show you shining at this feast,
And she shall scant show well that now seems best.

ROMEO

I'll go along, no such sight to be shown,
But to rejoice in splendour of mine own.   *Exeunt* 100

67

LADY CAPULET

Nurse, where's my daughter? Call her forth to me.

NURSE

Now, by my maidenhead at twelve year old,
I bade her come. What, lamb! What, ladybird! –
God forbid! – Where's this girl? What, Juliet!

Enter Juliet

JULIET

How now? Who calls?

NURSE

Your mother.

JULIET

Madam, I am here. What is your will?

LADY CAPULET

This is the matter – Nurse, give leave awhile.
We must talk in secret. – Nurse, come back again.
10   I have remembered me, thou's hear our counsel.
Thou knowest my daughter's of a pretty age.

NURSE

Faith, I can tell her age unto an hour.

LADY CAPULET

She's not fourteen.

NURSE   I'll lay fourteen of my teeth –
And yet, to my teen be it spoken, I have but four –
She's not fourteen. How long is it now
To Lammastide?

LADY CAPULET

                              A fortnight and odd days.

NURSE

Even or odd, of all days in the year,
Come Lammas Eve at night shall she be fourteen.
Susan and she – God rest all Christian souls! –
20   Were of an age. Well, Susan is with God.

She was too good for me. But, as I said,
On Lammas Eve at night shall she be fourteen.
That shall she, marry! I remember it well.
'Tis since the earthquake now eleven years;
And she was weaned – I never shall forget it –
Of all the days of the year, upon that day.
For I had then laid wormwood to my dug,
Sitting in the sun under the dovehouse wall.
My lord and you were then at Mantua.
Nay, I do bear a brain. But, as I said,   30
When it did taste the wormwood on the nipple
Of my dug and felt it bitter, pretty fool,
To see it tetchy and fall out wi' th' dug!
Shake, quoth the dovehouse! 'Twas no need, I trow,
To bid me trudge.
And since that time it is eleven years.
For then she could stand high-lone. Nay, by th'rood,
She could have run and waddled all about.
For even the day before she broke her brow.
And then my husband – God be with his soul!   40
'A was a merry man – took up the child.
'Yea,' quoth he, 'dost thou fall upon thy face?
Thou wilt fall backward when thou hast more wit.
Wilt thou not, Jule?' And, by my holidam,
The pretty wretch left crying and said 'Ay'.
To see now how a jest shall come about!
I warrant, an I should live a thousand years,
I never should forget it. 'Wilt thou not, Jule?' quoth he,
And, pretty fool, it stinted and said 'Ay'.

LADY CAPULET
Enough of this. I pray thee hold thy peace.   50

NURSE
Yes, madam. Yet I cannot choose but laugh
To think it should leave crying and say 'Ay'.

69

And yet, I warrant, it had upon it brow
A bump as big as a young cockerel's stone,
A perilous knock. And it cried bitterly.
'Yea,' quoth my husband, 'fallest upon thy face?
Thou wilt fall backward when thou comest to age.
Wilt thou not, Jule?' It stinted, and said 'Ay'.

JULIET
And stint thou too, I pray thee, Nurse, say I.

NURSE
60 Peace, I have done. God mark thee to his grace!
Thou wast the prettiest babe that e'er I nursed.
An I might live to see thee married once,
I have my wish.

LADY CAPULET
Marry, that 'marry' is the very theme
I came to talk of. Tell me, daughter Juliet,
How stands your dispositions to be married?

JULIET
It is an honour that I dream not of.

NURSE
An honour! Were not I thine only nurse,
I would say thou hadst sucked wisdom from thy teat.

LADY CAPULET
70 Well, think of marriage now. Younger than you,
Here in Verona, ladies of esteem
Are made already mothers. By my count,
I was your mother much upon these years
That you are now a maid. Thus then in brief:
The valiant Paris seeks you for his love.

NURSE
A man, young lady! Lady, such a man
As all the world – why, he's a man of wax.

LADY CAPULET
Verona's summer hath not such a flower.

NURSE

Nay, he's a flower; in faith, a very flower.

LADY CAPULET

What say you? Can you love the gentleman?　　　　80
This night you shall behold him at our feast.
Read o'er the volume of young Paris' face,
And find delight writ there with beauty's pen.
Examine every married lineament,
And see how one another lends content.
And what obscured in this fair volume lies
Find written in the margent of his eyes.
This precious book of love, this unbound lover,
To beautify him only lacks a cover.
The fish lives in the sea, and 'tis much pride　　　90
For fair without the fair within to hide.
That book in many's eyes doth share the glory,
That in gold clasps locks in the golden story.
So shall you share all that he doth possess,
By having him making yourself no less.

NURSE

No less? Nay, bigger! Women grow by men.

LADY CAPULET

Speak briefly, can you like of Paris' love?

JULIET

I'll look to like, if looking liking move.
But no more deep will I endart mine eye
Than your consent gives strength to make it fly.　　100

Enter Servingman

SERVINGMAN Madam, the guests are come, supper served
up, you called, my young lady asked for, the Nurse
cursed in the pantry, and everything in extremity. I
must hence to wait. I beseech you follow straight.

LADY CAPULET

We follow thee.　　　　　　　　　　*Exit Servingman*

　　　Juliet, the County stays.

71

NURSE

Go, girl, seek happy nights to happy days.   *Exeunt*

I.4   *Enter Romeo, Mercutio, Benvolio, with five or six*
           other maskers, and torchbearers

ROMEO

What, shall this speech be spoke for our excuse?
Or shall we on without apology?

BENVOLIO

The date is out of such prolixity.
We'll have no Cupid hoodwinked with a scarf,
Bearing a Tartar's painted bow of lath,
Scaring the ladies like a crowkeeper,
Nor no without-book prologue, faintly spoke
After the prompter, for our entrance.
But, let them measure us by what they will,
10   We'll measure them a measure and be gone.

ROMEO

Give me a torch. I am not for this ambling.
Being but heavy, I will bear the light.

MERCUTIO

Nay, gentle Romeo, we must have you dance.

ROMEO

Not I, believe me. You have dancing shoes
With nimble soles. I have a soul of lead
So stakes me to the ground I cannot move.

MERCUTIO

You are a lover. Borrow Cupid's wings
And soar with them above a common bound.

ROMEO

I am too sore empiercèd with his shaft
20   To soar with his light feathers; and so bound
I cannot bound a pitch above dull woe.

72

Under love's heavy burden do I sink.

MERCUTIO

And, to sink in it, should you burden love –
Too great oppression for a tender thing.

ROMEO

Is love a tender thing? It is too rough,
Too rude, too boisterous, and it pricks like thorn.

MERCUTIO

If love be rough with you, be rough with love.
Prick love for pricking, and you beat love down.
Give me a case to put my visage in.
A visor for a visor! What care I   30
What curious eye doth quote deformities?
Here are the beetle brows shall blush for me.

BENVOLIO

Come, knock and enter; and no sooner in
But every man betake him to his legs.

ROMEO

A torch for me! Let wantons light of heart
Tickle the senseless rushes with their heels.
For I am proverbed with a grandsire phrase –
I'll be a candle-holder and look on;
The game was ne'er so fair, and I am done.

MERCUTIO

Tut, dun's the mouse, the constable's own word!   40
If thou art Dun, we'll draw thee from the mire
Of – save your reverence – love, wherein thou stickest
Up to the ears. Come, we burn daylight, ho!

ROMEO

Nay, that's not so.

MERCUTIO   I mean, sir, in delay
We waste our lights in vain, like lamps by day.
Take our good meaning, for our judgement sits
Five times in that ere once in our five wits.

ROMEO

And we mean well in going to this masque,
But 'tis no wit to go.

MERCUTIO   Why, may one ask?

ROMEO

I dreamt a dream tonight.

50 MERCUTIO   And so did I.

ROMEO

Well, what was yours?

MERCUTIO   That dreamers often lie.

ROMEO

In bed asleep, while they do dream things true.

MERCUTIO

O, then I see Queen Mab hath been with you.
She is the fairies' midwife, and she comes
In shape no bigger than an agate stone
On the forefinger of an alderman,
Drawn with a team of little atomies
Over men's noses as they lie asleep.
Her chariot is an empty hazelnut,
60 Made by the joiner squirrel or old grub,
Time out o'mind the fairies' coachmakers.
Her wagon spokes made of long spinners' legs;
The cover, of the wings of grasshoppers;
Her traces, of the smallest spider web;
Her collars, of the moonshine's watery beams;
Her whip, of cricket's bone; the lash, of film;
Her wagoner, a small grey-coated gnat,
Not half so big as a round little worm
Pricked from the lazy finger of a maid.
70 And in this state she gallops night by night
Through lovers' brains, and then they dream of love;
O'er courtiers' knees, that dream on curtsies straight;
O'er lawyers' fingers, who straight dream on fees;

74

O'er ladies' lips, who straight on kisses dream,
Which oft the angry Mab with blisters plagues,
Because their breaths with sweetmeats tainted are.
Sometime she gallops o'er a courtier's nose,
And then dreams he of smelling out a suit.
And sometime comes she with a tithe-pig's tail
Tickling a parson's nose as 'a lies asleep;   80
Then he dreams of another benefice.
Sometime she driveth o'er a soldier's neck;
And then dreams he of cutting foreign throats,
Of breaches, ambuscados, Spanish blades,
Of healths five fathom deep; and then anon
Drums in his ear, at which he starts and wakes,
And being thus frighted, swears a prayer or two
And sleeps again. This is that very Mab
That plaits the manes of horses in the night
And bakes the elf-locks in foul sluttish hairs,   90
Which once untangled much misfortune bodes.
This is the hag, when maids lie on their backs,
That presses them and learns them first to bear,
Making them women of good carriage.
This is she –
ROMEO   Peace, peace, Mercutio, peace!
Thou talkest of nothing.
MERCUTIO   True. I talk of dreams;
Which are the children of an idle brain,
Begot of nothing but vain fantasy;
Which is as thin of substance as the air,
And more inconstant than the wind, who woos   100
Even now the frozen bosom of the North
And, being angered, puffs away from thence,
Turning his side to the dew-dropping South.
BENVOLIO
This wind you talk of blows us from ourselves.

75

Supper is done, and we shall come too late.

ROMEO
I fear, too early. For my mind misgives
Some consequence, yet hanging in the stars,
Shall bitterly begin his fearful date
With this night's revels and expire the term
110 Of a despisèd life, closed in my breast,
By some vile forfeit of untimely death.
But He that hath the steerage of my course
Direct my sail! On, lusty gentlemen!

BENVOLIO
Strike, drum.

I.5   *They march about the stage; and Servingmen come*
forth with napkins

FIRST SERVINGMAN Where's Potpan, that he helps not
to take away? He shift a trencher! He scrape a trencher!

SECOND SERVINGMAN When good manners shall lie all
in one or two men's hands, and they unwashed too, 'tis
a foul thing.

FIRST SERVINGMAN Away with the joint-stools; remove
the court-cupboard; look to the plate. Good thou, save
me a piece of marchpane; and, as thou loves me, let the
porter let in Susan Grindstone and Nell.

Exit Second Servingman

10   Anthony, and Potpan!
Enter two more Servingmen

THIRD SERVINGMAN Ay, boy, ready.

FIRST SERVINGMAN You are looked for and called for,
asked for and sought for, in the Great Chamber.

FOURTH SERVINGMAN We cannot be here and there too.
Cheerly, boys! Be brisk a while, and the longer liver
take all.

Exeunt Third and Fourth Servingmen

Enter Capulet, his wife, Juliet, Tybalt, Nurse, and all
the guests and gentlewomen to the maskers

CAPULET

Welcome, gentlemen! Ladies that have their toes
Unplagued with corns will walk a bout with you.
Ah, my mistresses, which of you all
Will now deny to dance? She that makes dainty,   20
She, I'll swear, hath corns. Am I come near ye now?
Welcome, gentlemen! I have seen the day
That I have worn a visor and could tell
A whispering tale in a fair lady's ear,
Such as would please. 'Tis gone, 'tis gone, 'tis gone!
You are welcome, gentlemen! Come, musicians, play.

Music plays, and they dance

A hall, a hall! Give room! and foot it, girls.
More light, you knaves! and turn the tables up;
And quench the fire, the room is grown too hot.
Ah, sirrah, this unlooked-for sport comes well.   30
Nay, sit, nay, sit, good cousin Capulet,
For you and I are past our dancing days.
How long is't now since last yourself and I
Were in a mask?

COUSIN CAPULET

                        By'r Lady, thirty years.

CAPULET

What, man? 'Tis not so much, 'tis not so much.
'Tis since the nuptial of Lucentio,
Come Pentecost as quickly as it will,
Some five-and-twenty years; and then we masked.

COUSIN CAPULET

'Tis more, 'tis more. His son is elder, sir.
His son is thirty.

CAPULET   Will you tell me that?   40
His son was but a ward two years ago.

77

ROMEO (*to Servingman*)
    What lady's that, which doth enrich the hand
    Of yonder knight?
SERVINGMAN   I know not, sir.
ROMEO
    O, she doth teach the torches to burn bright!
    It seems she hangs upon the cheek of night
    As a rich jewel in an Ethiop's ear –
    Beauty too rich for use, for earth too dear!
    So shows a snowy dove trooping with crows
    As yonder lady o'er her fellows shows.
50 The measure done, I'll watch her place of stand
    And, touching hers, make blessèd my rude hand.
    Did my heart love till now? Forswear it, sight!
    For I ne'er saw true beauty till this night.
TYBALT
    This, by his voice, should be a Montague.
    Fetch me my rapier, boy. What, dares the slave
    Come hither, covered with an antic face,
    To fleer and scorn at our solemnity?
    Now, by the stock and honour of my kin,
    To strike him dead I hold it not a sin.
CAPULET
60 Why, how now, kinsman? Wherefore storm you so?
TYBALT
    Uncle, this is a Montague, our foe.
    A villain, that is hither come in spite
    To scorn at our solemnity this night.
CAPULET
    Young Romeo is it?
TYBALT   'Tis he, that villain Romeo.
CAPULET
    Content thee, gentle coz, let him alone.
    'A bears him like a portly gentleman.

And, to say truth, Verona brags of him
To be a virtuous and well-governed youth.
I would not for the wealth of all this town
Here in my house do him disparagement.   70
Therefore be patient; take no note of him.
It is my will, the which if thou respect,
Show a fair presence and put off these frowns,
An ill-beseeming semblance for a feast.

TYBALT

It fits when such a villain is a guest.
I'll not endure him.

CAPULET   He shall be endured.
What, goodman boy! I say he shall. Go to!
Am I the master here, or you? Go to!
You'll not endure him! God shall mend my soul!
You'll make a mutiny among my guests!   80
You will set cock-a-hoop! You'll be the man!

TYBALT

Why, uncle, 'tis a shame.

CAPULET   Go to, go to!
You are a saucy boy. Is't so, indeed?
This trick may chance to scathe you. I know what.
You must contrary me! Marry, 'tis time –
Well said, my hearts! – You are a princox, go!
Be quiet, or – More light, more light! – For shame!
I'll make you quiet, what! – Cheerly, my hearts!

TYBALT

Patience perforce with wilful choler meeting
Makes my flesh tremble in their different greeting.   90
I will withdraw. But this intrusion shall,
Now seeming sweet, convert to bitterest gall. *Exit Tybalt*

ROMEO

If I profane with my unworthiest hand
    This holy shrine, the gentle sin is this.

    My lips, two blushing pilgrims, ready stand
      To smooth that rough touch with a tender kiss.

JULIET
    Good pilgrim, you do wrong your hand too much,
      Which mannerly devotion shows in this.
    For saints have hands that pilgrims' hands do touch,
100   And palm to palm is holy palmers' kiss.

ROMEO
    Have not saints lips, and holy palmers too?

JULIET
    Ay, pilgrim, lips that they must use in prayer.

ROMEO
    O, then, dear saint, let lips do what hands do!
      They pray: grant thou, lest faith turn to despair.

JULIET
    Saints do not move, though grant for prayers' sake.

ROMEO
    Then move not while my prayer's effect I take.
      He kisses her
    Thus from my lips, by thine my sin is purged.

JULIET
    Then have my lips the sin that they have took.

ROMEO
    Sin from my lips? O trespass sweetly urged!
      Give me my sin again.
      He kisses her

110 **JULIET**   You kiss by th'book.

NURSE
    Madam, your mother craves a word with you.

ROMEO
    What is her mother?

NURSE   Marry, bachelor,
    Her mother is the lady of the house,
    And a good lady, and a wise and virtuous.

I nursed her daughter that you talked withal.
I tell you, he that can lay hold of her
Shall have the chinks.

ROMEO   Is she a Capulet?
O dear account! My life is my foe's debt.

BENVOLIO
Away, be gone. The sport is at the best.

ROMEO
Ay, so I fear. The more is my unrest.   120

CAPULET
Nay, gentlemen, prepare not to be gone.
We have a trifling foolish banquet towards.
        They whisper in his ear
Is it e'en so? Why then, I thank you all.
I thank you, honest gentlemen. Good night.
More torches here! Come on then, let's to bed.
Ah, sirrah, by my fay, it waxes late.
I'll to my rest.   *Exeunt all but Juliet and Nurse*

JULIET
Come hither, Nurse. What is yond gentleman?

NURSE
The son and heir of old Tiberio.

JULIET
What's he that now is going out of door?   130

NURSE
Marry, that, I think, be young Petruchio.

JULIET
What's he that follows here, that would not dance?

NURSE
I know not.

JULIET
Go ask his name. – If he be marrièd,
My grave is like to be my wedding bed.

NURSE

    His name is Romeo, and a Montague,
    The only son of your great enemy.

JULIET

    My only love, sprung from my only hate!
    Too early seen unknown, and known too late!
140   Prodigious birth of love it is to me
    That I must love a loathèd enemy.

NURSE

    What's this, what's this?

JULIET   A rhyme I learnt even now
    Of one I danced withal.

        One calls within: 'Juliet'

NURSE   Anon, anon!
    Come, let's away. The strangers all are gone.   *Exeunt*

*

II   *Enter Chorus*

CHORUS

    Now old desire doth in his deathbed lie,
      And young affection gapes to be his heir.
    That fair for which love groaned for and would die,
      With tender Juliet matched, is now not fair.
    Now Romeo is beloved and loves again,
      Alike bewitchèd by the charm of looks.
    But to his foe supposed he must complain,
      And she steal love's sweet bait from fearful hooks.
    Being held a foe, he may not have access
10   To breathe such vows as lovers use to swear,
    And she as much in love, her means much less
      To meet her new belovèd anywhere.
    But passion lends them power, time means, to meet,
    Tempering extremities with extreme sweet.   *Exit*

Enter Romeo alone

ROMEO
Can I go forward when my heart is here?
Turn back, dull earth, and find thy centre out.

Enter Benvolio with Mercutio. Romeo withdraws

BENVOLIO
Romeo! My cousin Romeo! Romeo!

MERCUTIO   He is wise,
And, on my life, hath stolen him home to bed.

BENVOLIO
He ran this way and leapt this orchard wall.
Call, good Mercutio.

MERCUTIO   Nay, I'll conjure too.
Romeo! Humours! Madman! Passion! Lover!
Appear thou in the likeness of a sigh.
Speak but one rhyme, and I am satisfied.
Cry but 'Ay me!' Pronounce but 'love' and 'dove'.   10
Speak to my gossip Venus one fair word,
One nickname for her purblind son and heir,
Young Abraham Cupid, he that shot so trim
When King Cophetua loved the beggar maid.
He heareth not, he stirreth not, he moveth not.
The ape is dead, and I must conjure him.
I conjure thee by Rosaline's bright eyes,
By her high forehead and her scarlet lip,
By her fine foot, straight leg, and quivering thigh,
And the demesnes that there adjacent lie,   20
That in thy likeness thou appear to us!

BENVOLIO
An if he hear thee, thou wilt anger him.

MERCUTIO
This cannot anger him. 'Twould anger him
To raise a spirit in his mistress' circle
Of some strange nature, letting it there stand

Till she had laid it and conjured it down.
That were some spite. My invocation
Is fair and honest. In his mistress' name,
I conjure only but to raise up him.

BENVOLIO

30 Come, he hath hid himself among these trees
To be consorted with the humorous night.
Blind is his love and best befits the dark.

MERCUTIO

If love be blind, love cannot hit the mark.
Now will he sit under a medlar tree
And wish his mistress were that kind of fruit
As maids call medlars when they laugh alone.
O, Romeo, that she were, O that she were
An open-arse and thou a poppering pear!
Romeo, good night. I'll to my truckle-bed.
40 This field-bed is too cold for me to sleep.
Come, shall we go?

BENVOLIO   Go then, for 'tis in vain
To seek him here that means not to be found.

Exeunt Benvolio and Mercutio

II.2 ROMEO (*coming forward*)
He jests at scars that never felt a wound.
        Enter Juliet above
But soft! What light through yonder window breaks?
It is the East, and Juliet is the sun!
Arise, fair sun, and kill the envious moon,
Who is already sick and pale with grief
That thou her maid art far more fair than she.
Be not her maid, since she is envious.
Her vestal livery is but sick and green,
And none but fools do wear it. Cast it off.
10 It is my lady. O, it is my love!
O that she knew she were!

She speaks. Yet she says nothing. What of that?
Her eye discourses. I will answer it.
I am too bold. 'Tis not to me she speaks.
Two of the fairest stars in all the heaven,
Having some business, do entreat her eyes
To twinkle in their spheres till they return.
What if her eyes were there, they in her head?
The brightness of her cheek would shame those stars
As daylight doth a lamp. Her eyes in heaven   20
Would through the airy region stream so bright
That birds would sing and think it were not night.
See how she leans her cheek upon her hand!
O that I were a glove upon that hand,
That I might touch that cheek!

JULIET   Ay me!
ROMEO   She speaks.
O, speak again, bright angel! – for thou art
As glorious to this night, being o'er my head,
As is a wingèd messenger of heaven
Unto the white-upturnèd wondering eyes
Of mortals that fall back to gaze on him   30
When he bestrides the lazy, puffing clouds
And sails upon the bosom of the air.

JULIET
O Romeo, Romeo! – wherefore art thou Romeo?
Deny thy father and refuse thy name.
Or, if thou wilt not, be but sworn my love,
And I'll no longer be a Capulet.

ROMEO (aside)
Shall I hear more, or shall I speak at this?

JULIET
'Tis but thy name that is my enemy.
Thou art thyself, though not a Montague.
What's Montague? It is nor hand nor foot   40

Nor arm nor face nor any other part
Belonging to a man. O, be some other name!
What's in a name? That which we call a rose
By any other word would smell as sweet.
So Romeo would, were he not Romeo called,
Retain that dear perfection which he owes
Without that title. Romeo, doff thy name;
And for thy name, which is no part of thee,
Take all myself.

ROMEO   I take thee at thy word.
50   Call me but love, and I'll be new baptized.
Henceforth I never will be Romeo.

JULIET
What man art thou that, thus bescreened in night,
So stumblest on my counsel?

ROMEO   By a name
I know not how to tell thee who I am.
My name, dear saint, is hateful to myself,
Because it is an enemy to thee.
Had I it written, I would tear the word.

JULIET
My ears have yet not drunk a hundred words
Of thy tongue's uttering, yet I know the sound.
60   Art thou not Romeo, and a Montague?

ROMEO
Neither, fair maid, if either thee dislike.

JULIET
How camest thou hither, tell me, and wherefore?
The orchard walls are high and hard to climb,
And the place death, considering who thou art,
If any of my kinsmen find thee here.

ROMEO
With love's light wings did I o'erperch these walls.
For stony limits cannot hold love out,

And what love can do, that dares love attempt.
Therefore thy kinsmen are no stop to me.

JULIET

If they do see thee, they will murder thee.   70

ROMEO

Alack, there lies more peril in thine eye
Than twenty of their swords! Look thou but sweet,
And I am proof against their enmity.

JULIET

I would not for the world they saw thee here.

ROMEO

I have night's cloak to hide me from their eyes.
And but thou love me, let them find me here.
My life were better ended by their hate
Than death proroguèd, wanting of thy love.

JULIET

By whose direction foundest thou out this place?

ROMEO

By love, that first did prompt me to inquire.   80
He lent me counsel, and I lent him eyes.
I am no pilot; yet, wert thou as far
As that vast shore washed with the farthest sea,
I should adventure for such merchandise.

JULIET

Thou knowest the mask of night is on my face,
Else would a maiden blush bepaint my cheek
For that which thou hast heard me speak tonight.
Fain would I dwell on form – fain, fain deny
What I have spoke. But farewell compliment!
Dost thou love me? I know thou wilt say 'Ay'.   90
And I will take thy word. Yet, if thou swearest,
Thou mayst prove false. At lovers' perjuries,
They say, Jove laughs. O gentle Romeo,
If thou dost love, pronounce it faithfully.

Or if thou thinkest I am too quickly won,
I'll frown, and be perverse, and say thee nay,
So thou wilt woo. But else, not for the world.
In truth, fair Montague, I am too fond,
And therefore thou mayst think my 'haviour light.
100 But trust me, gentleman, I'll prove more true
Than those that have more cunning to be strange.
I should have been more strange, I must confess,
But that thou overheardest, ere I was ware,
My true-love passion. Therefore pardon me,
And not impute this yielding to light love,
Which the dark night hath so discoverèd.

ROMEO
Lady, by yonder blessèd moon I vow,
That tips with silver all these fruit-tree tops –

JULIET
O, swear not by the moon, th'inconstant moon,
110 That monthly changes in her circled orb,
Lest that thy love prove likewise variable.

ROMEO
What shall I swear by?

JULIET   Do not swear at all.
Or if thou wilt, swear by thy gracious self,
Which is the god of my idolatry,
And I'll believe thee.

ROMEO   If my heart's dear love –

JULIET
Well, do not swear. Although I joy in thee,
I have no joy of this contract tonight.
It is too rash, too unadvised, too sudden;
Too like the lightning, which doth cease to be
120 Ere one can say 'It lightens'. Sweet, good night!
This bud of love, by summer's ripening breath,
May prove a beauteous flower when next we meet.

Good night, good night! As sweet repose and rest
Come to thy heart as that within my breast!

ROMEO

O, wilt thou leave me so unsatisfied?

JULIET

What satisfaction canst thou have tonight?

ROMEO

Th'exchange of thy love's faithful vow for mine.

JULIET

I gave thee mine before thou didst request it.
And yet I would it were to give again.

ROMEO

Wouldst thou withdraw it? For what purpose, love?   130

JULIET

But to be frank and give it thee again.
And yet I wish but for the thing I have.
My bounty is as boundless as the sea,
My love as deep. The more I give to thee,
The more I have, for both are infinite.
I hear some noise within. Dear love, adieu!
        Nurse calls within
Anon, good Nurse! – Sweet Montague, be true.
Stay but a little, I will come again.   *Exit Juliet*

ROMEO

O blessèd, blessèd night! I am afeard,
Being in night, all this is but a dream,   140
Too flattering-sweet to be substantial.
        Enter Juliet above

JULIET

Three words, dear Romeo, and good night indeed.
If that thy bent of love be honourable,
Thy purpose marriage, send me word tomorrow,
By one that I'll procure to come to thee,
Where and what time thou wilt perform the rite,

And all my fortunes at thy foot I'll lay
And follow thee my lord throughout the world.

NURSE (*within*)
Madam!

JULIET

150 I come, anon – But if thou meanest not well,
I do beseech thee –

NURSE (*within*)   Madam!

JULIET   By and by I come –
To cease thy strife and leave me to my grief.
Tomorrow will I send.

ROMEO   So thrive my soul –

JULIET
A thousand times good night!   *Exit Juliet*

ROMEO
A thousand times the worse, to want thy light!
Love goes toward love as schoolboys from their books;
But love from love, toward school with heavy looks.

          Enter Juliet above again

JULIET
Hist! Romeo, hist! O for a falconer's voice,
To lure this tassel-gentle back again!

160 Bondage is hoarse and may not speak aloud,
Else would I tear the cave where Echo lies
And make her airy tongue more hoarse than mine
With repetition of 'My Romeo!'

ROMEO
It is my soul that calls upon my name.
How silver-sweet sound lovers' tongues by night,
Like softest music to attending ears!

JULIET
Romeo!

ROMEO   My nyas?

JULIET   What o'clock tomorrow
Shall I send to thee?

ROMEO   By the hour of nine.

JULIET

I will not fail. 'Tis twenty year till then.
I have forgot why I did call thee back.   170

ROMEO

Let me stand here till thou remember it.

JULIET

I shall forget, to have thee still stand there,
Remembering how I love thy company.

ROMEO

And I'll still stay, to have thee still forget,
Forgetting any other home but this.

JULIET

'Tis almost morning. I would have thee gone.
And yet no farther than a wanton's bird,
That lets it hop a little from his hand,
Like a poor prisoner in his twisted gyves,
And with a silken thread plucks it back again,   180
So loving-jealous of his liberty.

ROMEO

I would I were thy bird.

JULIET   Sweet, so would I.
Yet I should kill thee with much cherishing.
Good night, good night! Parting is such sweet sorrow
That I shall say goodnight till it be morrow.

                                          Exit Juliet

ROMEO

Sleep dwell upon thine eyes, peace in thy breast!
Would I were sleep and peace, so sweet to rest!
The grey-eyed morn smiles on the frowning night,
Chequering the eastern clouds with streaks of light,
And darkness fleckled like a drunkard reels   190
From forth day's pathway made by Titan's wheels.
Hence will I to my ghostly Friar's close cell,
His help to crave and my dear hap to tell.   *Exit*

Enter Friar Laurence alone, with a basket

FRIAR

Now, ere the sun advance his burning eye
The day to cheer and night's dank dew to dry,
I must up-fill this osier cage of ours
With baleful weeds and precious-juicèd flowers.
The earth that's nature's mother is her tomb.
What is her burying grave, that is her womb;
And from her womb children of divers kind
We sucking on her natural bosom find,
Many for many virtues excellent,

10 None but for some, and yet all different.
O mickle is the powerful grace that lies
In plants, herbs, stones, and their true qualities.
For naught so vile that on the earth doth live
But to the earth some special good doth give;
Nor aught so good but, strained from that fair use,
Revolts from true birth, stumbling on abuse.
Virtue itself turns vice, being misapplied,
And vice sometime's by action dignified.
Within the infant rind of this weak flower

20 Poison hath residence, and medicine power.
For this, being smelt, with that part cheers each part;
Being tasted, stays all senses with the heart.
Two such opposèd kings encamp them still
In man as well as herbs – grace and rude will.
And where the worser is predominant,
Full soon the canker death eats up that plant.

Enter Romeo

ROMEO

Good morrow, father.

FRIAR   Benedicite!
What early tongue so sweet saluteth me?
Young son, it argues a distempered head

92

So soon to bid good morrow to thy bed.   30
Care keeps his watch in every old man's eye,
And where care lodges, sleep will never lie.
But where unbruisèd youth with unstuffed brain
Doth couch his limbs, there golden sleep doth reign.
Therefore thy earliness doth me assure
Thou art uproused with some distemperature.
Or if not so, then here I hit it right –
Our Romeo hath not been in bed tonight.

ROMEO

The last is true. The sweeter rest was mine.

FRIAR

God pardon sin! Wast thou with Rosaline?   40

ROMEO

With Rosaline, my ghostly father? No.
I have forgot that name and that name's woe.

FRIAR

That's my good son! But where hast thou been then?

ROMEO

I'll tell thee ere thou ask it me again.
I have been feasting with mine enemy,
Where on a sudden one hath wounded me
That's by me wounded. Both our remedies
Within thy help and holy physic lies.
I bear no hatred, blessèd man, for, lo,
My intercession likewise steads my foe.   50

FRIAR

Be plain, good son, and homely in thy drift.
Riddling confession finds but riddling shrift.

ROMEO

Then plainly know my heart's dear love is set
On the fair daughter of rich Capulet.
As mine on hers, so hers is set on mine,
And all combined, save what thou must combine

By holy marriage. When, and where, and how
We met, we wooed, and made exchange of vow,
I'll tell thee as we pass. But this I pray,
60 That thou consent to marry us today.

FRIAR

Holy Saint Francis! What a change is here!
Is Rosaline, that thou didst love so dear,
So soon forsaken? Young men's love then lies
Not truly in their hearts, but in their eyes.
Jesu Maria! What a deal of brine
Hath washed thy sallow cheeks for Rosaline!
How much salt water thrown away in waste
To season love, that of it doth not taste!
The sun not yet thy sighs from heaven clears.
70 Thy old groans yet ring in mine ancient ears.
Lo, here upon thy cheek the stain doth sit
Of an old tear that is not washed off yet.
If e'er thou wast thyself, and these woes thine,
Thou and these woes were all for Rosaline.
And art thou changed? Pronounce this sentence then:
Women may fall when there's no strength in men.

ROMEO

Thou chidst me oft for loving Rosaline.

FRIAR

For doting, not for loving, pupil mine.

ROMEO

And badest me bury love.

FRIAR   Not in a grave
80 To lay one in, another out to have.

ROMEO

I pray thee chide me not. Her I love now
Doth grace for grace and love for love allow.
The other did not so.

FRIAR   O, she knew well

Thy love did read by rote, that could not spell.
But come, young waverer, come, go with me.
In one respect I'll thy assistant be.
For this alliance may so happy prove
To turn your households' rancour to pure love.

ROMEO

O, let us hence! I stand on sudden haste.

FRIAR

Wisely and slow. They stumble that run fast. *Exeunt* 90

4   *Enter Benvolio and Mercutio*

MERCUTIO Where the devil should this Romeo be? Came
he not home tonight?

BENVOLIO

Not to his father's. I spoke with his man.

MERCUTIO

Why, that same pale hard-hearted wench, that Rosaline,
Torments him so that he will sure run mad.

BENVOLIO

Tybalt, the kinsman to old Capulet,
Hath sent a letter to his father's house.

MERCUTIO A challenge, on my life.

BENVOLIO Romeo will answer it.

MERCUTIO Any man that can write may answer a letter. 10

BENVOLIO Nay, he will answer the letter's master, how he
dares, being dared.

MERCUTIO Alas, poor Romeo, he is already dead! –
stabbed with a white wench's black eye; run through the
ear with a love song; the very pin of his heart cleft with
the blind bow-boy's butt-shaft. And is he a man to encounter Tybalt?

BENVOLIO Why, what is Tybalt!

MERCUTIO More than Prince of Cats, I can tell you. O,

20 he's the courageous captain of compliments. He fights as
you sing pricksong: keeps time, distance, and proportion. He rests his minim rests, one, two, and the third in
your bosom. The very butcher of a silk button. A duellist, a duellist. A gentleman of the very first house, of the
first and second cause. Ah, the immortal *passado*! the
punto reverso! the *hay*!

BENVOLIO The what?

MERCUTIO The pox of such antic, lisping, affecting fantasticoes, these new tuners of accent! 'By Jesu, a very
30 good blade! a very tall man! a very good whore!' Why, is
not this a lamentable thing, grandsire, that we should be
thus afflicted with these strange flies, these fashion-
mongers, these 'pardon-me's', who stand so much on the
new form that they cannot sit at ease on the old bench?
O their bones, their bones!

Enter Romeo

BENVOLIO Here comes Romeo, here comes Romeo!

MERCUTIO Without his roe, like a dried herring. O flesh,
flesh, how art thou fishified! Now is he for the numbers
that Petrarch flowed in. Laura, to his lady, was a kitchen
40 wench – marry, she had a better love to berhyme her –
Dido a dowdy, Cleopatra a gypsy, Helen and Hero
hildings and harlots, Thisbe a grey eye or so, but not to
the purpose. Signor Romeo, *bon jour*. There's a French
salutation to your French slop. You gave us the counterfeit fairly last night.

ROMEO Good morrow to you both. What counterfeit did I
give you?

MERCUTIO The slip, sir, the slip. Can you not conceive?

ROMEO Pardon, good Mercutio. My business was great,
50 and in such a case as mine a man may strain courtesy.

MERCUTIO That's as much as to say, such a case as yours
constrains a man to bow in the hams.

ROMEO Meaning, to curtsy.

MERCUTIO Thou hast most kindly hit it.

ROMEO A most courteous exposition.

MERCUTIO Nay, I am the very pink of courtesy.

ROMEO Pink for flower.

MERCUTIO Right.

ROMEO Why, then is my pump well-flowered.

MERCUTIO Sure wit, follow me this jest now till thou hast 60
worn out thy pump, that, when the single sole of it
is worn, the jest may remain, after the wearing, solely
singular.

ROMEO O single-soled jest, solely singular for the single-
ness!

MERCUTIO Come between us, good Benvolio! My wits
faint.

ROMEO Swits and spurs, swits and spurs! or I'll cry a
match.

MERCUTIO Nay, if our wits run the wild-goose chase, I 70
am done. For thou hast more of the wild goose in one of
thy wits than, I am sure, I have in my whole five. Was I
with you there for the goose?

ROMEO Thou wast never with me for anything when
thou wast not there for the goose.

MERCUTIO I will bite thee by the ear for that jest.

ROMEO Nay, good goose, bite not.

MERCUTIO Thy wit is a very bitter sweeting. It is a most
sharp sauce.

ROMEO And is it not, then, well served in to a sweet 80
goose?

MERCUTIO O, here's a wit of cheverel, that stretches from
an inch narrow to an ell broad!

ROMEO I stretch it out for that word 'broad', which, added
to the goose, proves thee far and wide a broad goose.

MERCUTIO Why, is not this better now than groaning for

love? Now art thou sociable. Now art thou Romeo. Now
art thou what thou art, by art as well as by nature. For
this drivelling love is like a great natural that runs lolling
90 up and down to hide his bauble in a hole.

BENVOLIO Stop there, stop there!

MERCUTIO Thou desirest me to stop in my tale against
the hair.

BENVOLIO Thou wouldst else have made thy tale large.

MERCUTIO O, thou art deceived! I would have made it
short; for I was come to the whole depth of my tale, and
meant indeed to occupy the argument no longer.

ROMEO Here's goodly gear!

Enter Nurse and her man, Peter

A sail, a sail!

100 MERCUTIO Two, two. A shirt and a smock.

NURSE Peter!

PETER Anon.

NURSE My fan, Peter.

MERCUTIO Good Peter, to hide her face. For her fan's the
fairer face.

NURSE God ye good-morrow, gentlemen.

MERCUTIO God ye good-e'en, fair gentlewoman.

NURSE Is it good-e'en?

MERCUTIO 'Tis no less, I tell ye. For the bawdy hand of
110 the dial is now upon the prick of noon.

NURSE Out upon you! What a man are you!

ROMEO One, gentlewoman, that God hath made for himself to mar.

NURSE By my troth, it is well said. 'For himself to mar',
quoth 'a? Gentlemen, can any of you tell me where I
may find the young Romeo?

ROMEO I can tell you. But young Romeo will be older
when you have found him than he was when you sought
him. I am the youngest of that name, for fault of a
120 worse.

NURSE You say well.

MERCUTIO Yea, is the worst well? Very well took, i'faith,
wisely, wisely!

NURSE If you be he, sir, I desire some confidence with
you.

BENVOLIO She will endite him to some supper.

MERCUTIO A bawd, a bawd, a bawd! So ho!

ROMEO What hast thou found?

MERCUTIO No hare, sir; unless a hare, sir, in a lenten pie,
that is something stale and hoar ere it be spent.   130

He walks by them and sings

       An old hare hoar,
    And an old hare hoar,
   Is very good meat in Lent.
     But a hare that is hoar
     Is too much for a score
  When it hoars ere it be spent.

Romeo, will you come to your father's? We'll to dinner
thither.

ROMEO I will follow you.

MERCUTIO Farewell, ancient lady. Farewell. (*He sings*)   140
Lady, lady, lady.   *Exeunt Mercutio and Benvolio*

NURSE I pray you, sir, what saucy merchant was this that
was so full of his ropery?

ROMEO A gentleman, Nurse, that loves to hear himself
talk and will speak more in a minute than he will stand
to in a month.

NURSE An 'a speak anything against me, I'll take him
down, an 'a were lustier than he is, and twenty such
Jacks; and if I cannot, I'll find those that shall. Scurvy
knave! I am none of his flirt-gills. I am none of his   150
skains-mates. (*She turns to Peter her man*) And thou
must stand by too, and suffer every knave to use me at
his pleasure!

PETER I saw no man use you at his pleasure. If I had, my
weapon should quickly have been out. I warrant you,
I dare draw as soon as another man, if I see occasion in
a good quarrel, and the law on my side.

NURSE Now, afore God, I am so vexed that every part
about me quivers. Scurvy knave! Pray you, sir, a word;
160 and, as I told you, my young lady bid me inquire you
out. What she bid me say, I will keep to myself. But
first let me tell ye, if ye should lead her in a fool's paradise, as they say, it were a very gross kind of behaviour,
as they say. For the gentlewoman is young; and therefore, if you should deal double with her, truly it were an
ill thing to be offered to any gentlewoman, and very
weak dealing.

ROMEO Nurse, commend me to thy lady and mistress. I
protest unto thee –

170 NURSE Good heart, and i'faith I will tell her as much.
Lord, Lord! She will be a joyful woman.

ROMEO What wilt thou tell her, Nurse? Thou dost not
mark me.

NURSE I will tell her, sir, that you do protest, which, as I
take it, is a gentlemanlike offer.

ROMEO
Bid her devise
Some means to come to shrift this afternoon,
And there she shall at Friar Laurence' cell
Be shrived and married. Here is for thy pains.

NURSE
180 No, truly, sir. Not a penny.

ROMEO
Go to! I say you shall.

NURSE
This afternoon, sir? Well, she shall be there.

ROMEO

    And stay, good Nurse, behind the abbey wall.
    Within this hour my man shall be with thee
    And bring thee cords made like a tackled stair,
    Which to the high topgallant of my joy
    Must be my convoy in the secret night.
    Farewell. Be trusty, and I'll quit thy pains.
    Farewell. Commend me to thy mistress.

NURSE

    Now God in heaven bless thee! Hark you, sir.   190

ROMEO

    What sayest thou, my dear Nurse?

NURSE

    Is your man secret? Did you ne'er hear say,
    Two may keep counsel, putting one away?

ROMEO

    Warrant thee my man's as true as steel.

NURSE Well, sir, my mistress is the sweetest lady. Lord, Lord! when 'twas a little prating thing – O there is a nobleman in town, one Paris, that would fain lay knife aboard. But she, good soul, had as lief see a toad, a very toad, as see him. I anger her sometimes, and tell her that Paris is the properer man. But I'll warrant you, when I   200 say so, she looks as pale as any clout in the versal world. Doth not rosemary and Romeo begin both with a letter?

ROMEO Ay, Nurse. What of that? Both with an 'R'.

NURSE Ah, mocker! That's the dog's name. 'R' is for the – No, I know it begins with some other letter; and she hath the prettiest sententious of it, of you and rosemary, that it would do you good to hear it.

ROMEO Commend me to thy lady.   *Exit Romeo*

NURSE Ay, a thousand times. Peter!

PETER Anon.   210

NURSE Before, and apace.   *Exeunt*

JULIET

The clock struck nine when I did send the Nurse.
In half an hour she promised to return.
Perchance she cannot meet him. That's not so.
O, she is lame! Love's heralds should be thoughts,
Which ten times faster glides than the sun's beams
Driving back shadows over louring hills.
Therefore do nimble-pinioned doves draw love,
And therefore hath the wind-swift Cupid wings.
Now is the sun upon the highmost hill

10 Of this day's journey, and from nine till twelve
Is three long hours, yet she is not come.
Had she affections and warm youthful blood,
She would be as swift in motion as a ball.
My words would bandy her to my sweet love,
And his to me.
But old folks, many feign as they were dead –
Unwieldy, slow, heavy and pale as lead.

Enter Nurse and Peter

O God, she comes! O honey Nurse, what news?
Hast thou met with him? Send thy man away.

NURSE

20 Peter, stay at the gate.   *Exit Peter*

JULIET

Now, good sweet Nurse – O Lord, why lookest thou sad?
Though news be sad, yet tell them merrily.
If good, thou shamest the music of sweet news
By playing it to me with so sour a face.

NURSE

I am aweary. Give me leave a while.
Fie, how my bones ache! What a jaunce have I!

JULIET

I would thou hadst my bones, and I thy news.
Nay, come, I pray thee speak. Good, good Nurse, speak.

NURSE

    Jesu, what haste! Can you not stay a while?
    Do you not see that I am out of breath?   30

JULIET

    How art thou out of breath when thou hast breath
    To say to me that thou art out of breath?
    The excuse that thou dost make in this delay
    Is longer than the tale thou dost excuse.
    Is thy news good or bad? Answer to that.
    Say either, and I'll stay the circumstance.
    Let me be satisfied, is't good or bad?

NURSE Well, you have made a simple choice. You know
    not how to choose a man. Romeo? No, not he. Though
    his face be better than any man's, yet his leg excels all 40
    men's; and for a hand and a foot, and a body, though
    they be not to be talked on, yet they are past compare.
    He is not the flower of courtesy, but, I'll warrant him, as
    gentle as a lamb. Go thy ways, wench. Serve God. What,
    have you dined at home?

JULIET

    No, no. But all this did I know before.
    What says he of our marriage? What of that?

NURSE

    Lord, how my head aches! What a head have I!
    It beats as it would fall in twenty pieces.
    My back a't'other side – ah, my back, my back!   50
    Beshrew your heart for sending me about
    To catch my death with jaunceing up and down!

JULIET

    I'faith, I am sorry that thou art not well.
    Sweet, sweet, sweet Nurse, tell me, what says my love?

NURSE Your love says, like an honest gentleman, and a
    courteous, and a kind, and a handsome, and, I warrant,
    a virtuous – Where is your mother?

shriven — отпущение
исповедь   грехов
(sin)

JULIET

Where is my mother? Why, she is within.
Where should she be? How oddly thou repliest!
60 'Your love says, like an honest gentleman,
"Where is your mother?" '

NURSE   O God's Lady dear!
Are you so hot? Marry come up, I trow.
Is this the poultice for my aching bones?
Henceforward do your messages yourself.

JULIET

Here's such a coil! Come, what says Romeo?

NURSE

Have you got leave to go to shrift today?

JULIET

I have.

NURSE

Then hie you hence to Friar Laurence' cell.
There stays a husband to make you a wife.
70 Now comes the wanton blood up in your cheeks.
They'll be in scarlet straight at any news.
Hie you to church. I must another way,
To fetch a ladder, by the which your love
Must climb a bird's nest soon when it is dark.
I am the drudge, and toil in your delight.
But you shall bear the burden soon at night.
Go. I'll to dinner. Hie you to the cell.

JULIET

Hie to high fortune! Honest Nurse, farewell.   *Exeunt*

II.6   *Enter Friar Laurence and Romeo*

FRIAR

So smile the heavens upon this holy act
That after-hours with sorrow chide us not!

ROMEO

   Amen, amen! But come what sorrow can,
   It cannot countervail the exchange of joy
   That one short minute gives me in her sight.
   Do thou but close our hands with holy words,
   Then love-devouring death do what he dare –
   It is enough I may but call her mine.

FRIAR

   These violent delights have violent ends
   And in their triumph die, like fire and powder,   10
   Which as they kiss consume. The sweetest honey
   Is loathsome in his own deliciousness
   And in the taste confounds the appetite.
   Therefore love moderately. Long love doth so.
   Too swift arrives as tardy as too slow.
      Enter Juliet somewhat fast. She embraces Romeo
   Here comes the lady. O, so light a foot
   Will ne'er wear out the everlasting flint.
   A lover may bestride the gossamers
   That idles in the wanton summer air,
   And yet not fall. So light is vanity.   20

JULIET

   Good even to my ghostly confessor.

FRIAR

   Romeo shall thank thee, daughter, for us both.

JULIET

   As much to him, else is his thanks too much.

ROMEO

   Ah, Juliet, if the measure of thy joy
   Be heaped like mine, and that thy skill be more
   To blazon it, then sweeten with thy breath
   This neighbour air, and let rich music's tongue
   Unfold the imagined happiness that both
   Receive in either by this dear encounter.

JULIET

30   Conceit, more rich in matter than in words,
Brags of his substance, not of ornament.
They are but beggars that can count their worth.
But my true love is grown to such excess
I cannot sum up sum of half my wealth.

FRIAR

Come, come with me, and we will make short work.
For, by your leaves, you shall not stay alone
Till Holy Church incorporate two in one.   *Exeunt*

*

III.1   *Enter Mercutio, Benvolio, and their men*

BENVOLIO

I pray thee, good Mercutio, let's retire.
The day is hot, the Capels are abroad.
And if we meet we shall not 'scape a brawl,
For now, these hot days, is the mad blood stirring.

MERCUTIO Thou art like one of these fellows that, when
he enters the confines of a tavern, claps me his sword
upon the table and says 'God send me no need of thee!',
and by the operation of the second cup draws him on the
drawer, when indeed there is no need.

10 BENVOLIO Am I like such a fellow?

MERCUTIO Come, come, thou art as hot a Jack in thy
mood as any in Italy; and as soon moved to be moody,
and as soon moody to be moved.

BENVOLIO And what to?

MERCUTIO Nay, an there were two such, we should have
none shortly, for one would kill the other. Thou! Why,
thou wilt quarrel with a man that hath a hair more or a
hair less in his beard than thou hast. Thou wilt quarrel
with a man for cracking nuts, having no other reason but

106

because thou hast hazel eyes. What eye but such an eye 40
would spy out such a quarrel? Thy head is as full of
quarrels as an egg is full of meat; and yet thy head hath
been beaten as addle as an egg for quarrelling. Thou
hast quarrelled with a man for coughing in the street,
because he hath wakened thy dog that hath lain asleep in
the sun. Didst thou not fall out with a tailor for wearing
his new doublet before Easter; with another for tying
his new shoes with old riband? And yet thou wilt tutor
me from quarrelling!

BENVOLIO An I were so apt to quarrel as thou art, any 30
man should buy the fee simple of my life for an hour
and a quarter.

MERCUTIO The fee simple? O simple!

Enter Tybalt and others

BENVOLIO By my head, here comes the Capulets.

MERCUTIO By my heel, I care not.

TYBALT
Follow me close, for I will speak to them.
Gentlemen, good-e'en. A word with one of you.

MERCUTIO And but one word with one of us? Couple it
with something. Make it a word and a blow.

TYBALT You shall find me apt enough to that, sir, an you 40
will give me occasion.

MERCUTIO Could you not take some occasion without
giving?

TYBALT
Mercutio, thou consortest with Romeo.

MERCUTIO Consort? What, dost thou make us minstrels?
An thou make minstrels of us, look to hear nothing but
discords. Here's my fiddlestick. Here's that shall make
you dance. Zounds, consort!

BENVOLIO
We talk here in the public haunt of men.

50   Either withdraw unto some private place,
     Or reason coldly of your grievances,
     Or else depart. Here all eyes gaze on us.

MERCUTIO
     Men's eyes were made to look, and let them gaze.
     I will not budge for no man's pleasure, I.
              Enter Romeo

TYBALT
     Well, peace be with you, sir. Here comes my man.

MERCUTIO
     But I'll be hanged, sir, if he wear your livery.
     Marry, go before to field, he'll be your follower!
     Your worship in that sense may call him 'man'.

TYBALT
     Romeo, the love I bear thee can afford
60   No better term than this: thou art a villain.

ROMEO
     Tybalt, the reason that I have to love thee
     Doth much excuse the appertaining rage
     To such a greeting. Villain am I none.
     Therefore farewell, I see thou knowest me not.

TYBALT
     Boy, this shall not excuse the injuries
     That thou hast done me. Therefore turn and draw.

ROMEO
     I do protest I never injured thee,
     But love thee better than thou canst devise
     Till thou shalt know the reason of my love.
70   And so, good Capulet, which name I tender
     As dearly as mine own, be satisfied.

MERCUTIO
     O calm, dishonourable, vile submission!
     Alla stoccata carries it away.
              He draws

Tybalt, you ratcatcher, will you walk?

TYBALT

What wouldst thou have with me?

MERCUTIO Good King of Cats, nothing but one of your
nine lives. That I mean to make bold withal, and, as you
shall use me hereafter, dry-beat the rest of the eight.
Will you pluck your sword out of his pilcher by the ears?
Make haste, lest mine be about your ears ere it be out. 80

TYBALT

I am for you.
He draws

ROMEO

Gentle Mercutio, put thy rapier up.

MERCUTIO

Come, sir, your *passado*!
They fight

ROMEO

Draw, Benvolio. Beat down their weapons.
Gentlemen, for shame! Forbear this outrage!
Tybalt, Mercutio, the Prince expressly hath
Forbid this bandying in Verona streets.
Hold, Tybalt! Good Mercutio!
Tybalt under Romeo's arm thrusts Mercutio

A FOLLOWER

Away, Tybalt!
Exit Tybalt with his followers

MERCUTIO

I am hurt. 90
A plague a'both houses! I am sped.
Is he gone and hath nothing?

BENVOLIO   What, art thou hurt?

MERCUTIO

Ay, ay, a scratch, a scratch. Marry, 'tis enough.
Where is my page? Go, villain, fetch a surgeon.
Exit Page

ROMEO

Courage, man. The hurt cannot be much.

MERCUTIO No, 'tis not so deep as a well, nor so wide as
a church door. But 'tis enough. 'Twill serve. Ask for me
tomorrow, and you shall find me a grave man. I am peppered, I warrant, for this world. A plague a'both your
houses! Zounds, a dog, a rat, a mouse, a cat, to scratch
a man to death! A braggart, a rogue, a villain, that fights
by the book of arithmetic! Why the devil came you between us? I was hurt under your arm.

ROMEO

I thought all for the best.

MERCUTIO

Help me into some house, Benvolio,
Or I shall faint. A plague a'both your houses!
They have made worms' meat of me.
I have it, and soundly too. Your houses!

Exit Mercutio with Benvolio

ROMEO

This gentleman, the Prince's near ally,
My very friend, hath got this mortal hurt
In my behalf – my reputation stained
With Tybalt's slander – Tybalt, that an hour
Hath been my cousin. O sweet Juliet,
Thy beauty hath made me effeminate
And in my temper softened valour's steel!

Enter Benvolio

BENVOLIO

O Romeo, Romeo, brave Mercutio is dead!
That gallant spirit hath aspired the clouds,
Which too untimely here did scorn the earth.

ROMEO

This day's black fate on more days doth depend.
This but begins the woe others must end.

Enter Tybalt

BENVOLIO

Here comes the furious Tybalt back again.

ROMEO

Alive in triumph, and Mercutio slain!
Away to heaven respective lenity,
And fire-eyed fury be my conduct now!
Now, Tybalt, take the 'villain' back again
That late thou gavest me. For Mercutio's soul
Is but a little way above our heads,
Staying for thine to keep him company.
Either thou or I, or both, must go with him.

TYBALT

Thou, wretched boy, that didst consort him here, 130
Shalt with him hence.

ROMEO   This shall determine that.

They fight. Tybalt falls

BENVOLIO

Romeo, away, be gone!
The citizens are up, and Tybalt slain.
Stand not amazed. The Prince will doom thee death
If thou art taken. Hence, be gone, away!

ROMEO

O, I am fortune's fool!

BENVOLIO   Why dost thou stay?

Exit Romeo

Enter Citizens

CITIZENS

Which way ran he that killed Mercutio?
Tybalt, that murderer, which way ran he?

BENVOLIO

There lies that Tybalt.

CITIZEN   Up, sir, go with me.
I charge thee in the Prince's name obey. 140

III.1

Enter Prince, Montague, Capulet, their wives, and all

PRINCE

Where are the vile beginners of this fray?

BENVOLIO

O noble Prince, I can discover all
The unlucky manage of this fatal brawl.
There lies the man, slain by young Romeo,
That slew thy kinsman, brave Mercutio.

LADY CAPULET

Tybalt, my cousin! O my brother's child!
O Prince! O cousin! Husband! O, the blood is spilled
Of my dear kinsman! Prince, as thou art true,
For blood of ours shed blood of Montague.

150   O cousin, cousin!

PRINCE

Benvolio, who began this bloody fray?

BENVOLIO

Tybalt, here slain, whom Romeo's hand did slay.
Romeo, that spoke him fair, bid him bethink
How nice the quarrel was, and urged withal
Your high displeasure. All this – utterèd
With gentle breath, calm look, knees humbly bowed –
Could not take truce with the unruly spleen
Of Tybalt deaf to peace, but that he tilts
With piercing steel at bold Mercutio's breast;

160   Who, all as hot, turns deadly point to point,
And, with a martial scorn, with one hand beats
Cold death aside and with the other sends
It back to Tybalt, whose dexterity
Retorts it. Romeo he cries aloud,
'Hold, friends! Friends, part!' and swifter than his
        tongue
His agile arm beats down their fatal points,
And 'twixt them rushes; underneath whose arm

An envious thrust from Tybalt hit the life
Of stout Mercutio, and then Tybalt fled.
But by and by comes back to Romeo,   170
Who had but newly entertained revenge,
And to't they go like lightning. For, ere I
Could draw to part them, was stout Tybalt slain.
And as he fell, did Romeo turn and fly.
This is the truth, or let Benvolio die.

LADY CAPULET
He is a kinsman to the Montague.
Affection makes him false. He speaks not true.
Some twenty of them fought in this black strife,
And all those twenty could but kill one life.
I beg for justice, which thou, Prince, must give.   180
Romeo slew Tybalt. Romeo must not live.

PRINCE
Romeo slew him. He slew Mercutio.
Who now the price of his dear blood doth owe?

MONTAGUE
Not Romeo, Prince. He was Mercutio's friend;
His fault concludes but what the law should end,
The life of Tybalt.

PRINCE   And for that offence
Immediately we do exile him hence.
I have an interest in your hate's proceeding,
My blood for your rude brawls doth lie a-bleeding.
But I'll amerce you with so strong a fine   190
That you shall all repent the loss of mine.
I will be deaf to pleading and excuses.
Nor tears nor prayers shall purchase out abuses.
Therefore use none. Let Romeo hence in haste,
Else, when he is found, that hour is his last.
Bear hence this body, and attend our will.
Mercy but murders, pardoning those that kill. *Exeunt*

Enter Juliet alone

JULIET

> Gallop apace, you fiery-footed steeds,
> Towards Phoebus' lodging! Such a waggoner
> As Phaëton would whip you to the West
> And bring in cloudy night immediately.
> Spread thy close curtain, love-performing night,
> That runaway's eyes may wink, and Romeo
> Leap to these arms untalked of and unseen.
> Lovers can see to do their amorous rites
> By their own beauties; or, if love be blind,
> It best agrees with night. Come, civil night,
> Thou sober-suited matron, all in black,
> And learn me how to lose a winning match,
> Played for a pair of stainless maidenhoods.
> Hood my unmanned blood, bating in my cheeks,
> With thy black mantle till strange love grow bold,
> Think true love acted simple modesty.
> Come, night. Come, Romeo. Come, thou day in night;
> For thou wilt lie upon the wings of night
> Whiter than new snow upon a raven's back.
> Come, gentle night. Come, loving, black-browed night.
> Give me my Romeo. And when I shall die,
> Take him and cut him out in little stars,
> And he will make the face of heaven so fine
> That all the world will be in love with night
> And pay no worship to the garish sun.
> O I have bought the mansion of a love,
> But not possessed it; and though I am sold,
> Not yet enjoyed. So tedious is this day
> As is the night before some festival
> To an impatient child that hath new robes
> And may not wear them.

Enter Nurse, wringing her hands, with the ladder of cords

O here comes my Nurse,
And she brings news; and every tongue that speaks
But Romeo's name speaks heavenly eloquence.
Now, Nurse, what news? What, hast thou there the
    cords
That Romeo bid thee fetch?

NURSE   Ay, ay, the cords.

   She throws them down

JULIET
Ay me! what news? Why dost thou wring thy hands?

NURSE
Ah, weraday! He's dead, he's dead, he's dead!
We are undone, lady, we are undone!
Alack the day! he's gone, he's killed, he's dead!

JULIET
Can heaven be so envious?

NURSE   Romeo can,   40
Though heaven cannot. O Romeo, Romeo!
Who ever would have thought it? Romeo!

JULIET
What devil art thou that dost torment me thus?
This torture should be roared in dismal hell.
Hath Romeo slain himself? Say thou but 'Ay',
And that bare vowel 'I' shall poison more
Than the death-darting eye of cockatrice.
I am not I, if there be such an 'I'
Or those eyes shut that makes thee answer 'Ay'.
If he be slain, say 'Ay'; or if not, 'No'.   50
Brief sounds determine of my weal or woe.

NURSE
I saw the wound. I saw it with mine eyes –
God save the mark! – here on his manly breast.
A piteous corse, a bloody piteous corse;
Pale, pale as ashes, all bedaubed in blood,

All in gore-blood. I swounded at the sight.

JULIET

O, break, my heart! Poor bankrupt, break at once!
To prison, eyes; ne'er look on liberty!
Vile earth, to earth resign; end motion here,
60   And thou and Romeo press one heavy bier!

NURSE

O Tybalt, Tybalt, the best friend I had!
O courteous Tybalt, honest gentleman!
That ever I should live to see thee dead!

JULIET

What storm is this that blows so contrary?
Is Romeo slaughtered, and is Tybalt dead,
My dearest cousin and my dearer lord?
Then, dreadful trumpet, sound the General Doom!
For who is living, if those two are gone?

NURSE

Tybalt is gone, and Romeo banishèd;
70   Romeo that killed him, he is banishèd.

JULIET

O God! Did Romeo's hand shed Tybalt's blood?

NURSE

It did, it did! Alas the day, it did!

JULIET

O serpent heart, hid with a flowering face!
Did ever dragon keep so fair a cave?
Beautiful tyrant! fiend angelical!
Dove-feathered raven! Wolvish-ravening lamb!
Despisèd substance of divinest show!
Just opposite to what thou justly seemest –
A damnèd saint, an honourable villain!
80   O nature, what hadst thou to do in hell
When thou didst bower the spirit of a fiend
In mortal paradise of such sweet flesh?

Was ever book containing such vile matter
So fairly bound? O, that deceit should dwell
In such a gorgeous palace!

NURSE   There's no trust,
No faith, no honesty in men; all perjured,
All forsworn, all naught, all dissemblers.
Ah, where's my man? Give me some aqua vitae.
These griefs, these woes, these sorrows make me old.
Shame come to Romeo!

JULIET   Blistered be thy tongue   90
For such a wish! He was not born to shame.
Upon his brow shame is ashamed to sit.
For 'tis a throne where honour may be crowned
Sole monarch of the universal earth.
O, what a beast was I to chide at him!

NURSE
Will you speak well of him that killed your cousin?

JULIET
Shall I speak ill of him that is my husband?
Ah, poor my lord, what tongue shall smooth thy name
When I, thy three-hours wife, have mangled it?
But wherefore, villain, didst thou kill my cousin?   100
That villain cousin would have killed my husband.
Back, foolish tears, back to your native spring!
Your tributary drops belong to woe,
Which you, mistaking, offer up to joy.
My husband lives, that Tybalt would have slain;
And Tybalt's dead, that would have slain my husband.
All this is comfort. Wherefore weep I then?
Some word there was, worser than Tybalt's death,
That murdered me. I would forget it fain.
But O, it presses to my memory   110
Like damnèd guilty deeds to sinners' minds!
'Tybalt is dead, and Romeo – banishèd.'

That 'banishèd', that one word 'banishèd',
Hath slain ten thousand Tybalts. Tybalt's death
Was woe enough, if it had ended there;
Or, if sour woe delights in fellowship
And needly will be ranked with other griefs,
Why followed not, when she said 'Tybalt's dead',
Thy father, or thy mother, nay, or both,
120 Which modern lamentation might have moved?
But with a rearward following Tybalt's death,
'Romeo is banishèd' – to speak that word
Is father, mother, Tybalt, Romeo, Juliet,
All slain, all dead. 'Romeo is banishèd' –
There is no end, no limit, measure, bound,
In that word's death. No words can that woe sound.
Where is my father and my mother, Nurse?

NURSE

Weeping and wailing over Tybalt's corse.
Will you go to them? I will bring you thither.

JULIET

130 Wash they his wounds with tears. Mine shall be spent,
When theirs are dry, for Romeo's banishment.
Take up those cords. Poor ropes, you are beguiled,
Both you and I, for Romeo is exiled.
He made you for a highway to my bed,
But I, a maid, die maiden-widowèd.
Come, cords. Come, nurse. I'll to my wedding bed,
And death, not Romeo, take my maidenhead!

NURSE

Hie to your chamber. I'll find Romeo
To comfort you. I wot well where he is.
140 Hark ye, your Romeo will be here at night.
I'll to him. He is hid at Laurence' cell.

JULIET

O, find him! Give this ring to my true knight

118

And bid him come to take his last farewell.

Exit Juliet with Nurse

Enter Friar Laurence   III.3

FRIAR

Romeo, come forth. Come forth, thou fearful man.
Affliction is enamoured of thy parts,
And thou art wedded to calamity.

Enter Romeo

ROMEO

Father, what news? What is the Prince's doom?
What sorrow craves acquaintance at my hand
That I yet know not?

FRIAR   Too familiar

Is my dear son with such sour company.
I bring thee tidings of the Prince's doom.

ROMEO

What less than doomsday is the Prince's doom?

FRIAR

A gentler judgement vanished from his lips: 10
Not body's death, but body's banishment.

ROMEO

Ha, banishment? Be merciful, say 'death'.
For exile hath more terror in his look,
Much more than death. Do not say 'banishment'.

FRIAR

Hence from Verona art thou banishèd.
Be patient, for the world is broad and wide.

ROMEO

There is no world without Verona walls,
But purgatory, torture, hell itself.
Hence banishèd is banished from the world,
And world's exile is death. Then 'banishèd'   20

Is death mistermed. Calling death 'banishèd',
Thou cuttest my head off with a golden axe
And smilest upon the stroke that murders me.

FRIAR

O deadly sin! O rude unthankfulness!
Thy fault our law calls death. But the kind Prince,
Taking thy part, hath rushed aside the law,
And turned that black word 'death' to banishment.
This is dear mercy, and thou seest it not.

ROMEO

'Tis torture, and not mercy. Heaven is here,
30   Where Juliet lives. And every cat and dog
And little mouse, every unworthy thing,
Live here in heaven and may look on her.
But Romeo may not. More validity,
More honourable state, more courtship lives
In carrion flies than Romeo. They may seize
On the white wonder of dear Juliet's hand
And steal immortal blessing from her lips,
Who, even in pure and vestal modesty,
Still blush, as thinking their own kisses sin.
40   This may flies do, when I from this must fly.
And sayest thou yet that exile is not death?
But Romeo may not, he is banishèd.
Flies may do this but I from this must fly.
They are free men. But I am banishèd.
Hadst thou no poison mixed, no sharp-ground knife,
No sudden mean of death, though ne'er so mean,
But 'banishèd' to kill me – 'banishèd'?
O Friar, the damnèd use that word in hell.
Howling attends it! How hast thou the heart,
50   Being a divine, a ghostly confessor,
A sin-absolver, and my friend professed,
To mangle me with that word 'banishèd'?

FRIAR

Thou fond mad man, hear me a little speak.

ROMEO

O, thou wilt speak again of banishment.

FRIAR

I'll give thee armour to keep off that word –
Adversity's sweet milk, philosophy,
To comfort thee, though thou art banishèd.

ROMEO

Yet 'banishèd'? Hang up philosophy!
Unless philosophy can make a Juliet,
Displant a town, reverse a prince's doom,   60
It helps not, it prevails not. Talk no more.

FRIAR

O, then I see that madmen have no ears.

ROMEO

How should they, when that wise men have no eyes?

FRIAR

Let me dispute with thee of thy estate.

ROMEO

Thou canst not speak of that thou dost not feel.
Wert thou as young as I, Juliet thy love,
An hour but married, Tybalt murderèd,
Doting like me, and like me banishèd,
Then mightst thou speak; then mightst thou tear thy
          hair,
And fall upon the ground, as I do now,   70
Taking the measure of an unmade grave.
          Knock

FRIAR

Arise. One knocks. Good Romeo, hide thyself.

ROMEO

Not I; unless the breath of heartsick groans
Mist-like infold me from the search of eyes.

III.3

Knock

FRIAR

Hark, how they knock! – Who's there? – Romeo, arise.
Thou wilt be taken. – Stay awhile! – Stand up.
Knock
Run to my study. – By and by! – God's will,
What simpleness is this! – I come, I come!
Knock
Who knocks so hard? Whence come you? What's your
will?

NURSE

80 Let me come in, and you shall know my errand.
I come from Lady Juliet.

FRIAR   Welcome then.
Enter Nurse

NURSE

O holy Friar, O, tell me, holy Friar,
Where's my lady's lord, where's Romeo?

FRIAR

There on the ground, with his own tears made drunk.

NURSE

O, he is even in my mistress' case,
Just in her case! O woeful sympathy!
Piteous predicament! Even so lies she,
Blubbering and weeping, weeping and blubbering.
Stand up, stand up! Stand, an you be a man.
90 For Juliet's sake, for her sake, rise and stand!
Why should you fall into so deep an O?
He rises

ROMEO

Nurse –

NURSE   Ah sir! ah sir! Death's the end of all.

ROMEO

Spakest thou of Juliet? How is it with her?

Doth not she think me an old murderer,
Now I have stained the childhood of our joy
With blood removed but little from her own?
Where is she? and how doth she? and what says
My concealed lady to our cancelled love?

NURSE

O, she says nothing, sir, but weeps and weeps,
And now falls on her bed, and then starts up,   100
And Tybalt calls, and then on Romeo cries,
And then down falls again.

ROMEO   As if that name,
Shot from the deadly level of a gun,
Did murder her; as that name's cursèd hand
Murdered her kinsman. O, tell me, Friar, tell me,
In what vile part of this anatomy
Doth my name lodge? Tell me, that I may sack
The hateful mansion.

    He offers to stab himself, and the Nurse snatches the
    dagger away

FRIAR   Hold thy desperate hand.
Art thou a man? Thy form cries out thou art.
Thy tears are womanish. Thy wild acts denote   110
The unreasonable fury of a beast.
Unseemly woman in a seeming man!
And ill-beseeming beast in seeming both!
Thou hast amazed me. By my holy order,
I thought thy disposition better tempered.
Hast thou slain Tybalt? Wilt thou slay thyself?
And slay thy lady that in thy life lives,
By doing damnèd hate upon thyself?
Why railest thou on thy birth, the heaven, and earth?
Since birth and heaven and earth, all three, do meet   120
In thee at once; which thou at once wouldst lose.
Fie, fie, thou shamest thy shape, thy love, thy wit,

Which, like a usurer, aboundest in all,
And usest none in that true use indeed
Which should bedeck thy shape, thy love, thy wit.
Thy noble shape is but a form of wax,
Digressing from the valour of a man;
Thy dear love sworn but hollow perjury,
Killing that love which thou hast vowed to cherish;
130   Thy wit, that ornament to shape and love,
Misshapen in the conduct of them both,
Like powder in a skilless soldier's flask
Is set afire by thine own ignorance,
And thou dismembered with thine own defence.
What, rouse thee, man! Thy Juliet is alive,
For whose dear sake thou wast but lately dead.
There art thou happy. Tybalt would kill thee,
But thou slewest Tybalt. There art thou happy.
The law, that threatened death, becomes thy friend
140   And turns it to exile. There art thou happy.
A pack of blessings light upon thy back.
Happiness courts thee in her best array.
But, like a mishavèd and sullen wench,
Thou pouts upon thy fortune and thy love.
Take heed, take heed, for such die miserable.
Go, get thee to thy love, as was decreed.
Ascend her chamber. Hence and comfort her.
But look thou stay not till the Watch be set,
For then thou canst not pass to Mantua,
150   Where thou shalt live till we can find a time
To blaze your marriage, reconcile your friends,
Beg pardon of the Prince, and call thee back
With twenty hundred thousand times more joy
Than thou wentest forth in lamentation.
Go before, Nurse. Commend me to thy lady,
And bid her hasten all the house to bed,

Which heavy sorrow makes them apt unto.
Romeo is coming.

NURSE

O Lord, I could have stayed here all the night
To hear good counsel. O, what learning is! –   160
My lord, I'll tell my lady you will come.

ROMEO

Do so, and bid my sweet prepare to chide.

The Nurse begins to go in and turns back again

NURSE

Here, sir, a ring she bid me give you, sir.
Hie you, make haste, for it grows very late. *Exit Nurse*

ROMEO

How well my comfort is revived by this!

FRIAR

Go hence. Good night. And here stands all your state:
Either be gone before the Watch be set,
Or by the break of day disguised from hence.
Sojourn in Mantua. I'll find out your man,
And he shall signify from time to time   170
Every good hap to you that chances here.
Give me thy hand. 'Tis late. Farewell. Good night.

ROMEO

But that a joy past joy calls out on me,
It were a grief so brief to part with thee.
Farewell.   *Exeunt*

Enter old Capulet, his wife, and Paris   III.4

CAPULET

Things have fallen out, sir, so unluckily
That we have had no time to move our daughter.
Look you, she loved her kinsman Tybalt dearly,
And so did I. Well, we were born to die.

125

'Tis very late. She'll not come down tonight.
I promise you, but for your company,
I would have been abed an hour ago.

PARIS

These times of woe afford no times to woo.
Madam, good night. Commend me to your daughter.

LADY CAPULET

10   I will, and know her mind early tomorrow.
Tonight she's mewed up to her heaviness.

Paris offers to go in and Capulet calls him again

CAPULET

Sir Paris, I will make a desperate tender
Of my child's love. I think she will be ruled
In all respects by me. Nay more, I doubt it not.
Wife, go you to her ere you go to bed.
Acquaint her here of my son Paris' love,
And bid her – mark you me? – on Wednesday next –
But soft! what day is this?

PARIS   Monday, my lord.

CAPULET

Monday! Ha, ha! Well, Wednesday is too soon.
20   A'Thursday let it be. A'Thursday, tell her,
She shall be married to this noble earl.
Will you be ready? Do you like this haste?
We'll keep no great ado – a friend or two.
For hark you, Tybalt being slain so late,
It may be thought we held him carelessly,
Being our kinsman, if we revel much.
Therefore we'll have some half a dozen friends,
And there an end. But what say you to Thursday?

PARIS

My lord, I would that Thursday were tomorrow.

CAPULET

30   Well, get you gone. A'Thursday be it, then.

Go you to Juliet ere you go to bed.
Prepare her, wife, against this wedding day.
Farewell, my lord. – Light to my chamber, ho!
Afore me, it is so very late that we
May call it early by and by. Good night.   *Exeunt*

Enter Romeo and Juliet aloft, at the window   III.5

JULIET
  Wilt thou be gone? It is not yet near day.
  It was the nightingale, and not the lark,
  That pierced the fearful hollow of thine ear.
  Nightly she sings on yond pomegranate tree.
  Believe me, love, it was the nightingale.

ROMEO
  It was the lark, the herald of the morn;
  No nightingale. Look, love, what envious streaks
  Do lace the severing clouds in yonder East.
  Night's candles are burnt out, and jocund day
  Stands tiptoe on the misty mountain tops.
  I must be gone and live, or stay and die.

JULIET
  Yond light is not daylight; I know it, I.
  It is some meteor that the sun exhales
  To be to thee this night a torchbearer
  And light thee on thy way to Mantua.
  Therefore stay yet. Thou needest not to be gone.

ROMEO
  Let me be ta'en, let me be put to death.
  I am content, so thou wilt have it so.
  I'll say yon grey is not the morning's eye;
  'Tis but the pale reflex of Cynthia's brow.   20
  Nor that is not the lark whose notes do beat

The vaulty heaven so high above our heads.
I have more care to stay than will to go.
Come, death, and welcome! Juliet wills it so.
How is't, my soul? Let's talk. It is not day.

JULIET

It is, it is! Hie hence, be gone, away!
It is the lark that sings so out of tune,
Straining harsh discords and unpleasing sharps.
Some say the lark makes sweet division.
30   This doth not so, for she divideth us.
Some say the lark and loathèd toad change eyes.
O, now I would they had changed voices too,
Since arm from arm that voice doth us affray,
Hunting thee hence with hunt's-up to the day.
O, now be gone! More light and light it grows.

ROMEO

More light and light: more dark and dark our woes.
Enter Nurse hastily

NURSE

Madam!

JULIET

Nurse?

NURSE

Your lady mother is coming to your chamber.
40   The day is broke. Be wary. Look about.   *Exit Nurse*

JULIET

Then, window, let day in, and let life out.

ROMEO

Farewell, farewell! One kiss, and I'll descend.
He goes down

JULIET

Art thou gone so, love-lord, aye husband-friend?
I must hear from thee every day in the hour,
For in a minute there are many days.

O by this count I shall be much in years
Ere I again behold my Romeo.

ROMEO
Farewell!
I will omit no opportunity
That may convey my greetings, love, to thee.　50

JULIET
O, thinkest thou we shall ever meet again?

ROMEO
I doubt it not; and all these woes shall serve
For sweet discourses in our times to come.

JULIET
O God, I have an ill-divining soul!
Methinks I see thee, now thou art so low,
As one dead in the bottom of a tomb.
Either my eyesight fails, or thou lookest pale.

ROMEO
And trust me, love, in my eye so do you.
Dry sorrow drinks our blood. Adieu, adieu! *Exit Romeo*

JULIET
O Fortune, Fortune! All men call thee fickle.　60
If thou art fickle, what dost thou with him
That is renowned for faith? Be fickle, Fortune,
For then I hope thou wilt not keep him long
But send him back.

　　　She goes down from the window
　　　Enter Juliet's mother

LADY CAPULET　　Ho, daughter! Are you up?

JULIET
Who is't that calls? It is my lady mother.
Is she not down so late, or up so early?
What unaccustomed cause procures her hither?

LADY CAPULET
Why, how now, Juliet?

JULIET   Madam, I am not well.

LADY CAPULET

Evermore weeping for your cousin's death?
70   What, wilt thou wash him from his grave with tears?
An if thou couldst, thou couldst not make him live.
Therefore have done. Some grief shows much of love;
But much of grief shows still some want of wit.

JULIET

Yet let me weep for such a feeling loss.

LADY CAPULET

So shall you feel the loss, but not the friend
Which you weep for.

JULIET   Feeling so the loss,
I cannot choose but ever weep the friend.

LADY CAPULET

Well, girl, thou weepest not so much for his death
As that the villain lives which slaughtered him.

JULIET

What villain, madam?

80 LADY CAPULET   That same villain Romeo.

JULIET (*aside*)

Villain and he be many miles asunder. –
God pardon! I do, with all my heart.
And yet no man like he doth grieve my heart.

LADY CAPULET

That is because the traitor murderer lives.

JULIET

Ay, madam, from the reach of these my hands.
Would none but I might venge my cousin's death!

LADY CAPULET

We will have vengeance for it, fear thou not.
Then weep no more. I'll send to one in Mantua,
Where that same banished runagate doth live,
90   Shall give him such an unaccustomed dram

130

That he shall soon keep Tybalt company.
And then I hope thou wilt be satisfied.

JULIET

Indeed I never shall be satisfied
With Romeo till I behold him – dead –
Is my poor heart so for a kinsman vexed.
Madam, if you could find out but a man
To bear a poison, I would temper it –
That Romeo should, upon receipt thereof,
Soon sleep in quiet. O, how my heart abhors
To hear him named and cannot come to him,   100
To wreak the love I bore my cousin
Upon his body that hath slaughtered him!

LADY CAPULET

Find thou the means, and I'll find such a man.
But now I'll tell thee joyful tidings, girl.

JULIET

And joy comes well in such a needy time.
What are they, beseech your ladyship?

LADY CAPULET

Well, well, thou hast a careful father, child.
One who, to put thee from thy heaviness,
Hath sorted out a sudden day of joy
That thou expects not nor I looked not for.   110

JULIET

Madam, in happy time! What day is that?

LADY CAPULET

Marry, my child, early next Thursday morn
The gallant, young, and noble gentleman,
The County Paris, at Saint Peter's Church,
Shall happily make thee there a joyful bride.

JULIET

Now by Saint Peter's Church, and Peter too,
He shall not make me there a joyful bride!

I wonder at this haste, that I must wed
Ere he that should be husband comes to woo.
120 I pray you tell my lord and father, madam,
I will not marry yet; and when I do, I swear
It shall be Romeo, whom you know I hate,
Rather than Paris. These are news indeed!

LADY CAPULET

Here comes your father. Tell him so yourself,
And see how he will take it at your hands.
Enter Capulet and Nurse

CAPULET

When the sun sets the earth doth drizzle dew,
But for the sunset of my brother's son
It rains downright.
How now? A conduit, girl? What, still in tears?
130 Evermore showering? In one little body
Thou counterfeitest a bark, a sea, a wind.
For still thy eyes, which I may call the sea,
Do ebb and flow with tears. The bark thy body is,
Sailing in this salt flood. The winds, thy sighs,
Who, raging with thy tears and they with them,
Without a sudden calm will overset
Thy tempest-tossèd body. How now, wife?
Have you delivered to her our decree?

LADY CAPULET

Ay, sir. But she will none, she gives you thanks.
140 I would the fool were married to her grave!

CAPULET

Soft! Take me with you, take me with you, wife.
How? Will she none? Doth she not give us thanks?
Is she not proud? Doth she not count her blest,
Unworthy as she is, that we have wrought
So worthy a gentleman to be her bride?

JULIET

Not proud you have, but thankful that you have.

Proud can I never be of what I hate,
But thankful even for hate that is meant love.

CAPULET

How, how, how, how, chopped logic? What is this?
'Proud' – and 'I thank you' – and 'I thank you not' –   150
And yet 'not proud'? Mistress minion you,
Thank me no thankings, nor proud me no prouds,
But settle your fine joints 'gainst Thursday next
To go with Paris to Saint Peter's Church,
Or I will drag thee on a hurdle thither.
Out, you green-sickness carrion! Out, you baggage!
You tallow-face!

LADY CAPULET   Fie, fie! What, are you mad?

JULIET

Good father, I beseech you on my knees,
Hear me with patience but to speak a word.

CAPULET

Hang thee, young baggage! Disobedient wretch!   160
I tell thee what – get thee to church a'Thursday
Or never after look me in the face.
Speak not, reply not, do not answer me!
My fingers itch. Wife, we scarce thought us blest
That God had lent us but this only child.
But now I see this one is one too much,
And that we have a curse in having her.
Out on her, hilding!

NURSE   God in heaven bless her!
You are to blame, my lord, to rate her so.

CAPULET

And why, my Lady Wisdom? Hold your tongue,   170
Good Prudence. Smatter with your gossips, go!

NURSE

I speak no treason.

CAPULET   O, God-i-good-e'en!

NURSE

May not one speak?

CAPULET   Peace, you mumbling fool!

Utter your gravity o'er a gossip's bowl,

For here we need it not.

LADY CAPULET   You are too hot.

CAPULET

God's bread! It makes me mad.

Day, night; hour, tide, time; work, play;

Alone, in company; still my care hath been

To have her matched. And having now provided

180 A gentleman of noble parentage,

Of fair demesnes, youthful, and nobly trained,

Stuffed, as they say, with honourable parts,

Proportioned as one's thought would wish a man –

And then to have a wretched puling fool,

A whining mammet, in her fortune's tender,

To answer 'I'll not wed, I cannot love;

I am too young, I pray you pardon me'!

But, an you will not wed, I'll pardon you!

Graze where you will, you shall not house with me.

190 Look to't, think on't. I do not use to jest.

Thursday is near. Lay hand on heart. Advise.

An you be mine, I'll give you to my friend.

An you be not, hang, beg, starve, die in the streets,

For, by my soul, I'll ne'er acknowledge thee,

Nor what is mine shall never do thee good.

Trust to't. Bethink you. I'll not be forsworn. *Exit Capulet*

JULIET

Is there no pity sitting in the clouds

That sees into the bottom of my grief?

O sweet my mother, cast me not away!

200 Delay this marriage for a month, a week.

Or if you do not, make the bridal bed

In that dim monument where Tybalt lies.

LADY CAPULET

Talk not to me, for I'll not speak a word.
Do as thou wilt, for I have done with thee.

Exit Lady Capulet

JULIET

O God! – O Nurse, how shall this be prevented?
My husband is on earth, my faith in heaven.
How shall that faith return again to earth
Unless that husband send it me from heaven
By leaving earth? Comfort me, counsel me.
Alack, alack, that heaven should practise stratagems   210
Upon so soft a subject as myself!
What sayest thou? Hast thou not a word of joy?
Some comfort, Nurse.

NURSE   Faith, here it is.

Romeo is banished; and all the world to nothing
That he dares ne'er come back to challenge you.
Or if he do, it needs must be by stealth.
Then, since the case so stands as now it doth,
I think it best you married with the County.
O, he's a lovely gentleman!
Romeo's a dishclout to him. An eagle, madam,   220
Hath not so green, so quick, so fair an eye
As Paris hath. Beshrew my very heart,
I think you are happy in this second match,
For it excels your first; or if it did not,
Your first is dead – or 'twere as good he were
As living here and you no use of him.

JULIET

Speakest thou from thy heart?

NURSE

And from my soul too. Else beshrew them both.

JULIET

Amen!

135

NURSE

230   What?

JULIET

Well, thou hast comforted me marvellous much.
Go in; and tell my lady I am gone,
Having displeased my father, to Laurence' cell,
To make confession and to be absolved.

NURSE

Marry, I will; and this is wisely done.   *Exit Nurse*

JULIET

Ancient damnation! O most wicked fiend!
Is it more sin to wish me thus forsworn,
Or to dispraise my lord with that same tongue
Which she hath praised him with above compare
240   So many thousand times? Go, counsellor!
Thou and my bosom henceforth shall be twain.
I'll to the Friar to know his remedy.
If all else fail, myself have power to die.   *Exit*

IV.1   *Enter Friar Laurence and County Paris*

FRIAR

On Thursday, sir? The time is very short.

PARIS

My father Capulet will have it so,
And I am nothing slow to slack his haste.

FRIAR

You say you do not know the lady's mind.
Uneven is the course. I like it not.

PARIS

Immoderately she weeps for Tybalt's death,
And therefore have I little talked of love;

136

For Venus smiles not in a house of tears.
Now, sir, her father counts it dangerous
That she do give her sorrow so much sway,   10
And in his wisdom hastes our marriage
To stop the inundation of her tears,
Which, too much minded by herself alone,
May be put from her by society.
Now do you know the reason of this haste.

FRIAR (*aside*)
I would I knew not why it should be slowed. –
Look, sir, here comes the lady toward my cell.
        Enter Juliet

PARIS
Happily met, my lady and my wife!

JULIET
That may be, sir, when I may be a wife.

PARIS
That 'may be' must be, love, on Thursday next.   20

JULIET
What must be shall be.

FRIAR   That's a certain text.

PARIS
Come you to make confession to this father?

JULIET
To answer that, I should confess to you.

PARIS
Do not deny to him that you love me.

JULIET
I will confess to you that I love him.

PARIS
So will ye, I am sure, that you love me.

JULIET
If I do so, it will be of more price,
Being spoke behind your back, than to your face.

PARIS

   Poor soul, thy face is much abused with tears.

JULIET

30   The tears have got small victory by that,
   For it was bad enough before their spite.

PARIS

   Thou wrongest it more than tears with that report.

JULIET

   That is no slander, sir, which is a truth.
   And what I spake, I spake it to my face.

PARIS

   Thy face is mine, and thou hast slandered it.

JULIET

   It may be so, for it is not mine own. –
   Are you at leisure, holy father, now,
   Or shall I come to you at evening mass?

FRIAR

   My leisure serves me, pensive daughter, now. –
40   My lord, we must entreat the time alone.

PARIS

   God shield I should disturb devotion! –
   Juliet, on Thursday early will I rouse ye.
   Till then, adieu, and keep this holy kiss.   *Exit Paris*

JULIET

   O shut the door! and when thou hast done so,
   Come weep with me. Past hope, past cure, past help!

FRIAR

   O, Juliet, I already know thy grief.
   It strains me past the compass of my wits.
   I hear thou must, and nothing may prorogue it,
   On Thursday next be married to this County.

JULIET

50   Tell me not, Friar, that thou hearest of this,
   Unless thou tell me how I may prevent it.

If in thy wisdom thou canst give no help,
Do thou but call my resolution wise
And with this knife I'll help it presently.
God joined my heart and Romeo's, thou our hands;
And ere this hand, by thee to Romeo's sealed,
Shall be the label to another deed,
Or my true heart with treacherous revolt
Turn to another, this shall slay them both.
Therefore, out of thy long-experienced time,   60
Give me some present counsel; or, behold,
'Twixt my extremes and me this bloody knife
Shall play the umpire, arbitrating that
Which the commission of thy years and art
Could to no issue of true honour bring.
Be not so long to speak. I long to die
If what thou speakest speak not of remedy.

FRIAR

Hold, daughter. I do spy a kind of hope,
Which craves as desperate an execution
As that is desperate which we would prevent.   70
If, rather than to marry County Paris,
Thou hast the strength of will to slay thyself,
Then is it likely thou wilt undertake
A thing like death to chide away this shame,
That copest with death himself to 'scape from it.
And, if thou darest, I'll give thee remedy.

JULIET

O bid me leap, rather than marry Paris,
From off the battlements of any tower,
Or walk in thievish ways, or bid me lurk
Where serpents are. Chain me with roaring bears,   80
Or hide me nightly in a charnel house,
O'ercovered quite with dead men's rattling bones,
With reeky shanks and yellow chapless skulls.

Or bid me go into a new-made grave
And hide me with a dead man in his tomb –
Things that, to hear them told, have made me tremble –
And I will do it without fear or doubt,
To live an unstained wife to my sweet love.

FRIAR

Hold, then. Go home, be merry, give consent
90   To marry Paris. Wednesday is tomorrow.
Tomorrow night look that thou lie alone.
Let not the Nurse lie with thee in thy chamber.
Take thou this vial, being then in bed,
And this distilling liquor drink thou off;
When presently through all thy veins shall run
A cold and drowsy humour. For no pulse
Shall keep his native progress, but surcease.
No warmth, no breath, shall testify thou livest.
The roses in thy lips and cheeks shall fade
100   To wanny ashes, thy eyes' windows fall
Like death when he shuts up the day of life.
Each part, deprived of supple government,
Shall, stiff and stark and cold, appear like death.
And in this borrowed likeness of shrunk death
Thou shalt continue two-and-forty hours,
And then awake as from a pleasant sleep.
Now, when the bridegroom in the morning comes
To rouse thee from thy bed, there art thou dead.
Then, as the manner of our country is,
110   In thy best robes uncovered on the bier
Thou shalt be borne to that same ancient vault
Where all the kindred of the Capulets lie.
In the meantime, against thou shalt awake,
Shall Romeo by my letters know our drift.
And hither shall he come. And he and I
Will watch thy waking, and that very night

Shall Romeo bear thee hence to Mantua.
And this shall free thee from this present shame,
If no inconstant toy nor womanish fear
Abate thy valour in the acting it.   120

JULIET
Give me, give me! O tell not me of fear!

FRIAR
Hold. Get you gone. Be strong and prosperous
In this resolve. I'll send a friar with speed
To Mantua, with my letters to thy lord.

JULIET
Love give me strength, and strength shall help afford.
Farewell, dear father.   *Exeunt*

Enter Capulet, Lady Capulet, Nurse, and two or three   IV.2
    Servingmen

CAPULET
So many guests invite as here are writ. *Exit a Servingman*
Sirrah, go hire me twenty cunning cooks.

SERVINGMAN You shall have none ill, sir. For I'll try if
they can lick their fingers.

CAPULET How! Canst thou try them so?

SERVINGMAN Marry, sir, 'tis an ill cook that cannot lick
his own fingers. Therefore he that cannot lick his fingers
goes not with me.

CAPULET
Go, begone.   *Exit Servingman*
We shall be much unfurnished for this time.   10
What, is my daughter gone to Friar Laurence?

NURSE
Ay, forsooth.

CAPULET
Well, he may chance to do some good on her.

141

A peevish self-willed harlotry it is.
Enter Juliet

NURSE
See where she comes from shrift with merry look.

CAPULET
How now, my headstrong! Where have you been
    gadding?

JULIET
Where I have learnt me to repent the sin
Of disobedient opposition
To you and your behests, and am enjoined
20 By holy Laurence to fall prostrate here
To beg your pardon. Pardon, I beseech you!
Henceforward I am ever ruled by you.

CAPULET
Send for the County. Go tell him of this.
I'll have this knot knit up tomorrow morning.

JULIET
I met the youthful lord at Laurence' cell
And gave him what becomèd love I might,
Not stepping o'er the bounds of modesty.

CAPULET
Why, I am glad on't. This is well. Stand up.
This is as't should be. Let me see, the County.
30 Ay, marry, go, I say, and fetch him hither.
Now, afore God, this reverend holy Friar,
All our whole city is much bound to him.

JULIET
Nurse, will you go with me into my closet
To help me sort such needful ornaments
As you think fit to furnish me tomorrow?

LADY CAPULET
No, not till Thursday. There is time enough.

CAPULET

Go, Nurse, go with her. We'll to church tomorrow.

Exeunt Juliet and Nurse

LADY CAPULET

We shall be short in our provision.

'Tis now near night.

CAPULET   Tush, I will stir about,

And all things shall be well, I warrant thee, wife.   40

Go thou to Juliet, help to deck up her.

I'll not to bed tonight. Let me alone.

I'll play the housewife for this once. What, ho!

They are all forth. Well, I will walk myself

To County Paris, to prepare up him

Against tomorrow. My heart is wondrous light,

Since this same wayward girl is so reclaimed.   *Exeunt*

Enter Juliet and Nurse   IV.3

JULIET

Ay, those attires are best. But, gentle Nurse,

I pray thee leave me to myself tonight.

For I have need of many orisons

To move the heavens to smile upon my state,

Which, well thou knowest, is cross and full of sin.

Enter Lady Capulet

LADY CAPULET

What, are you busy, ho? Need you my help?

JULIET

No, madam. We have culled such necessaries

As are behoveful for our state tomorrow.

So please you, let me now be left alone,

And let the Nurse this night sit up with you.   10

For I am sure you have your hands full all

In this so sudden business.

LADY CAPULET   Good night.
    Go thee to bed, and rest. For thou hast need.
                            Exeunt Lady Capulet and Nurse

JULIET
    Farewell! God knows when we shall meet again.
    I have a faint cold fear thrills through my veins
    That almost freezes up the heat of life.
    I'll call them back again to comfort me.
    Nurse! – What should she do here?
    My dismal scene I needs must act alone.
20 Come, vial.
    What if this mixture do not work at all?
    Shall I be married then tomorrow morning?
    No, no! This shall forbid it. Lie thou there.
        She lays down a knife
    What if it be a poison which the Friar
    Subtly hath ministered to have me dead,
    Lest in this marriage he should be dishonoured
    Because he married me before to Romeo?
    I fear it is. And yet methinks it should not,
    For he hath still been tried a holy man.
30 How if, when I am laid into the tomb,
    I wake before the time that Romeo
    Come to redeem me? There's a fearful point!
    Shall I not then be stifled in the vault,
    To whose foul mouth no healthsome air breathes in,
    And there die strangled ere my Romeo comes?
    Or, if I live, is it not very like
    The horrible conceit of death and night,
    Together with the terror of the place –
    As in a vault, an ancient receptacle
40 Where for this many hundred years the bones
    Of all my buried ancestors are packed;
    Where bloody Tybalt, yet but green in earth,

Lies festering in his shroud; where, as they say,
At some hours in the night spirits resort –
Alack, alack, is it not like that I,
So early waking – what with loathsome smells,
And shrieks like mandrakes torn out of the earth,
That living mortals, hearing them, run mad –
O, if I wake, shall I not be distraught,
Environèd with all these hideous fears,   50
And madly play with my forefathers' joints,
And pluck the mangled Tybalt from his shroud,
And, in this rage, with some great kinsman's bone
As with a club dash out my desperate brains?
O, look! Methinks I see my cousin's ghost
Seeking out Romeo, that did spit his body
Upon a rapier's point. Stay, Tybalt, stay!
Romeo, Romeo, Romeo.
Here's drink. I drink to thee.
    She falls upon her bed within the curtains

    Enter Lady Capulet and Nurse, with herbs   IV.4

LADY CAPULET
  Hold, take these keys and fetch more spices, Nurse.

NURSE
  They call for dates and quinces in the pastry.
    Enter Capulet

CAPULET
  Come, stir, stir, stir! The second cock hath crowed.
  The curfew bell hath rung. 'Tis three o'clock.
  Look to the baked meats, good Angelica.
  Spare not for cost.

NURSE   Go, you cot-quean, go.
  Get you to bed! Faith, you'll be sick tomorrow
  For this night's watching.

CAPULET

    No, not a whit. What, I have watched ere now

10   All night for lesser cause, and ne'er been sick.

LADY CAPULET

    Ay, you have been a mouse-hunt in your time.

    But I will watch you from such watching now.

                  Exeunt Lady Capulet and Nurse

CAPULET

    A jealous hood, a jealous hood!

        Enter three or four Servingmen with spits and logs and
        baskets

                    Now, fellow,

    What is there?

FIRST SERVINGMAN

    Things for the cook, sir; but I know not what.

CAPULET

    Make haste, make haste.   *Exit First Servingman*

                Sirrah, fetch drier logs.

    Call Peter. He will show thee where they are.

SECOND SERVINGMAN

    I have a head, sir, that will find out logs

    And never trouble Peter for the matter.

CAPULET

20   Mass! and well said. A merry whoreson, ha!

    Thou shalt be loggerhead.   *Exit Second Servingman*

                Good Father! 'tis day.

    The County will be here with music straight,

    For so he said he would.

        Music plays

                  I hear him near.

    Nurse! Wife! What, ho! What, Nurse, I say!

        Enter Nurse

    Go waken Juliet. Go and trim her up.

    I'll go and chat with Paris. Hie, make haste,

Make haste! The bridegroom he is come already.
Make haste, I say.   *Exit Capulet*
    Nurse goes to curtains   IV.5

NURSE
Mistress! What, mistress! Juliet! Fast, I warrant her, she.
Why, lamb! Why, lady! Fie, you slug-abed!
Why, love, I say! Madam! Sweetheart! Why, bride!
What, not a word? You take your pennyworths now.
Sleep for a week. For the next night, I warrant,
The County Paris hath set up his rest
That you shall rest but little. God forgive me!
Marry, and amen! How sound is she asleep!
I needs must wake her. Madam, madam, madam!
Ay, let the County take you in your bed.   10
He'll fright you up, i'faith. Will it not be?
What, dressed, and in your clothes, and down again?
I must needs wake you. Lady! lady! lady!
Alas, alas! Help, help! My lady's dead!
O weraday that ever I was born!
Some aqua vitae, ho! My lord! My lady!
    Enter Lady Capulet

LADY CAPULET
What noise is here?

NURSE   O lamentable day!

LADY CAPULET
What is the matter?

NURSE   Look, look! O heavy day!

LADY CAPULET
O me, O me! My child, my only life!
Revive, look up, or I will die with thee!   20
Help, help! Call help.
    Enter Capulet

CAPULET
For shame, bring Juliet forth. Her lord is come.

147

NURSE

She's dead, deceased. She's dead, alack the day!

LADY CAPULET

Alack the day, she's dead, she's dead, she's dead!

CAPULET

Ha! let me see her. Out alas! she's cold,
Her blood is settled, and her joints are stiff.
Life and these lips have long been separated.
Death lies on her like an untimely frost
Upon the sweetest flower of all the field.

NURSE

O lamentable day!

30 **LADY CAPULET**   O woeful time!

CAPULET

Death, that hath ta'en her hence to make me wail,
Ties up my tongue and will not let me speak.

Enter Friar Laurence and the County Paris

FRIAR

Come, is the bride ready to go to church?

CAPULET

Ready to go, but never to return.
O son, the night before thy wedding day
Hath death lain with thy wife. There she lies,
Flower as she was, deflowerèd by him.
Death is my son-in-law. Death is my heir.
My daughter he hath wedded. I will die
40 And leave him all. Life, living, all is death's.

PARIS

Have I thought long to see this morning's face,
And doth it give me such a sight as this?

LADY CAPULET

Accursed, unhappy, wretched, hateful day!
Most miserable hour that e'er time saw
In lasting labour of his pilgrimage!

148

But one, poor one, one poor and loving child,
But one thing to rejoice and solace in,
And cruel death hath catched it from my sight.

NURSE

O woe! O woeful, woeful, woeful day!
Most lamentable day, most woeful day   50
That ever, ever I did yet behold!
O day, O day, O day! O hateful day!
Never was seen so black a day as this.
O woeful day! O woeful day!

PARIS

Beguiled, divorcèd, wrongèd, spited, slain!
Most detestable Death, by thee beguiled,
By cruel, cruel thee quite overthrown.
O love! O life! – not life, but love in death!

CAPULET

Despised, distressèd, hated, martyred, killed!
Uncomfortable time, why camest thou now   60
To murder, murder our solemnity?
O child! O child! my soul, and not my child!
Dead art thou – alack, my child is dead,
And with my child my joys are burièd!

FRIAR

Peace, ho, for shame! Confusion's cure lives not
In these confusions. Heaven and yourself
Had part in this fair maid. Now heaven hath all,
And all the better is it for the maid.
Your part in her you could not keep from death,
But heaven keeps his part in eternal life.   70
The most you sought was her promotion,
For 'twas your heaven she should be advanced.
And weep ye now, seeing she is advanced
Above the clouds, as high as heaven itself?
O, in this love, you love your child so ill

149

That you run mad, seeing that she is well.
She's not well married that lives married long,
But she's best married that dies married young.
Dry up your tears and stick your rosemary
80 On this fair corse, and, as the custom is,
In all her best array bear her to church.
For though fond nature bids us all lament,
Yet nature's tears are reason's merriment.

CAPULET

All things that we ordainèd festival
Turn from their office to black funeral.
Our instruments to melancholy bells;
Our wedding cheer to a sad burial feast;
Our solemn hymns to sullen dirges change;
Our bridal flowers serve for a buried corse;
90 And all things change them to the contrary.

FRIAR

Sir, go you in; and, madam, go with him;
And go, Sir Paris. Every one prepare
To follow this fair corse unto her grave.
The heavens do lour upon you for some ill.
Move them no more by crossing their high will.

*Exeunt all except the Nurse, casting
rosemary on her and shutting the curtains
Enter Musicians*

FIRST MUSICIAN

Faith, we may put up our pipes and be gone.

NURSE

Honest good fellows, ah, put up, put up!
For well you know this is a pitiful case.

FIDDLER

Ay, by my troth, the case may be amended. *Exit Nurse
Enter Peter*

100 PETER Musicians, O musicians, 'Heart's ease', 'Heart's

ease'! O, an you will have me live, play 'Heart's ease'.

FIDDLER Why 'Heart's ease'?

PETER O musicians, because my heart itself plays 'My heart is full'. O play me some merry dump to comfort me.

FIRST MUSICIAN Not a dump we! 'Tis no time to play now.

PETER You will not then?

FIRST MUSICIAN No.

PETER I will then give it you soundly.   110

FIRST MUSICIAN What will you give us?

PETER No money, on my faith, but the gleek. I will give you the minstrel.

FIRST MUSICIAN Then will I give you the serving-creature.

PETER Then will I lay the serving-creature's dagger on your pate. I will carry no crotchets. I'll re you, I'll fa you. Do you note me?

FIRST MUSICIAN An you re us and fa us, you note us.

SECOND MUSICIAN Pray you put up your dagger, and   120
put out your wit.

PETER Then have at you with my wit! I will dry-beat you with an iron wit, and put up my iron dagger. Answer me like men.

    'When griping griefs the heart doth wound,
       And doleful dumps the mind oppress,
      Then music with her silver sound' –
Why 'silver sound'? Why 'music with her silver sound'?
What say you, Simon Catling?

FIRST MUSICIAN Marry, sir, because silver hath a sweet   130
sound.

PETER Pretty! What say you, Hugh Rebeck?

SECOND MUSICIAN I say 'silver sound' because musicians sound for silver.

PETER Pretty too! What say you, James Soundpost?

THIRD MUSICIAN Faith, I know not what to say.

PETER O, I cry you mercy! You are the singer. I will say
for you. It is 'music with her silver sound' because musicians have no gold for sounding.

140   'Then music with her silver sound
             With speedy help doth lend redress.' *Exit Peter*

FIRST MUSICIAN What a pestilent knave is this same!

SECOND MUSICIAN Hang him, Jack! Come, we'll in here,
tarry for the mourners, and stay dinner.   *Exeunt*

*

V.1   *Enter Romeo*

ROMEO

If I may trust the flattering truth of sleep,
My dreams presage some joyful news at hand.
My bosom's lord sits lightly in his throne,
And all this day an unaccustomed spirit
Lifts me above the ground with cheerful thoughts.
I dreamt my lady came and found me dead –
Strange dream that gives a dead man leave to think! –
And breathed such life with kisses in my lips
That I revived and was an emperor.

10   Ah me! how sweet is love itself possessed,
When but love's shadows are so rich in joy!
        Enter Balthasar, Romeo's man, booted
News from Verona! How now, Balthasar?
Dost thou not bring me letters from the Friar?
How doth my lady? Is my father well?
How doth my lady Juliet? That I ask again,
For nothing can be ill if she be well.

BALTHASAR

Then she is well, and nothing can be ill.
Her body sleeps in Capel's monument,
And her immortal part with angels lives.
I saw her laid low in her kindred's vault   20
And presently took post to tell it you.
O, pardon me for bringing these ill news,
Since you did leave it for my office, sir.

ROMEO

Is it e'en so? Then I defy you, stars!
Thou knowest my lodging. Get me ink and paper,
And hire posthorses. I will hence tonight.

BALTHASAR

I do beseech you, sir, have patience.
Your looks are pale and wild and do import
Some misadventure.   Tush, thou art deceived.

ROMEO

Leave me and do the thing I bid thee do.   30
Hast thou no letters to me from the Friar?

BALTHASAR

No, my good lord.

ROMEO   No matter. Get thee gone
And hire those horses. I'll be with thee straight.

Exit Balthasar

Well, Juliet, I will lie with thee tonight.
Let's see for means. O mischief, thou art swift
To enter in the thoughts of desperate men.
I do remember an apothecary,
And hereabouts 'a dwells, which late I noted
In tattered weeds, with overwhelming brows,
Culling of simples. Meagre were his looks.   40
Sharp misery had worn him to the bones.
And in his needy shop a tortoise hung,
An alligator stuffed, and other skins

153

Of ill-shaped fishes; and about his shelves
A beggarly account of empty boxes,
Green earthen pots, bladders, and musty seeds,
Remnants of packthread, and old cakes of roses
Were thinly scattered, to make up a show.
Noting this penury, to myself I said,
50 'An if a man did need a poison now
Whose sale is present death in Mantua,
Here lives a caitiff wretch would sell it him.'
O, this same thought did but forerun my need,
And this same needy man must sell it me.
As I remember, this should be the house.
Being holiday, the beggar's shop is shut.
What, ho! Apothecary!

Enter Apothecary

APOTHECARY   Who calls so loud?

ROMEO

Come hither, man. I see that thou art poor.
Hold, there is forty ducats. Let me have
60 A dram of poison, such soon-speeding gear
As will disperse itself through all the veins,
That the life-weary taker may fall dead
And that the trunk may be discharged of breath
As violently as hasty powder fired
Doth hurry from the fatal cannon's womb.

APOTHECARY

Such mortal drugs I have. But Mantua's law
Is death to any he that utters them.

ROMEO

Art thou so bare and full of wretchedness
And fearest to die? Famine is in thy cheeks.
70 Need and oppression starveth in thy eyes.
Contempt and beggary hangs upon thy back.
The world is not thy friend, nor the world's law.

The world affords no law to make thee rich.
Then be not poor, but break it and take this.

APOTHECARY

My poverty but not my will consents.

ROMEO

I pay thy poverty and not thy will.

APOTHECARY

Put this in any liquid thing you will
And drink it off, and if you had the strength
Of twenty men it would dispatch you straight.

ROMEO

There is thy gold – worse poison to men's souls,   80
Doing more murder in this loathsome world,
Than these poor compounds that thou mayst not sell.
I sell thee poison. Thou hast sold me none.
Farewell. Buy food and get thyself in flesh.
Come, cordial and not poison, go with me
To Juliet's grave. For there must I use thee.   *Exeunt*

Enter Friar John   V.2

FRIAR JOHN Holy Franciscan Friar, brother, ho!
    Enter Friar Laurence

FRIAR LAURENCE

This same should be the voice of Friar John.
Welcome from Mantua. What says Romeo?
Or, if his mind be writ, give me his letter.

JOHN

Going to find a bare-foot brother out,
One of our order, to associate me
Here in this city visiting the sick,
And finding him, the searchers of the town,
Suspecting that we both were in a house
Where the infectious pestilence did reign,   10

Sealed up the doors, and would not let us forth,
So that my speed to Mantua there was stayed.

LAURENCE
Who bare my letter, then, to Romeo?

JOHN
I could not send it – here it is again –
Nor get a messenger to bring it thee,
So fearful were they of infection.

LAURENCE
Unhappy fortune! By my brotherhood,
The letter was not nice, but full of charge,
Of dear import; and the neglecting it
20   May do much danger. Friar John, go hence.
Get me an iron crow and bring it straight
Unto my cell.

JOHN   Brother, I'll go and bring it thee.

Exit Friar John

LAURENCE
Now must I to the monument alone.
Within this three hours will fair Juliet wake.
She will beshrew me much that Romeo
Hath had no notice of these accidents.
But I will write again to Mantua,
And keep her at my cell till Romeo come.
Poor living corse, closed in a dead man's tomb!   *Exit*

V.3   *Enter Paris and his Page, with flowers and sweet water*

PARIS
Give me thy torch, boy. Hence, and stand aloof.
Yet put it out, for I would not be seen.
Under yond yew trees lay thee all along,
Holding thy ear close to the hollow ground.
So shall no foot upon the churchyard tread,

Being loose, unfirm, with digging up of graves,
But thou shalt hear it. Whistle then to me,
As signal that thou hearest something approach.
Give me those flowers. Do as I bid thee, go.

PAGE (*aside*)

I am almost afraid to stand alone 10
Here in the churchyard. Yet I will adventure. *Page retires*

PARIS

Sweet flower, with flowers thy bridal bed I strew –
    O woe! thy canopy is dust and stones –
Which with sweet water nightly I will dew;
    Or, wanting that, with tears distilled by moans.
The obsequies that I for thee will keep
Nightly shall be to strew thy grave and weep.
        Page whistles
The boy gives warning something doth approach.
What cursèd foot wanders this way tonight
To cross my obsequies and true love's rite? 20
What, with a torch? Muffle me, night, awhile. *Paris retires*
        *Enter Romeo and Balthasar, with a torch, a mattock,
        and a crow of iron*

ROMEO

Give me that mattock and the wrenching iron.
Hold, take this letter. Early in the morning
See thou deliver it to my lord and father.
Give me the light. Upon thy life I charge thee,
Whate'er thou hearest or seest, stand all aloof
And do not interrupt me in my course.
Why I descend into this bed of death
Is partly to behold my lady's face,
But chiefly to take thence from her dead finger 30
A precious ring, a ring that I must use
In dear employment. Therefore hence, be gone.
But if thou, jealous, dost return to pry

In what I farther shall intend to do,
By heaven, I will tear thee joint by joint
And strew this hungry churchyard with thy limbs.
The time and my intents are savage-wild,
More fierce and more inexorable far
Than empty tigers or the roaring sea.

BALTHASAR

40 I will be gone, sir, and not trouble ye.

ROMEO

So shalt thou show me friendship. Take thou that.
Live, and be prosperous; and farewell, good fellow.

BALTHASAR (*aside*)

For all this same, I'll hide me hereabout.
His looks I fear, and his intents I doubt. *Balthasar retires*

ROMEO

Thou detestable maw, thou womb of death,
Gorged with the dearest morsel of the earth,
Thus I enforce thy rotten jaws to open,
And in despite I'll cram thee with more food.
        Romeo begins to open the tomb

PARIS

This is that banished haughty Montague
50 That murdered my love's cousin – with which grief
It is supposèd the fair creature died –
And here is come to do some villainous shame
To the dead bodies. I will apprehend him.
Stop thy unhallowed toil, vile Montague!
Can vengeance be pursued further than death?
Condemnèd villain, I do apprehend thee.
Obey, and go with me. For thou must die.

ROMEO

I must indeed; and therefore came I hither.
Good gentle youth, tempt not a desperate man.
60 Fly hence and leave me. Think upon these gone.

Let them affright thee. I beseech thee, youth,
Put not another sin upon my head
By urging me to fury. O, be gone!
By heaven, I love thee better than myself,
For I come hither armed against myself.
Stay not, be gone. Live, and hereafter say
A madman's mercy bid thee run away.

PARIS

I do defy thy conjuration
And apprehend thee for a felon here.

ROMEO

Wilt thou provoke me? Then have at thee, boy!   70
      They fight

PAGE

O Lord, they fight! I will go call the Watch. *Exit Page*
      Paris falls

PARIS

O, I am slain! If thou be merciful,
Open the tomb, lay me with Juliet.   *Paris dies*

ROMEO

In faith, I will. Let me peruse this face.
Mercutio's kinsman, noble County Paris!
What said my man when my betossèd soul
Did not attend him as we rode? I think
He told me Paris should have married Juliet.
Said he not so? Or did I dream it so?
Or am I mad, hearing him talk of Juliet,   80
To think it was so? O, give me thy hand,
One writ with me in sour misfortune's book.
I'll bury thee in a triumphant grave.
A grave? O, no, a lantern, slaughtered youth.
      He opens the tomb
For here lies Juliet, and her beauty makes
This vault a feasting presence full of light.

Death, lie thou there, by a dead man interred.
He lays him in the tomb
How oft when men are at the point of death
Have they been merry! which their keepers call
90 A lightning before death. O how may I
Call this a lightning? O my love, my wife!
Death, that hath sucked the honey of thy breath,
Hath had no power yet upon thy beauty.
Thou art not conquered. Beauty's ensign yet
Is crimson in thy lips and in thy cheeks,
And death's pale flag is not advancèd there.
Tybalt, liest thou there in thy bloody sheet?
O, what more favour can I do to thee
Than with that hand that cut thy youth in twain
100 To sunder his that was thine enemy?
Forgive me, cousin! Ah, dear Juliet,
Why art thou yet so fair? Shall I believe
That unsubstantial death is amorous,
And that the lean abhorrèd monster keeps
Thee here in dark to be his paramour?
For fear of that I still will stay with thee
And never from this palace of dim night
Depart again. Here, here will I remain
With worms that are thy chambermaids. O here
110 Will I set up my everlasting rest
And shake the yoke of inauspicious stars
From this world-wearied flesh. Eyes, look your last!
Arms, take your last embrace! and, lips, O you
The doors of breath, seal with a righteous kiss
A dateless bargain to engrossing death!
Come, bitter conduct, come, unsavoury guide!
Thou desperate pilot, now at once run on
The dashing rocks thy seasick weary bark!
Here's to my love! (*He drinks*) O true Apothecary!

Thy drugs are quick. Thus with a kiss I die.   *He falls* 120
    Enter Friar Laurence, with lantern, crow, and spade

FRIAR

Saint Francis be my speed! How oft tonight
Have my old feet stumbled at graves! Who's there?

BALTHASAR

Here's one, a friend, and one that knows you well.

FRIAR

Bliss be upon you! Tell me, good my friend,
What torch is yond that vainly lends his light
To grubs and eyeless skulls? As I discern,
It burneth in the Capels' monument.

BALTHASAR

It doth so, holy sir; and there's my master,
One that you love.

FRIAR   Who is it?

BALTHASAR   Romeo.

FRIAR

How long hath he been there?

BALTHASAR   Full half an hour.   130

FRIAR

Go with me to the vault.

BALTHASAR   I dare not, sir.
My master knows not but I am gone hence,
And fearfully did menace me with death
If I did stay to look on his intents.

FRIAR

Stay then; I'll go alone. Fear comes upon me.
O much I fear some ill unthrifty thing.

BALTHASAR

As I did sleep under this yew tree here,
I dreamt my master and another fought,
And that my master slew him.

FRIAR   Romeo!

He stoops and looks on the blood and weapons

140   Alack, alack, what blood is this which stains
The stony entrance of this sepulchre?
What mean these masterless and gory swords
To lie discoloured by this place of peace?

He enters the tomb

Romeo! O, pale! Who else? What, Paris too?
And steeped in blood? Ah, what an unkind hour
Is guilty of this lamentable chance!
The lady stirs.

Juliet rises

JULIET

O comfortable Friar! Where is my lord?
I do remember well where I should be,
150   And there I am. Where is my Romeo?

FRIAR

I hear some noise. Lady, come from that nest
Of death, contagion, and unnatural sleep.
A greater power than we can contradict
Hath thwarted our intents. Come, come away.
Thy husband in thy bosom there lies dead;
And Paris too. Come, I'll dispose of thee
Among a sisterhood of holy nuns.
Stay not to question, for the Watch is coming.
Come, go, good Juliet. I dare no longer stay.

JULIET

160   Go, get thee hence, for I will not away.   *Exit Friar*
What's here? A cup, closed in my true love's hand?
Poison, I see, hath been his timeless end.
O churl! drunk all, and left no friendly drop
To help me after? I will kiss thy lips.
Haply some poison yet doth hang on them
To make me die with a restorative.

She kisses him

Thy lips are warm!

162

WATCHMAN (*within*)

Lead, boy. Which way?

JULIET

Yea, noise? Then I'll be brief. O happy dagger!

She snatches Romeo's dagger

This is thy sheath; there rust, and let me die.   17c

She stabs herself and falls

Enter Paris's Page and the Watch

PAGE

This is the place. There, where the torch doth burn.

FIRST WATCHMAN

The ground is bloody. Search about the churchyard.

Go, some of you. Whoe'er you find attach.

Exeunt some of the Watch

Pitiful sight! Here lies the County slain!

And Juliet bleeding, warm, and newly dead,

Who here hath lain this two days burièd.

Go, tell the Prince. Run to the Capulets.

Raise up the Montagues. Some others search.

Exeunt others of the Watch

We see the ground whereon these woes do lie,

But the true ground of all these piteous woes   180

We cannot without circumstance descry.

Enter some of the Watch, with Balthasar

SECOND WATCHMAN

Here's Romeo's man. We found him in the churchyard.

FIRST WATCHMAN

Hold him in safety till the Prince come hither.

Enter Friar Laurence and another of the Watch

THIRD WATCHMAN

Here is a Friar that trembles, sighs, and weeps.

We took this mattock and this spade from him

As he was coming from this churchyard's side.

FIRST WATCHMAN

A great suspicion! Stay the Friar too.

Enter the Prince and attendants

PRINCE

What misadventure is so early up,
That calls our person from our morning rest?
Enter Capulet and his wife with others

CAPULET

190   What should it be, that is so shrieked abroad?

LADY CAPULET

O the people in the street cry 'Romeo',
Some 'Juliet', and some 'Paris'; and all run
With open outcry toward our monument.

PRINCE

What fear is this which startles in your ears?

FIRST WATCHMAN

Sovereign, here lies the County Paris slain;
And Romeo dead; and Juliet, dead before,
Warm and new killed.

PRINCE

Search, seek, and know, how this foul murder comes.

FIRST WATCHMAN

Here is a Friar, and slaughtered Romeo's man,
200   With instruments upon them fit to open
These dead men's tombs.

CAPULET

O heavens! O wife, look how our daughter bleeds!
This dagger hath mista'en, for, lo, his house
Is empty on the back of Montague,
And it mis-sheathèd in my daughter's bosom!

LADY CAPULET

O me! This sight of death is as a bell
That warns my old age to a sepulchre.
Enter Montague and others

PRINCE

Come, Montague. For thou art early up

To see thy son and heir now early down.

MONTAGUE

Alas, my liege, my wife is dead tonight! 210
Grief of my son's exile hath stopped her breath.
What further woe conspires against mine age?

PRINCE

Look, and thou shalt see.

MONTAGUE

O thou untaught! what manners is in this,
To press before thy father to a grave?

PRINCE

Seal up the mouth of outrage for a while,
Till we can clear these ambiguities
And know their spring, their head, their true descent.
And then will I be general of your woes
And lead you, even to death. Meantime forbear, 220
And let mischance be slave to patience.
Bring forth the parties of suspicion.

FRIAR

I am the greatest, able to do least,
Yet most suspected, as the time and place
Doth make against me, of this direful murder.
And here I stand, both to impeach and purge
Myself condemnèd and myself excused.

PRINCE

Then say at once what thou dost know in this.

FRIAR

I will be brief, for my short date of breath
Is not so long as is a tedious tale. 230
Romeo, there dead, was husband to that Juliet;
And she, there dead, that Romeo's faithful wife.
I married them; and their stolen marriage day
Was Tybalt's doomsday, whose untimely death
Banished the new-made bridegroom from this city;

For whom, and not for Tybalt, Juliet pined.
You, to remove that siege of grief from her,
Betrothed and would have married her perforce
To County Paris. Then comes she to me
240 And with wild looks bid me devise some mean
To rid her from this second marriage,
Or in my cell there would she kill herself.
Then gave I her – so tutored by my art –
A sleeping potion; which so took effect
As I intended, for it wrought on her
The form of death. Meantime I writ to Romeo
That he should hither come as this dire night
To help to take her from her borrowed grave,
Being the time the potion's force should cease.
250 But he which bore my letter, Friar John,
Was stayed by accident and yesternight
Returned my letter back. Then all alone
At the prefixèd hour of her waking
Came I to take her from her kindred's vault;
Meaning to keep her closely at my cell
Till I conveniently could send to Romeo.
But when I came, some minute ere the time
Of her awakening, here untimely lay
The noble Paris and true Romeo dead.
260 She wakes; and I entreated her come forth
And bear this work of heaven with patience.
But then a noise did scare me from the tomb,
And she, too desperate, would not go with me,
But, as it seems, did violence on herself.
All this I know; and to the marriage
Her nurse is privy; and if aught in this
Miscarried by my fault, let my old life
Be sacrificed, some hour before his time,
Unto the rigour of severest law.

PRINCE

We still have known thee for a holy man.   270
Where's Romeo's man? What can he say to this?

BALTHASAR

I brought my master news of Juliet's death;
And then in post he came from Mantua
To this same place, to this same monument.
This letter he early bid me give his father,
And threatened me with death, going in the vault,
If I departed not and left him there.

PRINCE

Give me the letter. I will look on it.
Where is the County's page that raised the Watch?
Sirrah, what made your master in this place?   280

PAGE

He came with flowers to strew his lady's grave,
And bid me stand aloof, and so I did.
Anon comes one with light to ope the tomb,
And by and by my master drew on him.
And then I ran away to call the Watch.

PRINCE

This letter doth make good the Friar's words,
Their course of love, the tidings of her death.
And here he writes that he did buy a poison
Of a poor pothecary, and therewithal
Came to this vault to die, and lie with Juliet.   290
Where be these enemies? Capulet, Montague,
See what a scourge is laid upon your hate,
That heaven finds means to kill your joys with love.
And I, for winking at your discords too,
Have lost a brace of kinsmen. All are punished.

CAPULET

O brother Montague, give me thy hand.
This is my daughter's jointure, for no more

167

Can I demand.

MONTAGUE   But I can give thee more.
For I will raise her statue in pure gold,
That whiles Verona by that name is known,
There shall no figure at such rate be set
As that of true and faithful Juliet.

CAPULET
As rich shall Romeo's by his lady's lie,
Poor sacrifices of our enmity!

PRINCE
A glooming peace this morning with it brings.
    The sun for sorrow will not show his head.
Go hence, to have more talk of these sad things.
    Some shall be pardoned, and some punishèd.
For never was a story of more woe
Than this of Juliet and her Romeo.   *Exeunt*

COMMENTARY

In these notes the early editions of *Romeo and Juliet* are referred to as follows:

Q1 the first edition (1597), commonly called the 'Bad Quarto';

Q2 the second edition (1599), the 'Good Quarto', which is our principal text for the play;

Q3 the reprint of 1609;

Q4 the undated reprint (now known to have appeared in 1622);

F the folio edition of Shakespeare's plays (1623).

Only the more substantial variants are discussed here, and the readings of the early editions are usually given in *modern spelling*. For further details and lists of variants in the original spelling see 'An Account of the Text', pages 279–95 below.

The Prologue

The first Chorus (a sonnet) has generally been used in the theatre, often spoken by the actor who plays the role of the Prince of Verona. It contains fine phrases which effectively set the tone of the play: *fair Verona, star-crossed lovers, misadventured piteous overthrows, death-marked love*; and even if it is inadequate as a summary of the plot, it gives the right emphasis. The first four lines describe the family feud. The second four introduce the two lovers whose deaths, though not clearly attributed to the feud, bring about its end. The next three lines summarize in different words the previous eight. Line 12 says that the above is a plot summary of the play about to be performed, and the final couplet humbly asks for the patience and favour of the audience. The Prologue confines itself strictly to the tragic theme of the play; there is no hint of the comic element (the Nurse and Mercutio) or of the efforts at reconciliation by the Friar.

Between Acts I and II is another Chorus in the form of a sonnet; see note on p. 203.

Q1 (1597) includes a clumsy version of Chorus 1 (but not Chorus 2), which suggests that this prologue was spoken in early performances (see p. 287). Both choruses appear in Q2 (1599). Curiously this text omits Q1's jeer at a *without-book prologue, faintly spoke* (see note on I.4.7–8). The F text (1623) is a direct reprint of Q3 (1609); but whereas Q3 (following Q2) gives both choruses, F omits the first. There is no evidence to explain this. It may have been left out accidentally, owing to some defect in the copy of Q3 used by the printer of F. But possibly it was omitted by a deliberate decision; if so, its exclusion by his trustworthy friends suggests that it was not written by Shakespeare (and in that case the inclusion of Chorus 2, also unauthentic, was simply overlooked by those who excluded Chorus 1).

2   *Verona.* This famous Italian city had already appeared in Shakespeare's plays. *The Two Gentlemen of Verona* has its early scenes set there. Petruchio in *The Taming of the Shrew* is a gentleman of Verona and comes thence to Padua. The whole of *Romeo and Juliet* (apart from V.1, which is in Mantua) is set in Verona: in the streets (I.1, 2, and 4, II.4, III.1), in the Capulet house and garden (I.3 and 5, II.1, 2, and 5, III.2, 4, and 5, IV.2, 3, 4, and 5), in Friar Laurence's cell (II.3 and 6, III.3, IV.1, V.2), or in the churchyard by the Capulet monument (V.3). The changes of scene are indicated to the audience by the words of the speakers, by simple changes of costume (such as cloaks for outdoor scenes), or by simple properties (such as chairs for indoor scenes).

3   *ancient grudge.* The origin of the feud between the two families is not explained. The sympathies of the

audience are not therefore engaged on one side or the
other.

3   *mutiny* outburst of violence

4   *civil blood makes civil hands.* In the first instance *civil*
         does not merely mean (as in the second) 'belonging to
         citizens' but has behind it such phrases as 'civil war',
         'civil strife'.

6   *star-crossed* destined by the stars to be thwarted. There
         are numerous references to the fateful influence of the
         stars in this play. See Introduction, pp. 19–22.

8   *Doth* (plural)

9   *passage* course

12   *two hours' traffic.* An Elizabethan play seems to have
         been regarded as lasting approximately two hours.
         Many of the surviving texts of plays are clearly longer
         than that, and the phrase *two hours* is perhaps to be
         interpreted vaguely, and as emphasizing that the enter-
         tainment is free from tediousness.
         traffic business

14   *What here shall miss* what may seem to you to be inade-
         quate in this performance
         our toil the actors' efforts

The Play

.1   (stage direction) *Sampson and Gregory.* Sampson is a
         boaster and, Capulet-wise, makes a virtue of quarrel-
         ling; Gregory is more of a tactician. Although Gregory
         is twice addressed (lines 1 and 61), the audience is
         never told Sampson's name.
         with swords and bucklers. The servants are armed and
         ready for trouble. But the play begins like a comedy.

1   *carry coals* perform menial tasks, be humiliated

2   *colliers* (a term of abuse). The puns on *collier, choler,
         collar* (hangman's noose) continue.

3   *draw* (swords)

5, 6   *moved* aroused (similarly *move(s)* in lines 7 and 10). But
         in line 9 Gregory interprets *To move* as 'to run away'.

11   *take the wall* keep to the clean side of the path, nearest the wall

15   *weaker vessels* ('ye husbands, dwell with them . . . giving honour unto the wife, as unto the weaker vessel', 1 Peter 3.7)
      thrust to the wall (in amorous assault)

21   *civil.* Sampson is using the word ironically or obscenely. In Q4 it was changed to *cruel*, which is followed by many editors.

25   *sense* meaning. But in line 26 Gregory quibbles on *sense* as 'feeling'.

27   *to stand* (with a bawdy quibble)

30   *poor-John* dried salted hake (probably with a bawdy quibble, as not being *flesh* that would *stand*)

30–31 *Here comes of the house* here come (some) of the house

31   (stage direction) The second servingman is not named in the Quartos. Some editors identify him with Balthasar, Romeo's servant, who appears in V.1 and 3. But, in any case, the audience never learns the name of Abram, who is so called only in the speech prefixes.

40   *list* please

41   *bite my thumb at.* This was an insulting gesture, made by inserting the thumbnail into the mouth and jerking it from the upper teeth, making a click.

57–8 *one of my master's kinsmen.* Presumably this is Tybalt (who comes in abruptly at line 64); but Benvolio, a Montague, enters first.

62   *washing* swashing, slashing

63–8 *Part, fools! . . . part these men with me.* Benvolio is characterized as a peace-maker (see III.1.1–4, 49–52 and notes). His name ('well-wishing') suggests his role.

65   *What, art thou drawn . . .* By the introduction of Tybalt, with his unmotivated quarrelsomeness, thus early in the play Shakespeare prepares us for the fatal conflict between him and Romeo which is to be the turning-point of the action.

heartless hinds cowardly yokels or menials (presumably punning on female deer without their harts)

72–4   *Clubs, bills, and partisans! . . . Down with the Montagues!* Attributed to *Offi.* in Q2, but the words appear to be uttered by various members of the crowd, rather than by one officer.

72   *bills, and partisans* kinds of pikes used by guards, the bill having a curved blade and the partisan a broad head with (sometimes) a side projection

74   (stage direction) *gown* night-gown (the modern 'dressing-gown'). This indicates that the time is early morning and Capulet is not yet properly dressed for going outside his house.

75   *long sword* (an old-fashioned weapon in Shakespeare's time)

76   *A crutch, a crutch!* Capulet is at once established as an old man and his younger wife (see note on I.3.73–4) as having a tart tongue. The Prince emphasizes the point by calling him *old Capulet* at line 90. Lady Montague's determined words (line 80) contrast with Lady Capulet's sarcasm.

78   *in spite of me* to scorn me

80   *Escalus.* The name is given as *Eskales* in Q2. Otherwise in entries (III.1.140 and V.3.187) and in dialogue he is *the Prince.* Brooke called him 'Escalus' and Painter 'the Lord Bartholomew of Escala'. This represents the name of the famous rulers of Verona, the family della Scala. It was in the times of Bartolommeo della Scala (early fourteenth century) that Luigi da Porto, and following him Bandello, had placed the story of Romeo and Julietta. (See 'Further Reading', p. 46.)

81–103 *Rebellious subjects, enemies to peace . . . all men depart.* The grave sonorous language of the Prince, with its excess of adjectives and its elaborate imagery (*purple fountains issuing from your veins*), reminds us of many passages in the historical plays on themes of civil dissension which Shakespeare was writing in these years.

82   *Profaners of this neighbour-stainèd steel* misusers of your swords by staining them with the blood of your neighbours

85   *purple*. This adjective, meaning 'dark red' rather than a mixture of blue and red, was commonly used of blood.

87   *mistempered* (a pun). They are tempered (on the anvil) with evil intent and intemperately used.

89, 91   *Three ... thrice*. See second note on line 104 below.

95   *Cankered with peace* grown rusty through disuse (in the same way as hate has malignantly affected the hearts of the two families)

97   *Your lives shall pay the forfeit of the peace* you will be executed as a penalty for your having broken the peace (a compressed expression)

102   *Free-town*. Shakespeare found this name in Brooke's *Romeus and Juliet*, where it translates the Italian *Villa Franca*, the name of Capulet's castle.

104   *set ... new abroach* caused to be stirring once again (*abroach* is used of a cask of liquor pierced and left running)

        ancient quarrel. Like the *ancient grudge* of the Prologue and the Prince's *Three ... thrice* (lines 89, 91), this gives an extension of time. Montague's words at lines 104–5 show, perhaps, that his heart is not really in the quarrel.

109–12   *The fiery Tybalt ...* Benvolio's description of Tybalt's way of fighting (which already has a touch of sarcasm in it: *hissed him in scorn*) prepares for Mercutio's more derisive account in II.4.19–26.

114   *on part and part* some on each side

116–17   *O where is Romeo? ...* Romeo is engagingly introduced into the play by these eager inquiries by his mother.

118–30   *Madam, an hour before the worshipped sun ...* Benvolio's poetical manner here is a striking change from his preceding account of the fight, and contrasts equally with his subsequent conversations with Romeo and Mercutio.

174

120   *drive* (pronounced 'driv') is past tense (similarly *write* has past tense *writ* as well as *wrote*); in Q3 it was changed to the commoner form *drave*.

121   *sycamore*. This tree was traditionally dedicated to melancholy lovers; compare the song Desdemona borrows from 'poor Barbary' in *Othello*, IV.3.39 ('The poor soul sat sighing by a sycamore tree').

122   *westward rooteth from this city side* grows to the west from this side of the city

126-7   *my own,* | *Which then most sought where most might not be found* my own (affections or inclinations) which, at that time, particularly sought (prompted me to seek) places where the least number of people might be found

129   *humour* mood

130   *who* him who

136   *Aurora*. The goddess of the dawn was married to Tithonus, whose 'bed' she was imagined to leave in the morning.

137   *heavy son* (quibbling on *light* in this line and on *sun* in line 134)

145   *importuned* (three syllables, with accent on the second)

153   *sun*. This is an emendation of Q2 *same*.

156   *So please you* if you please

159   *To hear true shrift* as to hear a true confession from Romeo

160   *Is the day so young?* Romeo is surprised to be addressed with a 'good morning', for he thought the day was much further advanced.

161   *new struck nine*. Indications of the time of day are numerous in the play

171   *whose view is muffled*. Cupid is often shown as having light bandages over his eyes.

172   *Should without eyes see pathways to his will* should, though blind, see clearly the ways to bring about what he wants

173   *Where shall we dine?* An unloverlike question, especially at nine o'clock in the morning – unless it indicates

Romeo's distracted state of mind. But perhaps he wishes to divert Benvolio's curiosity about his love.

175 *much to-do with hate, but more with love* much turmoil in the streets over the feud, but a greater turmoil within me because of love. The noun *to-do* (bustle, turmoil) was an Elizabethan usage as well as a modern colloquial one.

176–82 *Why then, O brawling love, O loving hate . . . no love in this.* Romeo speaks in the commonplace antithetical language of contemporary love poetry. This gives a feeling of artificiality to his passion.

177 *O anything, of nothing first create!* This is a paradoxical treatment of the old saying that 'nothing can come of nothing' (*nil posse creari de nihilo*).

183 *coz.* This is a short form of 'cousin', used in familiar speech when addressing a kinsman.

187–8 *Which thou wilt propagate, to have it pressed | With more of thine. pressed* connects with *oppression* in line 184 and develops the image of sexual embrace leading to 'propagation'.

190 *made.* Q1 has *raised*, which is often adopted by editors.

191 *purged* purified, the smoke becoming less thick

193–4 *A madness most discreet, | A choking gall and a preserving sweet.* Many of Romeo's fanciful statements about love bear no relation to his subsequent experience with Juliet.

195 *Soft!* Wait a moment!

199 *in sadness* seriously. Apparently Benvolio does not know whether to take Romeo's love-expostulations seriously.

209 *Dian's wit* the wisdom of the goddess Diana (who guarded herself from love and remained chaste)

210 *in strong proof* with strong armour

211 *uncharmed.* This is the reading from Q2. Q1 has *unharmed*, which is easier but probably mistaken.

214 *ope her lap to saint-seducing gold.* It is curious that Romeo, for all his idealistic protestations, should have entertained the idea of buying Rosaline's chastity. The

image is that of Danaë, who was taken by Jupiter in a shower of gold.

216 *when she dies, with beauty dies her store.* This is the theme of the first seventeen of Shakespeare's *Sonnets.*

218 *sparing* economy of love

221 *too* excessively

222 *To merit bliss by making me despair* in deserving heavenly bliss by her continence, while involving me in the deadly sin of despair

224 *I live dead* I go on living, but in a half-dead condition

229 *To call hers, exquisite, in question more* to bring her exquisite beauty into my thoughts even more

234–6 *Show me a mistress that is passing fair, | What doth her beauty serve but as a note | Where I may read who passed that passing fair?* when I see a surpassingly beautiful woman, it only serves to remind me of her who surpasses that surpassing beauty

238 *I'll pay that doctrine* I'll teach you that lesson as a debt of friendship

I.2 At the entry of Capulet and Paris we break in on their conversation. As we have last seen Capulet being taken off by the Prince (I.1.99), the discussion with Paris is naturally about the injunction against the quarrel.

(stage direction) *Paris.* He is named at line 16. He is usually called a *Count* or *County*, but he is *Sir Paris* at III.4.12 and *this noble earl* at III.4.21 (perhaps because Brooke says 'County Paris cleped he was; an earl he had to sire', line 1883). It is stated that, as well as being the Prince's kinsman (V.3.295), he is Mercutio's (V.3.75).

1–5 *But Montague is bound as well as I . . . at odds so long.* This sensible attitude to the family feud shows that the time is ripe for reconciliation, if only the young men and servants stop giving provocation.

1 *bound* (to keep the peace)

3   *men so old*. Compare note on I.1.76.

4   *honourable reckoning* public esteem. Paris is adding the
     notion of rank and position to the years Capulet men-
     tioned.

5   *so long*. See note on I.1.104 (*ancient quarrel, ancient
     grudge*, and so on)

6   *my lord*. Paris addresses Juliet's father in an ingratiating
     manner. Compare III.4.18.

8   *My child*. We are not told Juliet's name until I.3.4;
     and since we are not told Rosaline's name until lines
     68 and 82 below, an audience which does not know the
     story would suppose that the object of Romeo's love-
     longings in the previous scene and of Paris's suit here
     is the heroine of the play.
     a stranger in the world. Juliet has led the secluded life of
     a girl growing up (and therefore, incidentally, she has
     no acquaintance with Romeo and the rest).

9   *change* (of the seasons)
     fourteen years. There is much emphasis on Juliet's age.
     Compare I.3.13–23. Marina in *Pericles* is fourteen.
     Miranda in *The Tempest* is fifteen.

10   *two more summers*. It is amusing to remember this
     later when Capulet is impatient for her marriage within
     a few days.
     summers. This implies that the season is now summer.
     At I.3.16 we are told it is mid-July (a fortnight before
     Lammastide). See note on I.5.29.

12   *Younger than she are happy mothers made*. Lady Capulet
     says much the same thing at I.3.70–72.

13   *marred* spoilt by bearing children (and perhaps he is
     also thinking of her being brought to death by bearing
     children too early. The loss of his other children
     (line 14) makes him anxious for his only-surviving
     daughter).
     made made mothers

14–15 *Earth hath swallowed all my hopes but she;* | *She's the
     hopeful lady of my earth*. Juliet's position as the Capulet

178

heiress is made clear, and repeated at various points in the play (I.5.117, III.5.164–6, IV.5.46).

14   *hopes* children which were his hope for posterity

15   *earth* his body or (perhaps) the inheritance. The repetition of *earth* from line 14, with a different meaning, is awkward when read; but perhaps it can be spoken effectively. It has been plausibly suggested that line 14 or 15 (and perhaps both of them) should be omitted, as being one of Shakespeare's 'false starts', imperfectly deleted in his manuscript and so accidentally printed. The touch of sentiment in Capulet's words is, however, very much in character.

16–19   *But woo her . . . fair according voice.* This indulgent attitude towards Juliet is not borne out by his subsequent dealings with her (especially III.5.141–96).

24   *my poor house.* It is characteristic of the hospitable Capulet to belittle, rather ostentatiously, his own possessions and activities. He disparages Juliet's merits (lines 32–3 below); he offers *a trifling foolish banquet* (I.5.122); and he says *We'll keep no great ado* for Juliet's marriage feast (III.4.23), which nevertheless needs *twenty cunning cooks* (IV.2.2).

25   *Earth-treading stars that make dark heaven light.* The ladies will be like stars walking on (or dancing on) the earth and reflecting light up into the sky, which would otherwise be dark.

26   *lusty young men.* Capulet's fancy is retrospective, full of memories of youth (compare I.5.22–5 and 31–41).

27   *well-apparelled April* (because in April the earth is newly clothed with leaves and plants and flowers)

28   *limping winter* (because winter only slowly departs to give place to spring)

29   *female buds.* So Q1. The reading of Q2 is *fennel buds*, which has been defended as referring to a herb which played a part in wedding ritual. But the connexion seems to be too remote.

31   *And like her most whose merit most shall be.* Capulet is

giving to Paris the same sort of advice as Benvolio gives
to Romeo at lines 81–98.

32–3   *Which, on more view of many, mine, being one,* | *May*
        stand in number, though in reckoning none and when you
        have had a more thorough view of many of the girls,
        my daughter, who will be one of those there, may be
        one of the number you will consider for first place –
        except, of course, for the old saying, that one isn't a
        number. (Capulet is, as usual, rather obviously under-
        valuing his own property.)

39   *meddle with* busy himself about (with a bawdy quibble;
        see II.1.34–6 and note)

40   *yard* yard measure (with a bawdy quibble)
        last (perhaps quibbling on 'the last thing I have men-
        tioned'; that is, his yard, too)
        pencil paint brush (probably continuing the quibble)

44   *In good time!* (here come some people to help me)
        (stage direction) Benvolio and Romeo enter continuing
        the conversation where we left them at the end of I.1.

45–50   *Tut, man, one fire burns out another's burning.* . . . | *And*
        the rank poison of the old will die. Benvolio speaks the
        sestet of a sonnet, with characteristic paradoxes. He
        recommends Romeo to fall in love a second time, for
        this will cure him of his first love; and events prove him
        to be right.

46   *another's anguish* the anguish of a second pain

47   *holp* helped (old past participle)
        backward turning turning in a reverse direction

48   *cures with another's languish* is cured by the languish-
        ment that comes from a second grief

51, 52 *your* (here a kind of indefinite article, meaning 'the kind
        of thing you know well')

51   *plantain leaf.* It was apparently used to tie over small
        cuts and grazes, to prevent the part becoming infected.
        Romeo brushes aside Benvolio's advice by taking *infec-*
        tion (line 49) literally, and mocking at everyday reme-
        dies for such a serious case as his is.

53 From about here until about I.3.35 the text of the
    second (or 'Good') Quarto was merely a reprint of the
    earlier 'Bad Quarto' and we can have little confidence
    in its accuracy in representing Shakespeare's words.
    (See 'An Account of the Text', p. 286.)

54-6 *Not mad, but bound more than a madman is* ... This
    describes the usual treatment of the insane in Shake-
    speare's time.

56 *Good-e'en* good evening (but the phrase could be used
    at any time after noon)

57 *God gi' good-e'en* may God grant you good evening

62 *Rest you merry.* The servant says good-bye, supposing
    from Romeo's cryptic answers that he has said he can-
    not read.

65 *Utruvio.* The editions at the end of the seventeenth
    century changed this to *Vitruvio* (a more common
    name). But there is some evidence for the existence
    of Utruvio as a name.

66 *Mercutio* (whom we are to meet as Romeo's friend in
    I.4, is invited to the Capulet party)

68 *My fair niece Rosaline.* We do not yet know that this is
    Romeo's beloved, but obviously the actor playing
    Romeo can reveal the impression the name makes on
    him. Capulet's niece is soon to be replaced by Capulet's
    daughter as Romeo's love.

69 *Tybalt,* whom we met as the fire-eater in I.1.65, will
    reappear ominously at the party (I.5.54–92).

72 *To supper?* The phrase is awkward and should perhaps
    be transferred to the next speech of the servant.

78 *the great rich Capulet.* The servants have a just idea of
    their master's position; compare the Nurse on *the
    chinks* at I.5.117, and Romeo's *rich Capulet* at II.3.54.

79 *crush* drink down

81 *this same ancient feast.* At line 20 Capulet calls it *an old
    accustomed feast.*

82 *Rosaline.* This is the first mention that Romeo's love is
    Rosaline. For all the audience knows, the love-language

hitherto might be directed towards the lady whose name appears in the title of the play.

84   *unattainted* unprejudiced

87–90   *When the devout religion of mine eye . . .* Romeo is presumptuous in his use of religious language for his love-situation.

89   *these, who, often drowned, could never die* these eyes of mine, which I often drowned with tears but which didn't die (go blind) in spite of the drownings. Romeo seems to be referring to the testing of those suspected of being in league with the devil, by means of trying to drown them: if they kept afloat they obviously had supernatural assistance and were *transparent heretics*.

90   *Transparent heretics*. His eyes are 'transparent' and the heretics are 'easily discovered'.

91–2   *One fairer than my love? . . .* Again Romeo's hyperbolical language courts disaster.

93–8   *Tut, you saw her fair, none else being by . . .* Precisely what Benvolio here proposes, and Romeo rejects, takes place when Romeo sees Juliet – as he himself admits (I.5.52–3).

94   *poised* weighed

95   *scales* (singular). Benvolio fantastically imagines Romeo's eyes as a pair of scales which ought to weigh the merits of two different ladies, one in each.

96   *Your lady's love against some other maid* the love you feel for Rosaline against the love you would feel at seeing the beauty of some other girl

98   *scant* scarcely

99   *I'll go along.* It is amusing to note that Romeo goes to the party to see Rosaline, and Juliet to see Paris (I.3.98).

I.3.1–35   These lines (like the ones in the preceding scene from about I.2.53) are reprinted in Q2 from Q1 and are therefore not to be taken as accurately representing Shakespeare's writing. From line 36 onwards, where the printer returned to a manuscript which was either Shakespeare's or a transcription of Shakespeare's, the verse becomes regular and the writing better organized.

2 *Now, by my maidenhead at twelve year old*. The Nurse's first words are characterful.

3 *ladybird*. This was probably already in Shakespeare's time a word for a light o'love. The Nurse remembers this after she has spoken and so adds an apology: *God forbid*. (Compare her *God forgive me! Marry, and amen!* at IV.5.7–8.) Or perhaps she merely means 'I hope nothing has happened to her.' The uncertain quality of the text here makes it impossible to be sure of the meaning of what Shakespeare originally wrote.

4 *Juliet*. About one-sixth of the play has passed before we are allowed to receive an impression of Juliet herself.

8 *give leave* leave us alone

10 *thou's* thou shalt

12 *an hour*. Q1, on which the text must be based here, reads *a houre*; this may indicate the Nurse's pronunciation with initial aspirate, but we can infer nothing confidently from a 'Bad Quarto'. The printer of Q2 changed it to *an houre*.

13 *She's not fourteen*. See Introduction, p. 16. The Nurse apparently retained her virginity at twelve (line 2 above), but we are not told how much longer.

14 *teen* grief (she quibbles on 'four' 'teen')

16 *Lammastide* the first of August (originally a harvest festival when the first loaves from the new corn were consecrated). The time of the year (high summer) and Juliet's age (she will be fourteen on 31 July, about a fortnight's time) are strongly impressed on the audience by these repetitions. Presumably Shakespeare deliberately gives a heroine named Juliet a birthday in July.

17 *Even or odd*. By *odd days* Lady Capulet meant 'a few more days', but the Nurse misunderstands this and says it doesn't matter whether the days are even or odd in number.

19–20   *Susan and she . . . | Were of an age.* Shakespeare thinks
        of the Nurse as one who had a daughter nearly fourteen
        years ago and who had suckled Juliet, for three years,
        until about eleven years ago. She is not, therefore, to be
        imagined as an aged crone but as, perhaps, in her early
        fifties.

19   *God rest all Christian souls!* (a pious ejaculation when
        the dead are mentioned)

23   *marry!* by Mary!

24   *since the earthquake now eleven years.* Some editors
        hoped that this would turn out to be a topical allusion
        and that the writing of the play could be dated eleven
        years after an earthquake – presumably in England,
        rather than in Italy. But it seems likely that the pre-
        ciseness of the Nurse's memory and her associations of
        events are due to Shakespeare's dramatic artistry rather
        than to real events. (There was a serious earthquake felt
        in England on 6 April 1580, and lesser ones in 1583 and
        1585.)

29   *Mantua.* See note on III.3.149.

30   *Nay, I do bear a brain* (perhaps) I have a good memory
        still

33   *tetchy* fretful

34   *Shake, quoth the dovehouse!* Presumably this refers to
        the earthquake which occurred that day. The move-
        ment of the personified building is expressed in words –
        a common practice of unsophisticated story-telling. But
        the text may be sketchy and abbreviated here (see first
        note on this scene).

        trow (pronunciation rhymes with 'slow') assure you

35   *To bid me trudge* 'to send me packing', to get me out of
        the way (because of the earthquake and because Juliet
        didn't want me as a wet-nurse any more)

37   *stand high-lone* (presumably) stand upright by herself
        by th'rood by the Cross on which Christ died

39   *broke her brow* cut the skin of her forehead

41   *'A* he

43   *fall backward* (ready for making love)
      wit understanding
44   *holidam* 'halidom', holiness
46   *come about* come true eventually (Juliet is now ready
      for marriage and so for love-making)
49   *stinted* ceased
53   *it brow* its brow ('its' was not much in use in Shake-
      speare's time; it does not appear to occur in the texts of
      his plays printed during his life, nor in the Authorized
      Version of the Bible (1611). The usual form was 'his'
      or occasionally 'it'.)
54   *stone* testicle
55   *perilous* (probably to be pronounced 'parlous')
59   *say I*. Juliet puns on the Nurse's *said 'Ay'* in the pre-
      vious line.
60   *God mark thee to his grace!* May God make you one of
      his elect!
62   *once* some day
66   *dispositions* (changed in F to *disposition*, but the plural
      form also was used in the seventeenth century and is
      probably correct here)
67, 68   *honour* is the reading of Q1. Q2 has *hour*, which could
      be defended in line 67, but it does not suit the Nurse's
      reply in lines 68–9.
68   *An honour!* The Nurse approves of Juliet's view of
      marriage and says she is a wise girl. But the *honour* of
      a woman was a word used in bawdy senses, and there
      may be an unwitting jest here.
69   *thy teat* the teat you sucked (the Nurse's own teat)
70–72   *Younger than you . . . | Are made already mothers*. This
      is exactly what Paris had said at I.2.12.
73–4   *I was your mother much upon these years | That you are
      now a maid*. This gives an indication that Lady Capulet
      is about twenty-eight. Capulet is clearly much older
      (compare I.1.76 and 90, I.2.3, I.5.22–5 and 31–41). But
      Lady Capulet's words could be spoken so that the
      audience interpreted them as untruthful: she is a lady

still pretending to be 'nearly thirty' in spite of her having a marriageable daughter. At V.3.206–7 she says (perhaps more truthfully): *This sight of death is as a bell | That warns my old age to a sepulchre*.

77   *a man of wax* 'a perfect picture of a man' (but, as usual, the Nurse slips, wittingly or unwittingly, into a bawdy quibble)

79   *Nay* (a kind of affirmative, introducing a stronger opinion than the one just stated)

81   *This night you shall behold him at our feast*. The episode is not represented in I.5, in spite of this promise.

82–93   *Read o'er the volume* . . . Lady Capulet begins an elaborate comparison of Paris with a manuscript book (*volume, writ, pen, content, margent, book, unbound, cover, clasps, story*). The contrast between these fancies and real passion is very effective.

84   *married* joined in harmony

85   *content* (accent on second syllable) (1) the 'contents' of the book; and (2) satisfaction

87   *written in the margent*. In sixteenth-century books annotations and interpretations of obscurities (the equivalent of modern footnotes) were generally printed in the margins.

88   *unbound lover*. Even Lady Capulet puns: Paris is like a book without its binding, and he is also not yet bound by the ties of marriage.

89   *cover* the cover of a book and the embraces of a wife

90–91   *The fish lives in the sea, and 'tis much pride | For fair without the fair within to hide*. (She imagines Juliet as the cover of the book which 'binds' Paris.) It is a fine and natural thing to give to a book with very good contents (Paris) a binding (Juliet) worthy of them. Such a book in a good binding is in its natural element as is a fish in the sea.

92–3   *That book in many's eyes doth share the glory, | That in gold clasps locks in the golden story*. (This carries on the imagery of lines 90–91.) There is a kind of book which is

esteemed, by many people, both because of its good
contents (*golden story*) and because of its rich binding
(*gold clasps*). As the binding and the contents share
equally in the *glory* (the admiration in which the book
is held), so will you and Paris share equally in honour
when you are united in marriage.

But by her allusions to *gold* and *golden* and *all that he
doth possess*, Lady Capulet also seems to be suggesting
that the marriage is one that is financially advantageous.

93   *clasps* the fastenings of the book-covers and the embraces of love

96   *bigger! Women grow by men* (by becoming pregnant)

98   *I'll look to like* I shall expect to like (she quibbles with
looking 'the act of seeing'). See note on I.2.99.

99-100   *But no more deep will I endart mine eye* ... These words
contain unwitting irony. For within a few hours Juliet
will have fallen in love and plighted her troth, regard-
less of her parents' *consent*, and next day her marriage
will be solemnized and consummated. In this scene
Juliet is an unawakened girl, submissive to her mother.

99   *endart* (presumably) bury as if it were an arrow

101-4   *Madam, the guests are come, supper served up ... follow
straight*. The sudden intrusion of vigorous prose for the
domestic anxieties is a lively contrast to the artificiali-
ties of Lady Capulet's discourse to her daughter. Compare similarly the comic servant's prose at I.2.38-44.

103   *cursed* (because she is not about her household duties;
see note on IV.4.5)

105   *County*. This two-syllabled form for 'Count' seems to
be due to the Italian *Conte*.

106   *happy nights*. The Nurse's usual thoughts are on sexual
matters.

I.4   (stage direction) *Mercutio*. He was mentioned in Capulet's letter (I.2.66), but he is not named to the audience
until line 95 below. The name, which Shakespeare took

from Brooke's poem, suggests that he is a 'mercurial' type, that is, sprightly, quick-witted, and volatile. Although a close friend of the Montagues, Romeo and Benvolio, he is invited to the Capulet party. His kinship with the Prince is alluded to at III.1.145 and 188–9, and V.3.295.

1–10   *What, shall this speech be spoke for our excuse? . . .* The attribution of these two speeches to Romeo and Benvolio is surprising. Lines 1–2 are in Benvolio's manner and 3–10 very much in Mercutio's; and line 10 seems contrary to Benvolio's words at lines 104–5.

The text of Q2 follows Q1 closely here (with the omission of lines 7–8) and may have been corrupted by it. Q1 makes errors in speech-prefixes: at line 53 it omits the prefix Mercutio and so attributes the Queen Mab speech to Benvolio; wrongly, as is clear from line 95.

A producer could perhaps be bolder than an editor and transfer the two speeches to Benvolio and Mercutio respectively.

1   *this speech.* Presumably Romeo and his friends have a formal speech ready to speak as an excuse for the intrusion of the maskers into Capulet's party. Examples in Shakespeare's plays are: *Love's Labour's Lost* V.2.158 (by Moth), *Timon of Athens* I.2.117 (by Cupid), *Henry VIII* I.4.65 (by the Chamberlain).

3   *The date is out of such prolixity* it is nowadays unfashionable to give these tedious speeches of apology on arriving uninvited at a masquerade

4   *Cupid* is commonly the 'presenter' of maskers (as in *Timon of Athens*; see note on line 1 above)
hoodwinked blind-folded

5   *Tartar's painted bow* (the name usually given to the short bow shaped like the outline of the upper lip – the traditional shape of Cupid's bow)
lath thin wood (that is, it was an imitation sword)

6   *crowkeeper* boy acting as a scarecrow

7–8   *Nor no without-book prologue, faintly spoke | After the prompter, for our entrance.* These two lines are only found in Q1. Perhaps they were cut at some time as being rather insulting to the speaker of the Prologue to *this* play. Benvolio describes the kind of prologue spoken (*without-book*, not read from a script) but so ill-learned that it is delivered without energy and only with the help of the prompter. Shakespeare generally speaks with a kind of mocking self-consciousness about the stage practices of his time.

8   *entrance* (three syllables)

9   *let them measure us by what they will* let the Capulets at the party judge us by whatever standard they like

10   *measure them a measure* mete out for them a dance (with quibbles on *measure* in the previous line)

12   *Being but heavy, I will bear the light.* Romeo continues his quibbles on *heavy* and *light*; compare I.1.178.

15   The pun on *sole* and *soul* occurs elsewhere in Shakespeare.

16   *So stakes me to the ground* (like a bull or a bear)

18–22   *And soar with them above a common bound . . . do I sink.* They get all the possible puns from *soar*, *sore*, and *bound* ('limit', 'leap', and 'chained').

21   *pitch* the height a falcon soars

23   *to sink in it, should you burden love.* Mercutio perverts Romeo's words, characteristically, into sexual quibbles: in order to make love you would have to be a burden on the woman you love. Compare *the mire | Of – save your reverence – love, wherein thou stickest* (lines 41–2)

24   *oppression.* Compare I.1.184.

26   *it pricks like thorn.* The nightingale was supposed to sing its love songs while pricking its breast against a thorn.

28   *Prick love for pricking, and you beat love down* give vent to love and satisfy it, and so will love be brought down (with sexual quibbles)

189

29   *case* mask

30   *visor* mask, and so also an ugly face

31   *quote* observe

32   *the beetle brows shall blush for me.* It seems that Mercutio's mask has large overhanging eyebrows and ruddy cheeks.

36   *rushes.* They were strewn on the floors of Elizabethan houses. It is probable that they were sometimes also used on the stage.

37-8 *I am proverbed with a grandsire phrase* . . . I have my worldly wisdom from a good old-fashioned proverb: the onlooker (or candle-holder) sees the best of the game

39   *The game was ne'er so fair* . . . The proverb recommended one to leave the gambling-table when the game was at its best; *game* seems to be a quibble on 'quarry' (his Rosaline) and 'gambling'.
      done. This is the reading of Q1. Q2 has *dum* (which cannot be right), amended in later quartos to *dun* ('dusky', and so 'gloomy'). The *done/dun* pun is also a quibble on *fair*.

40   *dun's the mouse* (apparently) keep quiet! (a proverbial phrase)
      the constable's own word what the constable says when he is on the alert to arrest someone

41   *Dun.* The allusion is to an ancient Christmas game of pulling Dun the horse (represented by a log of wood) out of the (imaginary) mire.

41-2 *the mire | Of – save your reverence – love.* Mercutio makes a mock apology for seeming to be about to utter an indecent word, though he continues his bawdy quibbles.

44   *Nay, that's not so.* Romeo, himself a chronic quibbler, pretends to be literal-minded, saying that it is now dark, not daytime; and Mercutio has to explain what he meant by *we burn daylight* (we waste time by delay). This part of the conversation and the stage-indication

of the carried torches makes the audience feel that the scene is taking place at night.

45   *like lamps.* Q2 reads *lights lights.* By omitting the final 's' on the first word, this could make sense punctuated thus: *We waste our lights, in vain [we] light lights by day.* The reading *like lamps* comes from Q1. Some editors take a word from each reading and prefer *light lamps* or *like lights.*

46   *Take our good meaning* accept the meaning intended by what we say (not a false meaning due to a misleadingly literal interpretation of the words)

46–7   *our judgement sits | Five times in that ere once in our five wits* our good sense is to be found in the intended meaning far more often than in the mere words which relate literally to what we experience through our *five wits* (the five senses)

48–9   *And we mean well in going to this masque, | But 'tis no wit to go.* Romeo continues to express his reluctance, picking up *meaning* (line 46) and *wits* (line 47): 'We may have good intentions in going to the Capulet party, but it is an unwise thing to do.'

50   *I dreamt a dream tonight.* Romeo does not get a chance to relate this dream, but presumably its nature is indicated by his speech at the end of the scene (lines 106–11). (Compare V.1.6–9, where he similarly has a foreboding dream, in that case related.)
  tonight last night

52   *In bed asleep.* Romeo takes Mercutio's *lie* 'tell untruth' as 'be prone on one's bed'.

53   *Queen Mab.* Apparently she is Shakespeare's invention, or, if she is not, this at any rate is his introduction of a country belief into literature.

54   *fairies' midwife.* Probably not the midwife who helps fairies to give birth to other fairies, but rather the one among the fairies who performs the duties of midwife, in 'delivering' the fancies of men, *the children of an idle brain* (line 97).

55   *agate stone* (commonly used for seal-rings; probably the reference is to the engraved figure in such an agate-ring)

57   *atomies* little atoms (tiny creatures). Q1 reads *Atomi*, which may be correct (Latin plural of *atomus*) and is supported by Q2 *ottamie* (with first letter misprinted). The Q2 reading was amended to *atomies* in the printing of Q3.

59–61 *Her chariot is an empty hazelnut . . . the fairies' coach-makers.* These three lines are printed after line 69 in Q2. But the sense of the passage seems to demand their transference here; otherwise the parts of the *chariot* are described before the chariot itself is mentioned.

60   *joiner squirrel or old grub.* The squirrel gnaws nuts and the grub bores holes in them.

62   *spinners* spiders

65   *moonshine's watery beams.* The moon was associated both with the tides and with dew.

66   *film* gossamer (curiously spelt *philome* in Q2)

68   *round little worm.* There was a proverbial expression that the idle hands of maidens breed maggots.

70   *state* stately progress

77   *courtier's.* The repetition of the instance of the courtiers (line 72) is a little awkward and perhaps indicates that some rewriting of this speech took place. Q1 reads *lawyer's*, which also does not seem right, as the lawyers had already appeared in line 73.

78   *suit* court-petition, for presenting which the courtier would expect a fee from the petitioner

79   *tithe-pig.* The legal due of the parson was the tenth of a litter of pigs.

84   *ambuscados* ambushes
      Spanish blades. The swords of Toledo were famous throughout Europe.

85   *healths five fathom deep* deep drinking

90   *bakes* makes them hard and matted
      elf-locks horses' hair so treated, it was supposed, by elves

91 *untangled* tangled up

92-4 *This is the hag, when maids lie on their backs,* | *That presses them ... good carriage.* Love dreams were formerly attributed to evil spirits who took the form of a sexual partner.

92 *hag* fairy, generally an evil one, producing nightmares

94 *carriage* (three syllables). He puns on 'bearing children', 'deportment', and 'bearing a lover's weight'.

100-103 *And more inconstant than the wind ... dew-dropping South.* The variable wind is imagined as a fickle lover who woos the North, but, having a cold reception there, in pique turns towards the more responsive South (which is *dew-dropping*, in contrast to the *frozen bosom* of the North).

104 *from ourselves* from what we intended to do (go to the Capulets' party)

106-13 *I fear, too early....* | *Direct my sail!* This is probably to be spoken as a soliloquy.

106 *my mind misgives.* See Introduction, p. 19.

107-11 *Some consequence ...* | *Shall bitterly begin his ... date* | *... and expire the term ...* The metaphor is legal. Romeo imagines that he has mortgaged his life from a date beginning that evening. The mortgage will be forfeit, and so he will lose his life.

108 *fearful date* period of time full of fear

109-10 *expire the term* | *Of* bring to an end

112 *He that hath the steerage of my course.* See Introduction pp. 22-4.
He God as Providence

I.5 Editors have marked a new scene here (and it is convenient to keep the numbering for reference purposes); but Mercutio and the others do not go out (*They march about the stage*), and they are met by the Capulet party, who enter at line 16 (*Enter ... to the maskers*).

1-5 *Where's Potpan, that he helps not ... 'tis a foul thing.*

Apparently the two Servingmen are trained house-servants and they speak sarcastically about inferior (perhaps hired) servants (Anthony and Potpan) who are shirking their work; *one or two* perhaps implies that the extra 'hands' are too few.

The part of the First Servingman is doubtless to be taken by the actor of the Clown in I.2.38–80 and I.3.101–4, Gregory or Sampson in I.1, and perhaps Peter.

2   *trencher* wooden dish

6   *joint-stools* stools made of parts fitted together by joiner's work

7   *court-cupboard* sideboard

         plate table-utensils (generally of pewter or silver)

8   *marchpane* marzipan

9   *Susan Grindstone and Nell* (girls coming to the servants' party to be held after the great folks have finished)

11, 14   The Third and Fourth Servingmen are presumably the Potpan and Anthony called at line 10.

13   *Great Chamber* the hall of a great house, used for social occasions

15–16   *the longer liver take all.* A proverbial expression, originally meaning, of course, that the survivor takes the whole property (as of a group of joint-tenants), but becoming a vaguely cheery saying that it doesn't matter what happens when you're dead.

16   (stage direction) *Enter Capulet . . . to the maskers.* There is no sign of Paris in this scene, in spite of Capulet's invitation at I.2.20–34 and Lady Capulet's statement to Juliet at I.3.81 (*This night you shall behold him at our feast*). Only Tybalt, not the gentle Paris, appears as the representative of opposition to Romeo.

17, 22   *Welcome, gentlemen!* Capulet addresses the maskers (Mercutio and his friends in disguise); and as usual he is hospitable.

18   *walk a bout* have a dance

20   *makes dainty* fastidiously hesitates to accept the invitation

21   *Am I come near ye now?* Have I not said something that
       strikes home?

27   *A hall, a hall!* Clear a space for dancing!

28   *you knaves!* (to his servants)
       turn the tables up. Probably they would be boards and
       trestles, easily packed up.

29   *quench the fire.* At I.3.16 we have been told that it is the
       middle of July – and in Italy. At IV.4.16 logs for the
       fire are being fetched. Shakespeare is perhaps thinking
       of a summer evening in England, not in Italy; or he
       may have been unwittingly influenced by his source: in
       Brooke's poem the Capulet party takes place at Christ-
       mas. But compare III.1.2 (*The day is hot*).

30   *sirrah.* It is not clear whom he addresses: perhaps
       cousin Capulet of the next line; perhaps himself.
       unlooked-for sport (the arrival of Mercutio and friends,
       uninvited guests, which made the dance possible)

31   *good cousin Capulet.* He is *Mine uncle Capulet* in the letter
       of invitation at I.2.67. But 'cousin' can be used in
       addressing any kinsman with familiarity or affection.

34   *Were in a mask wore a mask*
       thirty years. We remember that at I.3.73–4 his wife had
       informed us that she was about twenty-eight; again,
       the old age of Capulet is emphasized.

41   *a ward* a minor (a male ward ceased to be under
       guardianship at twenty-one)

43   *I know not, sir.* A surprising remark: the servant does
       not know who is the daughter of the house. Or perhaps
       it is a bit of 'stage-business': the servant is too busy or
       too supercilious to trouble to answer such a foolish (and
       absurdly phrased) question.

44   *she doth teach the torches to burn bright!* The onset of
       love does not deprive Romeo of his power of exagger-
       ated language.
       teach (because she is brighter than they are)

46   *Ethiop* (a common Elizabethan word for a black African)

47   *Beauty too rich for use, for earth too dear!* Her beauty is

too splendid for ordinary life, for 'the uses of this world'. Romeo's verbal quibbles are foreboding; we remember that at I.2.14 Capulet had said: *Earth hath swallowed all my hopes but she.*

48, 49   *shows* appears

48   *a snowy dove trooping with crows*. At I.2.86 Benvolio had said that, if Romeo will accompany him to the Capulet party, *I will make thee think thy swan a crow*.

49   *her fellows* the ladies who are her companions

50   *The measure done* when the dance is finished

51   *touching hers*. Romeo is already forming the image of Juliet as a statue of a saint, the touching of which will bless (lines 93–6 below).

52–3   *Did my heart love till now? Forswear it, sight! | For I ne'er saw true beauty till this night.* What Benvolio had foretold at I.2.81–98 has happened.

52   *Forswear it* deny the previous oath

54   *This, by his voice, should be a Montague*. Tybalt is allowed to overhear part of Romeo's soliloquy. It is not clear how he should recognize a Montague by his voice. But the theatrical convention is sufficient. We have seen Tybalt only for a few moments (speaking I.1.65–71), but it established him as the principal adversary Romeo would have to face. And while Romeo watches Juliet dancing, entranced by her beauty, Tybalt is threatening *To strike him dead.*

56   *covered with an antic face* masked. Such carnival masks were often comic or grotesque in appearance.

57   *fleer* sneer

57, 63   *solemnity* festive occasion

65   *Content thee* take it calmly

    gentle coz. Capulet begins courteously to Tybalt.

66–70   *'A bears him like a portly gentleman ... disparagement.* This striking testimonial from Capulet in favour of Romeo is evidence that, as Friar Laurence is to suggest, the family quarrel is not insoluble if only fire-eaters like Tybalt can be kept under control.

66   *portly* well-mannered (at this party)
70   *disparagement* indignity
74   *semblance* expression on the face
76–88 *He shall be endured ... I'll make you quiet, what!*
      Capulet preserves the peace at his party. But, when
      provoked by Tybalt's *I'll not endure him*, he displays
      the same quick temper as Tybalt himself, and so we
      are prepared for his later display of angry harshness
      towards Juliet.
77   *goodman boy!* This is a double insult: a yeoman (not a
      gentleman) and a youngster; the second insult is passed
      on by Tybalt to Romeo at III.1.65 and 130.
77, 78, 82 *Go to!* (an expression of impatience)
79   *God shall mend my soul!* (an impatient oath)
80   *mutiny* disturbance
81   *set cock-a-hoop.* The phrase is of obscure origin. In the
      earlier uses it seems to mean 'to drink recklessly', and
      so, generally, 'to abandon all restraint'.
      You'll be the man! (derisively) you'll play the big fellow!
83   *saucy* insolent (stronger than the modern meaning of
      the word: compare II.4.142)
      Is't so, indeed? (referring to Tybalt's *Why, uncle, 'tis a
      shame* or perhaps it is the first of Capulet's interruptions
      to speak to a guest, see note on line 86 below)
84   *This trick may chance to scathe you.* Presumably Capu-
      let is threatening Tybalt with some such punishment
      as a reduction of his money expectations. But, ironi-
      cally, his *trick* of quarrelling leads to his death at
      Romeo's hands.
      scathe injure
      I know what I know what I am doing
85   *contrary* (accent on second syllable)
      'tis time. It is not clear whether he is still addressing
      Tybalt or has turned to the company at large; probably
      the former. Perhaps it suggests some piece of stage
      business: Tybalt may bow with constrained respect to
      his uncle-in-law's commands.

86   *Well said, my hearts!* Capulet interrupts his reprimand-
      ing of Tybalt with words to his guests generally and to
      the servants. The exact division of these remarks is not
      always clear.

86, 88   *my hearts* my friends (the company)

86   *princox* pert young fellow

87   *For shame!* This might go with *More light, more light!*,
      but it seems more likely to be addressed to Tybalt.

89-92 *Patience perforce . . . bitterest gall.* Tybalt's rhyming
      couplets are the ominous prelude to the meeting of the
      two lovers. His menaces are fulfilled in III.1.59–60.

89-90 *Patience perforce with wilful choler meeting | Makes my
      flesh tremble* my having to restrain myself, since I have
      come up against Capulet's angry determination, causes
      my body to quiver

90   *in their different greeting* at the meeting of these opposite
      mental states (patience and anger)

92   *Now seeming sweet.* The punctuation of this text indi-
      cates that it is an adjectival phrase qualifying *intrusion*.
      Some editors prefer to omit the commas before and
      after the phrase and treat it as the object of *convert*.

93-106 *If I profane with my unworthiest hand . . .* In this duet
      Romeo and Juliet speak a sonnet, which is concluded
      by their kissing. They begin another sonnet (lines
      107–10), but Juliet half-breaks it with *You kiss by
      th'book*, and then they are interrupted by the Nurse
      (line 111).

      The artificial rhymed verse here provides a kind of
      music to accompany the meeting. It has a somewhat
      indefinite seriousness of metaphor which is perfectly
      appropriate, for the audience can give their full atten-
      tion to the lovers, without having too much concern
      with what they say. The religious phraseology (*holy
      shrine, sin, pilgrims, devotion, saints, holy palmers,
      prayer, faith, trespass*) gives a strong elevation to the
      dialogue. But although on one level it is artificial in
      tone, yet at the same time the whole thing is delicious

verbal fencing, in which Romeo smoothly makes his masculine audacity acceptable and Juliet gives feminine replies which restrain him without stopping him.

It is clear that Juliet has already been observing Romeo while she was dancing and he was standing aside. See note on line 132 below.

94 *holy shrine* her hand

sin. The meaning of this, the unanimous reading of the early editions, is rather difficult; perhaps *the gentle sin is this* means 'this is only a mild and unimportant sin'. Some editors accept an emendation to *fine* (penalty, forfeit). Another attractive emendation is *pain* (suffering due as a penance). But *sin* seems to anticipate lines 107-10 below, and at III.3.39 (in a passage with reminiscences of their words at this meeting) Romeo says that Juliet's lips *Still blush, as thinking their own kisses sin.*

95 *pilgrims* (because his lips intend to visit her hand, which he has just described as a *holy shrine*)

97 *pilgrim.* The emphasis on this word has led to the suggestion that Romeo is wearing the conventional pilgrim's garb (large hat, cloak, staff, scallop shell) as a fancy-dress disguise at the party. Mercutio and his friends are 'maskers', but there seems to be no evidence that they are wearing masquerade costumes. It is probable that there is a further quibble and that Shakespeare knew that the Italian *romeo* meant 'a pilgrim to Rome'. In the Italian dictionary of Shakespeare's contemporary, Florio, the word *romeo* is defined as 'a roamer, a wanderer, a palmer'.

you do wrong your hand too much your hand is not so rough as you say it is (and so there is no need of a kiss to smooth my hand)

98 *mannerly* proper

99 *For saints have hands that pilgrims' hands do touch* for the images of saints (and you seem to be addressing me as if I were a saint) have hands (as I have) which are

touched by the hands of pilgrims (and so a handclasp, instead of a kiss, is sufficient for us)

100   *And palm to palm is holy palmers' kiss.* She quibbles on palm (of the hand) and palmer (pilgrim, originally one who on return from the Holy Land bore a palm-branch or palm-leaf)

102   *prayer* is the emphasized word. Juliet has enticingly ambiguous answers in the fencing of their love-conversation. Here she seems to refute Romeo's argument by reapplying his imagery, but at the same time, perhaps, urges him to further *prayer* for her favour if he wants a kiss from her. She is learning quickly.

103   *let lips do what hands do !* let our lips, like our hands, press each other's (in a kiss)!

104   *They pray: grant thou, lest faith turn to despair.* My lips are indeed praying. You must grant their prayer. Otherwise my faith (my love for you) will turn to despair (which is an irreligious state of mind).

105   *Saints do not move, though grant for prayers' sake.* The statue of a saint (such as you call me) does not move (and take the initiative). But a saint may respond to prayers and grant what is asked for.

106   *Then move not while my prayer's effect I take* then keep still as a statue (don't resist) while I kiss you (and so *take* the answer to my prayer)

109   *urged* mentioned as an argument

110   *by th'book* expertly, as if by instructions in a book of etiquette. Shakespeare generally mocks at the books of instructions; compare Mercutio's scorn of Tybalt as one who *fights by the book of arithmetic* (III.1.101–2).

111   *Madam, your mother craves a word with you.* This may perhaps be played as merely a chaperon's wary intrusion; the Nurse has obviously been watching them (line 115).

112   *Marry, bachelor* good gracious, young man

115, 143   *withal* with

117   *Shall have the chinks.* The Nurse, as well as being

200

garrulous to a stranger, shows her mercenary interests.
There is the usual emphasis on Juliet's position as an
heiress (see note on I.2.14–15).

118   *O dear account!* a terrible reckoning to pay!
    My life is my foe's debt my life (since I love her so
much) is now owing to (dependent upon) my family foe

119   *The sport is at the best.* For the proverbial expression
compare I.4.39.

120   *Ay, so I fear* yes, for I fear that worse things are to
come
    unrest uneasiness

121   *gentlemen.* Capulet addresses the maskers.

122   *banquet* light refreshments (a dessert of, usually, sweetmeats, fruit, and wine)
    towards 'on the way', 'just coming'
    (stage direction) *They whisper in his ear.* This comes
from Q1 and seems to represent an appropriate piece of
stage business by which the maskers excuse themselves.
The audience can imagine their saying that they are
going to visit some other ladies, or something of the
sort – to give a meaning to Capulet's *Is it e'en so.*

124   *honest* honourable

125   *More torches here!* (to show his guests the way out or
their way home)

126   *sirrah* (speaking to himself, or perhaps to 'cousin
Capulet' – compare line 30)
    fay faith

128–32   *Come hither, Nurse. What is yond gentleman? . . . would
not dance?* Juliet does not ask about Romeo at once,
but leads up to the question by her inquiries about two
other men. She is rapidly learning love's pretty little
deceits.

129, 131   *The son and heir of old Tiberio . . . young Petruchio.*
Neither of these are mentioned in the letter of invitation
at I.2.64–9. Petruchio is a Capulet (compare note on
the III.1.33 stage direction) and so cannot be a masker.
(The name 'Petruchio' is pronounced with a soft 'ch'

sound, not a 'k' sound. The Elizabethan spelling 'Petruchio' represents the Italian *Petruccio*; and so to pronounce the name as 'Petrookio' because one knows that in Italian the symbol *ch* represents the 'k' sound is misapplied knowledge.)

132 *that would not dance*. Romeo had said (I.4.11–22 and 35–9) he had no intention of dancing. Juliet's words indicate that she had seen Romeo watching her while she was dancing with one of the guests (from line 42 to about line 86, which sounds like the end of the *measure*, for which Romeo is waiting).

134 *If he be marrièd* . . . Juliet now at once thinks of marriage, though at I.3.67 she had said that *It is an honour that I dream not of*.

135 *My grave is like to be my wedding bed*. This is the introduction of the theme of death as Juliet's lover. At III.2.137 she says: *death, not Romeo, take my maidenhead*. Compare IV.5.35–9 and V.3.102–5.

138 *My only love, sprung from my only hate!* the one man I love is the son of the one household I, as a Capulet, hate

139 *Too early seen unknown, and known too late!* I saw him too soon without knowing who he was, and fell in love with him; and, now that I have found out who he is, it is too late to do anything about it, for I am already in love

140 *Prodigious* monstrous and so ill-omened. Juliet, too, has her premonitions of disaster, at discovering with whom she has fallen in love.

142 *What's this?* Q2 reads *Whats tis?*, which may indicate a vulgar or dialectal form of the demonstrative pronoun.

143 *one I danced withal*. She cannot be referring to Romeo since she clearly did not dance with him (line 132), and the Nurse had seen her *talking* with Romeo (line 115). She is giving an evasive reply.

Anon at once

Chorus	See note on the Chorus-prologue to Act 1 (page 169). Dr Johnson justly commented: 'The use of this chorus is not easily discovered, it conduces nothing to the progress of the play, but relates what is already known, or what the next scenes will shew; and relates it without adding the improvement of any moral sentiment.' Although the Chorus-prologue is often spoken, the second Chorus has usually been abandoned by stage tradition. This may have already been so in Shakespeare's time, for in Q1 (which seems to derive from a theatre production) the Chorus-prologue appears, but the second Chorus does not.
1	*old desire* Romeo's former love for Rosaline
2	*young affection* his new love for Juliet
	gapes longs eagerly, as with open mouth
3	*That fair* (Rosaline)
	love the lover (Romeo)
6	*Alike bewitchèd* both he and she equally are enchanted by love
7	*his foe supposed* (Juliet, who is of the family of the Capulets and so supposed to be an enemy)
	complain make his lover's lamentations
8	*fearful* causing fear. Juliet is playing a risky game; she is like a fish trying to take the bait off the hook without being caught.
9	*access* (accent on second syllable)
10	*use* are accustomed
13	*time means* time lends them means
14	*Tempering extremities with extreme sweet* mitigating the hardship of their situation by means of the great sweetness of their meetings
	extreme (accent on first syllable)
II.1.1	*forward* (away from Juliet)
2	*dull earth* (his body)

thy centre (Juliet is now the centre of his world, since his heart is where she is)

6   *conjure* summon spirits by magical incantation. Mercutio begins a parody of the formulas of practical magic, including a list of names (line 7) by which a spirit is summoned.

7   *Humours* moods and affectations

10   *'Ay me!'* This phrase had almost been Romeo's first words on entering the play (I.1.161).

11   *my gossip Venus* my friend, the goddess of love

12   *purblind* dim-sighted

13   *Abraham Cupid.* This phrase is difficult. 'Abraham men' were beggars, and perhaps Cupid is imagined in the guise of a hypocritical beggar. The emendation to *Adam Cupid* has often been accepted, on the grounds of similarity with the sentence in *Much Ado About Nothing*: 'shoot at me, and he that hits me let him be clapped on the shoulder, and called Adam' (I.1.260). It has been suggested that *Young Abraham* is a paradox, as Abraham was the biblical patriarch: Cupid, too, is both a young boy and the oldest of the gods.
     trim. Q2 reads *true*. But the correctness of *trim* (from Q1) seems confirmed by the line in the old ballad on the subject of King Cophetua and the beggar maid: 'The blinded boy, that shoots so trim . . .'

14   *When King Cophetua loved the beggar maid.* The old ballad which told this story has been preserved in a printed text of 1612.

16   *The ape is dead* the poor creature is pretending to be lifeless

17–21 *I conjure thee . . . appear to us!* Mercutio continues his parody of the formulas of magical incantation.

20   *demesnes* domains

24   *raise a spirit* by magical power compel a spirit to appear (with bawdy quibble)
     circle magical circle (with bawdy quibble)

25   *strange* belonging to another person (not Romeo)

26   *laid it* by magical power appeased a spirit and com-
pelled it to cease to appear (with bawdy quibble)
conjured (two syllables; with accent on second syllable,
unlike lines 6, 16, 17, 29)

27   *were some spite* would be doing him some wrong
invocation (five syllables)

29   *to raise up him* make him, like a conjured spirit, appear
to us (with a bawdy quibble)

31   *be consorted with* be associated with
humorous humid, but punning on the meaning of
'humorous' as 'full of humour' (as in line 7 above)

34, 36   *medlar tree . . . medlars.* As 'to meddle' was a common
word for sexual activity, the word 'medlar' was an
obvious opportunity for bawdy puns about the sex-
organs.

38   *open-arse* a country-name for the medlar-fruit
poppering pear (with bawdy quibble) kind of pear
named after the Flemish town of Poperinghe

39   *truckle-bed* small bed on wheels ('truckles') which could
be pushed under another bed

40   *field-bed* bed on the ground (but punning on 'camp
bed')

II.2.1   (stage direction) (*coming forward*) Presumably Romeo
had moved to the back of the stage or retired behind a
pillar (*he hath hid himself among these trees*, II.1.30),
where he would be assumed to be unseen by Mercutio
and Benvolio but visible to the audience. He now comes
forward.

1   *He jests at scars that never felt a wound.* Romeo com-
pletes the couplet of which Benvolio had spoken the
first line.
He a man like Mercutio

2   *But soft! What light through yonder window breaks?* It is
remarkable that Shakespeare provides no transition,
beyond Romeo's single sentence at line 1, between

Mercutio's ribaldries and the appearance of Juliet at her window.

7   *Be not her maid* do not be a follower of the virgin-goddess Diana, cold to love and averse to marriage

8   *vestal* virgin
        sick and green (suggestive of the pallor of moonlight)

9   *none but fools do wear it* it is foolish to remain cold to love and the *pale* and *green* of such maidens remind one of the motley of court-jesters

11   *O that she knew she were!* ('my love' is understood)

15   *stars* planets (as is shown by the *spheres* of line 17)

16   *Having some business* having something to do away from home

17   *spheres* the concentric spheres in which (in the astronomy before Copernicus) the planets were supposed to move

18   *there* (in the spheres left by the two stars)
        they (the stars)

21   *region* (of the sky)

28   *wingèd messenger* angel

29   *white-upturnèd . . . eyes* eyes with the whites turned upwards

31   *lazy, puffing.* Q1 has the pleasant reading *lazy-pacing.* But *puffing* (Q2) makes good sense (swollen in bulk, 'puffed out').

33   *wherefore* why

34   *refuse* abjure

39   *though not a Montague* whatever you call yourself; even though you *do* take some name other than Montague. Some editors punctuate: *Thou art thyself though, not a Montague.*

40–42   *What's Montague? It is nor hand nor foot . . . Belonging to a man.* Romeo remembers this at III.3.106–7.

44   *word.* The Q1 reading *name* was included in many of the older editions of Shakespeare, and so became usual in the proverbial saying.

46   *owes* owns

48   *for thy name* in exchange for thy name

53   *counsel* self-communings

53-4   *By a name | I know not how to tell thee who I am* I do
not know by means of what name I am to tell you who
I am

55   *dear saint.* Romeo subtly refers to their earlier meeting.
He had addressed her as 'dear saint' at I.5.103.

61   *thee dislike* is unpleasing to you

62-5, 74, 79 *How camest thou hither, tell me, and wherefore?*
Juliet's questions and comments are all direct and practical. Romeo's answers are all vague and fantastic.

62   *wherefore* (accent on second syllable)

66   *o'erperch* fly over

68   *can* (emphasized)

76   *but* unless

78   *prorogued* deferred

82-4   *I am no pilot . . . adventure for such merchandise.* For the
imagery, see Introduction, p. 23.

83   *vast* large and empty

84   *adventure* venture (the word was especially used for
mercantile enterprise overseas)

85-7   *Thou knowest the mask . . . speak tonight.* Juliet is conscious of her tendency to blush. Compare III.2.14
(*Hood my unmanned blood, bating in my cheeks*). The
Nurse notices it (*Now comes the wanton blood up in your
cheeks*, II.5.70). Charles Darwin in his book *The Expression of the Emotions in Man and Animals* (1872) has
some interesting remarks about Juliet's blushing. Since
blushes may be excited in absolute solitude, the darkness would not prevent Juliet's blushing; Darwin concludes that Shakespeare may have erred or may have
meant that the blush was unseen, not that it was ab-
sent.

88   *Fain* gladly

       dwell on form preserve my formal behaviour

89   *farewell compliment!* Shakespeare's young women in
love thus overcome their conventional restraints and

female arts. Likewise Miranda in *The Tempest* exclaims 'Hence, bashful cunning!' (III.1.81), when declaring herself to Ferdinand.

compliment polite conventions

92–3 *At lovers' perjuries, | They say, Jove laughs.* A proverbial expression, which comes from the *Art of Love* of Ovid: *Juppiter ex alto perjuria ridet amantum* (i. 633).

97 *So thou wilt woo* if only you will woo me

98 *fond* somewhat foolishly in love

99 *'haviour* behaviour

101 *cunning.* See the quotation from *The Tempest* in note on line 89 above.

strange distant, reserved

106 *Which* (yielding)

107 *Lady, by yonder blessèd moon I vow.* Romeo is about to slip into the characteristic phrases of the affected lover, but Juliet promptly cuts short these protestations (line 109).

110 *circled orb* the sphere in which the moon moves (compare note on line 17 above)

111 *variable* (four syllables, with secondary accent on the third syllable and a light fourth syllable)

116–20 *Although I joy in thee, | I have no joy of this contract tonight* ... For Juliet's forebodings, see Introduction, p. 19.

117 *contract* (accent on second syllable) exchange of lovers' vows

118 *unadvised* without careful consideration

124 *as that* as to that heart which is

129 *I would it were to give again.* I wish I had it so that I could give it a second time.

141 *substantial* (four syllables)

143 *thy bent of love* the inclination of your love

144 *Thy purpose marriage.* As at I.5.134, her thoughts are immediately on marriage.

145 *By one that I'll procure to come to thee.* In a characteristically practical spirit Juliet arranges the means of communication.

145   *procure* arrange

150   *anon* very soon

151   *By and by* immediately

152   *strife* striving. The reading *suit* (which is found in Q4) is adopted, by many editors; but the Q2 *strife* is acceptable, meaning 'endeavour to woo me'.

153   *So thrive my soul* as my immortal soul may be saved from damnation

155   *to want thy light* lacking the light of your presence (see lines 2–4 above)

159   *tassel-gentle* male falcon

160   *Bondage is hoarse.* Because she is in bondage in her father's house, she has to whisper Romeo's name.

161   *tear the cave* rend the hollow vault of air

162   *airy tongue.* Echo has no real tongue but merely reverberates the air.

167   *nyas* a young hawk, still in its nest. Romeo carries on the reference to falconry, from *tassel-gentle* in line 159. In Q2 the word is spelt *Neece*; this was obscure to the printers of later Quartos and Folios and it was amended to *my dear* (Q4) or *my sweet* (F1). But the brilliant explanation of the word by J. Dover Wilson (1955) can hardly be doubted.

168   *By the hour of nine.* It is in fact noon (II 4 109–10) when the Nurse meets Romeo the following morning.

170–85   *I have forgot why I did call thee back . . . till it be morrow.* Granville-Barker writes: 'This is the commonplace made marvellous. What is it, indeed, but the well-worn comic theme of the lovers that cannot once for all say good-bye and part, turned to pure beauty by the alchemy of the poet?'

177   *wanton* young mischievous person

179   *gyves* shackles (now pronounced with a soft 'g', as in 'gypsy')

180   *And with a silken thread plucks it back again.* The metrical irregularity is expressive.

188–91 *The grey-eyed morn smiles on the frowning night . . .*
From forth day's pathway made by Titan's wheels. In
Q2 these four lines are printed twice; once here and
then again (with small changes) as the opening of the
Friar's speech in the next scene. Many editors leave
them with the Friar. But the wild imagery of the lines
is more characteristic of Romeo.

188 *grey-eyed.* Probably this means 'with blue eyes'. See
note on II.4.42.

190 *fleckled* dappled (with spots of light)

191 *From forth* out of the way of
Titan's wheels. The sun god, according to classical
mythology, was Hyperion, one of the Titans, and he
drove across the sky in his chariot (compare III.2.1–4).

192 *Hence* from here
ghostly spiritual
close narrow

193 *dear hap* precious piece of good fortune

II.3.1–26 *Now, ere the sun advance his burning eye . . . eats up that*
plant. This long rhyming soliloquy given to the Friar
enables him to impress himself upon the audience. He
is shown to be simple, good-humoured, and well-
meaning, but also willing (as he shows later, lines 87–8)
to suppose himself a manipulator of the fates of others.
The discussion of the power of herbs prepares us for
his offer of the potion that Juliet drinks; also for the
Apothecary's poison that slays Romeo. For the four
lines often printed at the opening of this scene (*The*
grey-eyed morn smiles . . . Titan's fiery wheels), see note
on II.2.188–91 above.

1 *advance* raise

2 *The day to cheer and night's dank dew to dry.* The pace
of this line seems at once to indicate the Friar's manner
of speech.

3 *osier cage* willow basket

5   *nature's mother* the mother of all natural things (including the *plants, herbs, stones* of line 12)

6   *her burying grave* the grave which buries all natural things

      that (stressed)

7   *her womb* the place where natural things are begotten

      children that is, plants

      divers various

8   *We sucking . . . find* we find sucking

10   *None but for some* there are no plants which are not useful for *some* purpose

11   *mickle* great

      grace divine power and effectiveness

12   *true qualities* inherent powers

13   *For naught so vile* for there is nothing so vile

14   *to the earth* to the inhabitants of the earth

15   *strained* perverted

      that fair use that proper and virtuous use intended by nature

16   *Revolts from true birth* denies the power for which it was created (emphasis on *true*)

      stumbling on abuse if it chances to be mistakenly abused

17–18 *Virtue itself turns vice, being misapplied, | And vice sometime's by action dignified.* This is a somewhat casuistical demonstration that good qualities can be applied in the wrong spirit to have ill effects, and that bad qualities rightly used can have good effects.

17   *turns* turns into

18   *vice sometime's by action dignified.* An evil quality may, occasionally, have our approval because it results, in certain circumstances, in a good action.

19   *Within the infant rind of this weak flower.* . . . Q2 indicates the entry of Romeo here, and some editors retain it at this place so that he overhears the Friar's meditation on poison, grace, and will (lines 19–26), with some ironical effect. But the marking of entries of characters

earlier than their first words is not unusual; and in production the Friar is generally allowed to complete his piece before the attention of the audience is diverted by Romeo's entrance.

20   *Poison hath residence, and medicine power* both poison and curative power are contained

21   *with that part* by means of smelling it
cheers each part revives each portion of the body

22   *stays.* Q1 reads *slays*, and this has been adopted by many editors on the grounds that the Friar is here talking about death (line 26), and so the anticipation of Juliet's suspended animation (see his words at IV.1.93–106) does not seem admissible. But *stays* need not refer to suspended animation: rather, 'to bring the heart to a standstill, and with it all the senses'.

23   *still* always

24   *grace and rude will* on the one hand, the capacity to receive divine grace; on the other, the impulse to give way to one's fleshly desires

25   *the worser* (rude will)

26   *canker* cankerworm

27   *Benedicite!* (five syllables, with accent on third syllable, which is pronounced to rhyme with 'nice', and final vowel as short 'i') may God bless you!

29   *argues* proves
distempered disturbed by an unhealthy mixture (or tempering) of the bodily humours

30   *good morrow* farewell (unlike the *Good morrow* of line 27, which is a greeting at meeting)

31   *keeps his watch* keeps awake

33   *unbruisèd* undamaged by the world
unstuffed not clogged up with troubles (like one's nose when 'stuffy')

36   *distemperature.* See note on 'distempered', line 29 above.

40, 41, 62, 66, 74, 77 *Rosaline.* The audience, in spite of the enchantments of the last scene, is not allowed to forget Rosaline, though Romeo has *forgot that name and that name's woe* – as Benvolio had prophesied in I.1.225–38. See again at II.4.4.

41   *ghostly* spiritual

42   *that name's woe* the woe that that name caused me

45   *mine enemy* (Capulet)

46   *one* (Juliet)

46, 47   *wounded* (with Cupid's arrows, but Romeo is quibbling on *enemy* and *foe*)

47   *That's* (Juliet) who is
    Both our remedies the remedy, for both of us

48   *holy physic* (his powers not as a physician but as a priest, who will heal them by the sacrament of marriage)
    lies (a plural form in Shakespeare's usage)

49   *I bear no hatred* (at having been wounded by my foe, Juliet)

50   *intercession* petition (the word usually had a religious suggestion in Elizabethan usage)
    steads benefits

51   *homely* straightforward

52   *shrift* absolution

54   *rich Capulet.* Compare I.2.78, and the Nurse's words to Romeo at I.5.116–17: *he that can lay hold of her | Shall have the chinks.*

56   *all combined* altogether united in heart

59   *as we pass* as you and I go along (as usual, Romeo is in a hurry: compare line 89 below)

61   *Holy Saint Francis!* Laurence is, of course, a Franciscan.

68   *To season love, that of it doth not taste* (you have tried) to 'preserve' love (by salting it down in your tears), but (in spite of the salting, your) love still has no flavour

75   *sentence* general maxim, proverbial saying

77   *chidst* (past tense, short vowel)

81–2   *Her I love now | Doth ...* she whom I love now does ...

82   *grace for grace* a mutual exchange of love's favours

84   *Thy love did read by rote, that could not spell.* Your

notions of love were like those of someone who could recite words of a text learnt by heart without actually being able to read the words.

85   *waverer* (three syllables)

86   *In one respect* on account of one thing

87–8   *this alliance may so happy prove | To turn your house-holds' rancour to pure love.* For the audience this is an ironical hope – the alliance *will*, but only by the death of the two lovers (see V.3.296–304).

89   *stand on* insist upon

II.4.2   *tonight* last night

4   *that same pale hard-hearted wench, that Rosaline.* See note on II.3.40.

6   *Tybalt.* The first shadow falls. We are now reminded of Tybalt's ominous threats at I.5.89–92 and again feel the irony of the Friar's hopefulness at II.3.87–8.

9, 11 *answer* appear in person in response to a challenge. But in line 10 Mercutio with a quibble takes the word merely as 'reply to a letter'.

11   *how* as

12   *dared* challenged

14   *white wench's black eye.* See Introduction, p. 12.

15   *the very pin of his heart* the 'bull's eye'

16   *blind bow-boy* Cupid
       butt-shaft blunt-headed arrow for practising archery

18   *Why, what is Tybalt!* This is not a question, asking for information, but a derisive comment on Tybalt's abilities. At I.1.108–12 Benvolio had already described with some sarcasm Tybalt's manner of fighting (*the winds . . . hissed him in scorn*).

19   *Prince of Cats.* Tybalt is his name in the medieval stories of Reynard the Fox. Similarly, in III.1.74–7 Mercutio calls him *King of Cats* and *ratcatcher* and mocks at his alleged *nine lives.*

20   *compliments* formalities of the duel

20–21   *as you sing pricksong* as orderly as one follows the printed music (not extempore) in singing

21   *proportion* rhythm

23   *butcher of a silk button*. A skilful fencer could, allegedly, touch any particular button on his opponent's garment.

24   *duellist*. This was apparently a novel term in Shakespeare's time; Mercutio mocks at the new-fangled word.
  first house best school of instruction

25   *first and second cause*. These are the steps by which a quarrel developed, ending in a duel. In *As You Like It* (V.4.48–108) Touchstone gives a satirical account of the seven 'causes': 'we quarrel in print, by the book, as you have books for good manners'.
  passado lunging thrust (from the Italian *passata*)

26   *punto reverso* backhanded thrust (from the Italian, literally 'point reversed')
  hay thrust through (from Italian *hai*, 'thou hast [it]')

28   *The pox of* the plague upon
  antic grotesque
  fantasticoes fops

29   *new tuners of accent* those who introduce novel kinds of language

30   *tall* brave

31   *grandsire* Benvolio (mockingly perhaps because he is rather serious and peace-loving)

32   *flies* parasites

33   *pardon-me's*. Q2 reads *pardons mees* and Q1 *pardonmees*. Some editors 'improve' the joke by giving the phrase an Italianate or Frenchified form: *perdona-mi's* or *pardonnez-moi's*; but it seems that it is the affected English phrase that Mercutio is jeering at.
  stand insist

34   *form* code of manners
  bench. He quibbles on the previous *form*, as he does on *stand* and *sit*.

35   *their bones* (presumably) their fastidious or sensitive

   bodies (with a quibble on French *bons*), which are uncomfortable on the old kind of furniture (*bench*)

37   *roe* (punning on the first syllable of Romeo, so that he
   is only 'half himself', as well as on 'roe', deer)

38   *flesh, how art thou fishified!* (continuing the quibble on
   roe – a man is being compared to a herring)
   for the numbers inclined to the composition of (metrical)
   poetry

38–9   *the numbers that Petrarch flowed in.* The sonnets that
   Petrarch (1304–74) wrote to his chaste love Laura de
   Noves were a model for love poetry throughout Europe.
   The poet celebrates her beauty and virtue, and laments
   somewhat tearfully (hence *flowed*) the pangs of his un-
   fulfilled love. Shakespeare often mentions critically or
   satirically the conventions of Petrarchan love-poetry,
   notably in Sonnet 130 (in praise of the lady's beauty).

39   *to his lady* in comparison with his lady

39–40   *Laura, to his lady, was a kitchen wench – marry, she had a*
   better love to berhyme her it was only because Laura had
   a lover better at making poetry than Romeo is that, in
   spite of her being a kitchen-wench in comparison with
   Rosaline, she is so famous

41   *Dido a dowdy.* Perhaps because Dido, the queen of
   Carthage and Aeneas's love, was a widow. There are
   jests about 'widow Dido' in *The Tempest*, II.1.71–96.
   The alliteration here (and in *Helen and Hero hildings*
   and harlots) is part of the jest at poetry.
   Cleopatra a gypsy. She is twice called a 'gypsy' in a
   derogatory way in *Antony and Cleopatra* (I.1.10 and
   IV.12.28). The Elizabethans seem to have imagined
   Cleopatra as, vaguely, a dark-complexioned Egyptian
   (in Shakespeare's play she has a 'tawny front' and is
   'with Phoebus' amorous pinches black') though she was,
   of course, of pure Macedonian blood. When the gypsies
   first appeared in England about the beginning of the
   sixteenth century they were commonly believed to be
   Egyptians in origin.

41   *Helen* (of Sparta, whose abduction by Paris was the cause of the Trojan war)

Hero (of Sestos, the beloved of Leander, who swam the Hellespont from Abydos to visit her and was drowned)

42   *hildings* good-for-nothings

Thisbe (the beloved of Pyramus, familiar to us from the playlet of the rude mechanicals in *A Midsummer Night's Dream*, which was probably written soon after *Romeo and Juliet*)

grey eye. Both grey and what we now call 'blue' eyes were, it seems, described as 'grey' in Shakespeare's time. Compare 'grey-eyed morn' in II.2.188. The phrase 'blue-eyed' was used of a person with dark shadows around the eyes due to weeping, sickness, and so on.

42-3   *not to the purpose* that is of no importance

44   *to your French slop* appropriate to your loose trousers. Presumably this indicates Romeo's costume.

48   *slip* counterfeit coin. Mercutio puns on the other meaning of *slip*, 'an evasive action'.

Can you not conceive? Can you not use your imagination?

50   *to bow in the hams.* Mercutio (as Romeo explains in the next line) puns on 'courtesy' and 'curtsy', which apparently had the same pronunciation.

53 85   *Meaning, to curtsy . . . a broad goose.* Romeo is now in high spirits and is the equal of Mercutio in making verbal jests. There is a series of associations: (1) *courtesy, curtsy, courteous*, leads to *pink of courtesy*; (2) *pink* is not only 'highest degree' but also the *flower* and perforated ornaments on a *pump* (shoe); (3) *pump* leads to *sole* and thence to *solely* (singularly) and perhaps 'soul', since 'single-souled', mean or contemptible, is a phrase like 'narrow-souled'.

54   *kindly* naturally

59   *pump well-flowered.* If *pink* is a flower, then the 'pinkings' (perforations of a decorative kind) of his shoes are 'flowerings'.

64   *single-soled* thin
      singleness simplicity, silliness

68   *Swits and spurs ...!* Urge your horse faster with switches and spurs ...!

68–9   *cry a match* claim the victory

70   *wild-goose chase* an erratic cross-country horse-race in which whoever takes the lead has to be followed by the others. Mercutio picks up the metaphor in Romeo's *swits and spurs*, and a series of jests on *goose* now begins, mostly sexual quibbles.

72–3   *Was I with you ...?* Did I manage to keep even with you ...?

73   *goose* (probably) whore

75   *for the goose* as the 'silly goose' of the company. (Romeo's jibe that Mercutio is the jester in any company he is with strikes home, as Mercutio's reply shows.)

76   *bite thee by the ear* (to show affection, but Mercutio speaks ironically)

78   *sweeting* sweet apple

80–81   *well served in to a sweet goose* (because a goose needs a sharp apple-sauce)

82   *cheverel* kid, easily stretched

83   *ell* forty-five inches

85   *broad goose* (with bawdy quibble)

87–8   *art ... art ... art* (quibbling on *thou art* and the *art* which is opposed to nature)

89   *natural* idiot (by nature; quibbling on the *nature* in the previous sentence)
      lolling with the tongue (or *bauble*) hanging out

90   *bauble* decorated stick carried by a professional fool (with a bawdy quibble)

92–3   *against the hair* against the grain. Mercutio puns indecently on *there* (line 91).

94   *thy tale large* (with a bawdy pun)

97   *occupy.* This was an indecent word in Shakespeare's time. Compare Doll Tearsheet in *2 Henry IV* (II.4.159):

'A captain! God's light, these villains will make the word as odious as the word "occupy", which was an excellent good word before it was ill sorted.'

98   *goodly gear* matter for mockery (referring to what has gone before)

99   *A sail, a sail!* This perhaps indicates that the Nurse is rather over-dressed. It has not been explained why she has taken three hours to come to meet Romeo.

100   *A shirt and a smock* a man and a woman

104-5   *the fairer face*. This is the Q2 reading. Q1 has *the fairer of the two*, adopted by some editors.

107   *God ye good-e'en* (God give you) good evening (or afternoon)

108   *Is it good-e'en?* Is it evening?

111   *Out upon you!* (expressing indignation). The Nurse reacts promptly to Mercutio's way of saying that the clock shows it is now midday.

112-13   *for himself to mar*. Q2 omits *for* (which is found in Q1), but as the Nurse repeats the phrase in line 114, its insertion is probably justified here.

115-16   *can any of you tell me where I may find the young Romeo?* Presumably Shakespeare has forgotten that the Nurse, having already spoken to the masked Romeo at the party, had been later sent by Juliet to identify him (I.5.112-17 and 132-7).

119   *for fault of* in default of

124   *confidence*. Presumably she blunders for 'conference'.

126   *endite* invite (perhaps a deliberately blundering word, following the Nurse's misuse of *confidence*)

127   *So ho!* huntsman's cry when the game (such as a hare) is sighted. Romeo therefore replies with *What hast thou found?* and Mercutio continues with jokes about *hare* (whore).

129   *lenten pie* one without meat, served in Lent

130   *stale and hoar* (both are quibbles on *whore*)
        spent used up

141   *Lady, lady, lady* (the refrain of an old ballad)

142   *I pray you, sir.* Some editors insert, before this, *Marry, farewell!* from Q1.

       saucy merchant insolent fellow (*saucy* had a strong meaning)

143   *ropery* rascality

145–6 *stand to* abide by

147–8 *take him down* humble him (with unwitting bawdy quibble)

149   *Jacks* low fellows (compare III.1.11 and IV.5.143)

150   *flirt-gills* fast girls

151   *skains-mates* knives-mates; that is, cut-throat fellows

152–5 *and suffer every knave to use me at his pleasure!* ... *weapon should quickly have been out.* As usual, the Nurse lapses into unintentional bawdry and Peter continues in the same vein.

157   *the law on my side.* Compare the anxiety of Sampson and Gregory in the quarrel in the opening scene (I.1.37 and 46).

160   *as I told you.* Apparently Romeo and the Nurse have been conversing apart during Mercutio's singing (lines 131–6).

160, 161 *bid* (past tense)

162   *lead her in a fool's paradise* seduce her

165   *deal double* deceive

167   *weak* contemptible

168, 189, 208 *commend me* give my best regards

169, 174 *protest* Romeo begins to say 'I swear . . .', but the Nurse takes *protest* in its colloquial sense of 'I make a declaration of love.'

177   *shrift* absolution

178   *Friar.* The word is sometimes two syllables, sometimes one syllable, in Shakespeare's verse.

179   *shrived* absolved

180   *No, truly, sir. Not a penny.* After a show of protest, the Nurse takes the money.

185   *tackled stair* rope ladder

186   *high topgallant* summit (literally, the highest platform

or sails on a ship, to which Romeo imagines himself
climbing by means of his rope ladder)

187   *convoy* conveyance

188   *quit* requite (with payment)

189   *mistress* (three syllables)

193   *Two may keep counsel, putting one away* two, but not
three, can keep a secret (a proverbial expression)

197-8   *lay knife aboard* make his claim for her (at table a diner
brought his own knife)

199   *I anger her sometimes.* Shakespeare here ignores the
time-scheme of the play; the Nurse could only have
heard about Romeo a few hours ago, but she talks as if
the affair had been going on for some time. Compare
Juliet's words at III.5.238-40 (and note).

201   *versal* universal (in the Nurse's language)

202   *rosemary and Romeo.* Compare the rosemary in IV.5.79
and 95 (stage direction).
    a letter the same letter. The Nurse cannot read or
write.

204   *the dog's name.* 'R' was commonly called the dog's
letter as its sound resembled a dog's growling. Probably
the r-sound was more strongly sounded in Shakespeare's pronunciation than it is at the present time in
standard (southern) English.

206   *sententious* (presumably) a blunder for 'sentences'

208   *Commend me to thy lady.* Romeo departs, apparently
not much interested in *the prettiest sententious* that the
Nurse wants to relate.

211   *Before, and apace.* Some editors insert, in front of this,
from Q1: *Peter, take my fan, and go*; but this is probably
a repetition from line 103 above.

I.5.1   *The clock struck nine* (as she and Romeo had agreed at
II.2.168; but it was noon when the Nurse met him,
II.4.110 and line 10 below)

5   *glides* (plural form)

221

6   *louring* (rhymes with 'flowering') looking dark and threatening

7   *pinioned* winged
     draw (in her chariot)
     love the goddess of love, Venus

9   *highmost* highest. It is midday and the sun is at its zenith.

11   *hours* (two syllables)

14   *bandy* toss back (as in tennis, carrying on the metaphor of *ball* in the previous line)

15   *And his to me* and his words would bandy her back to me

16   *old folks, many feign as they were dead* many old people act as if they were only half alive. In *feign as they were dead* we have a curious anticipation of Juliet's later ordeal. But the awkward lines could perhaps mean 'many people talk about old folks, in a fanciful way, as being dead . . .' There may, however, be something wrong with the text here: among the emendations proposed, *marry, fare* for *many feign* gives good sense.

25   *Give me leave* let me alone

26   *jaunce* jaunt (literally, prance)

29   *stay* wait

34   *excuse* (thyself from telling)

36   *stay the circumstance* wait for details

38   *simple* foolish

41   *body.* Q1 prints this as *baudie*, and some editors have seen this as evidence that a suggestive pun is intended, especially as the Nurse continues: *though they be not to be talked on* (which could, however, mean 'though they are not worth talking about').

44   *Go thy ways, wench. Serve God.* Conversational phrases meaning 'enough of that'.

50   *a't'other* on the other. The usual stage-business here is that Juliet rubs the Nurse's back.

51   *Beshrew* confound

52   *jauncing* jaunting (compare line 26 above)

55   *honest* honourable

62   *Marry come up, I trow* (expressions of impatience or wounded dignity here affected by the Nurse)

65   *coil* trouble

68, 72, 77, 78 *hie* hasten

70   *Now comes the wanton blood.* For Juliet's blushing, see note on II.2.85–7.

71   *They'll be in scarlet straight* your cheeks are always inclined to flush suddenly

72–3   *I must another way, | To fetch a ladder . . .* (as instructed by Romeo at II.4.183–7)

76   *bear the burden.* She quibbles on the meanings: 'carry the responsibility of work' and 'bear the weight of your lover'.

78   *Hie to high fortune!* Juliet quibbles, in her excited state of mind, but her height of fortune is ominous; the wheel will soon begin to turn.

II.6.1   *So smile the heavens* so may the heavens smile

3   *But come what sorrow can* but let whatever sorrow come that possibly may come

4   *It cannot countervail the exchange of joy* the sorrow will not be able to outweigh the joy for which it must be taken in exchange

7   *do* may do

9–15   *These violent delights have violent ends . . . as too slow.* The Friar gives his brief marriage-sermon on the theme of *Love moderately. Long love doth so.*

10   *fire and powder* (gunpowder). For the imagery see Introduction, pp. 31–2.

11–12   *The sweetest honey | Is loathsome in his own deliciousness* honey is sweet; but merely because the sweetness is so strongly delicious it has the possibility of becoming loathsome

13   *confounds* destroys

16–20   *Here comes the lady. O, so light a foot . . . So light is vanity*. These lines are difficult to interpret exactly, though they are theatrically very effective. The Friar stands apart, moralizing a little sadly, as Juliet enters and embraces Romeo – it is the first time they have touched each other since their first meeting, in spite of their declarations of mutual love. The Friar's words, *so light a foot | Will ne'er wear out the everlasting flint*, are generally felt by the audience to mean (vaguely) that a delicate creature like Juliet will not be able to stand up to the hard knocks of life, or (even) that she hasn't got long to live. The words will hardly bear this pathetic interpretation. The Friar is observing the buoyant bearing of Juliet as she comes to meet her lover: her feet scarcely seem to touch the ground. He then passes to the general statement that love has the effect of making a lover so exhilarated that he needs little support on the earth. In both instances (*ne'er wear out the everlasting flint* and *bestride the gossamers*) the Friar is using exaggerated images.

19   *idles* (plural form)

20   *vanity* the empty delights of this transitory world (the Friar speaks from the point of view of religion)

21   *confessor* (accent on first syllable)

23   *As much to him, else is his thanks too much* if Romeo is to give thanks on behalf of both of you, I must give him a greeting too, the same one as I gave to you

24-9   *if the measure of thy joy . . . by this dear encounter* if you are filled with joy as I am, and if you have greater skill than I have in describing it appropriately, then let your sweet and musical voice be heard, revealing the happiness which we receive from each other by our thus coming together

26   *blazon* to set out in appropriate colours (a heraldic term)

30-31   *Conceit, more rich in matter than in words, | Brags of his substance, not of ornament* imagination, when it is richer in substance than in mere words, makes a display of the reality (of feeling), not of the appearances

34 *I cannot sum up sum of half my wealth*. In order to make the line simpler, some editors rearrange the words as: *I cannot sum up half my sum of wealth*.

II.1 The contrast between the quiet close of the previous scene and the impending violence at the opening of this scene is theatrically striking.

 (stage direction) *Enter Mercutio, Benvolio, and their men*. The *men* include Mercutio's page, whom he addresses at line 94.

1–4 *I pray thee, good Mercutio, let's retire ... mad blood stirring*. Benvolio tries to be a peacemaker (as in I.1.63–8). See also lines 49–52 below, where he urges prudence.

2 *The day is hot*. See note on I.5.29.

 Capels Capulets (as in V.1.18 and V.3.127). The abbreviated form is found in Brooke's *Romeus and Juliet*.

3 *And if* perhaps *An if*: that is, merely a double form of 'if' (see lines 15, 30 below, where in the original text *an* is spelt *and*),

5 *Thou art like one of these fellows* ... Benvolio has been speaking in simple blank verse, but Mercutio changes to lively and characterful prose.

5–7 *when he enters the confines of a tavern, claps me his sword upon the table* ... The braggart ostentatiously lays aside his sword, but he is really issuing a defiance to all present in the tavern; his apparent prayer for peace is itself a kind of provocation.

6 *me*. This grammatical usage (an indefinite indirect object, which in the old grammar books used to be called the 'ethic dative') gives an air of familiarity and ease to the dialogue.

8 *operation* influence on the brain or body (that is, the second draught of liquor begins to work on him)

8–9 *draws him on the drawer* draws his sword on the tavern-servant

10   *I.* Ironically emphasized by Benvolio, for he regards the
      description as fitting Mercutio himself. Compare line 20
      below.

11   *Jack* fellow, chap (somewhat disparaging, as the Nurse
      uses it in II.4.149 and a Musician in IV.5.143)

12   *moved to be moody* inclined to anger

13   *moody to be moved* angry at being provoked

15   *two.* Mercutio puns on Benvolio's *to.*

20   *What eye but such an eye.* Presumably the second *eye* is
      a pun on *I* and Mercutio is amusedly accepting the self-
      description, referring to Benvolio's ironical 'I' in line 10.
      He does indeed behave very like this, a few lines later
      in the scene (lines 38–48), in reacting to Tybalt's
      provocative *consortest.* He ironically prepares the
      audience for his losing his life for his petty quarrel-
      someness.

22   *meat* food

23   *addle* rotten

27   *doublet* close-fitting jacket with short skirt
      before Easter (that is, during Lent, anticipating the
      Spring fashions)

27–8 *tying his new shoes* . . . This cause of offence appears to
      have no point except its triviality; *his new shoes* probably
      means 'the shoes supplied by him', rather than 'the
      shoes he wears'.

28   *riband.* Ribbons were used as shoe-laces.

28–9 *tutor me from* give me prudent instruction against

31   *fee simple* permanent lease, full possession

31–2 *for an hour and a quarter* (that is, he would be dead
      before that time had elapsed)

33   *simple* stupid
      (stage direction) *Enter Tybalt and others.* Q2 reads
      Enter Tybalt, Petruchio, and others. Petruchio (who
      otherwise does not appear in the play except as one of
      Capulet's guests named at I.5.131) may be intended to
      be the friend who speaks the warning *Away, Tybalt!*
      at line 89 below. Shakespeare occasionally introduces

among the entries a named character whom he subsequently does not need to use.

34   *comes*. The colloquial singular form of the verb (*preceding* a plural subject) expresses excitement better than the amended form 'come'. See I.1.30 for another instance.

35   *By my heel* (expressing both contempt and his intention of not 'taking to his heels')

37   *good-e'en* good evening (it is the same afternoon, nearly an hour after the marriage of the lovers – see line 112 below)

38   *And but one* only one

39   *Make it a word and a blow*. Mercutio is not a Montague; but he deliberately provokes and undertakes Tybalt.

41, 42   *occasion* excuse. Tybalt tries to preserve the etiquette of duelling, as it has been described by Mercutio in II.4.19–26.

45   *Consort*. Tybalt uses the word *consortest* in the sense of 'are often in the company of', and presumably wants to inquire where Romeo can be found. As Romeo had apparently not been home since the last evening's party, there could not yet have been any answer to the challenge mentioned in II.4.7. Probably Tybalt does not wish to undertake Mercutio – it is Romeo he is after, and he at once turns to him at line 55. But Mercutio interprets *consort* as an offensive musical metaphor and therefore as a challenge.

45, 46   *minstrels*. Apparently a somewhat derogatory word: menial or hired musical entertainers. In IV.5.113 Peter insults the musicians by giving them *the minstrel*.

47   *Here's my fiddlestick* (pointing to his sword)

48   *Zounds* by God's wounds (that is, Christ's on the Cross). The word is pronounced to rhyme with 'wounds'.

49–52   *We talk here in the public haunt of men . . . gaze on us*. Benvolio proposes three possible courses of action to avert the public quarrel. Some editors emend *Or* at the beginning of line 51 to *And*, giving Benvolio only two proposals. For Benvolio as peacemaker, compare I.1.63–8 and III.1.1–4. His firm language contrasts with Romeo's somewhat rash efforts in lines 82–8 below.

51   *reason coldly* discuss calmly

52   *depart* go away separately

55   *my man* the man I am looking for. Tybalt had been plotting his revenge on Romeo since the previous evening (I.5.91–2 and II.4.6–8).

56   *But I'll be hanged, sir, if he wear your livery.* Mercutio persists in his wilful misinterpreting of Tybalt's words. He takes *my man* as if it meant 'my manservant', and so carries on the jest about *livery* (servant's uniform) and *follower* (attendant, and one who will literally follow him to the duelling-place).

57   *field* a place for duelling

58   *Your worship* (with mocking politeness)
       'man' (a man of honour, and no coward)

59   *love.* The word is surprising, because Tybalt does not elsewhere use irony. Q1 reads the simpler word *hate* and some editors prefer it as more appropriate to Tybalt's direct character.

60   *thou art a villain.* This is the comprehensive insult, in the code of honour, about birth and conduct. The duel must follow. Compare I.5.62,64.

61–4   *Tybalt, the reason that I have to love thee ... thou knowest me not.* The confrontation of Romeo and Tybalt is a turning-point in the play. It is the one occasion when, in a crisis, Romeo shows self-restraint and good sense. Only the audience knows the meaning of his riddling speech.

62   *excuse the appertaining rage* excuse my not showing the rage which would be appropriate

65   *Boy.* The insulting word had been applied to Tybalt himself by Capulet at I.5.77 and 83.

67   *injured.* So Q1. Q2 has the old form of the word, *injuried.*

68   *devise* imagine

69   *Till thou shalt know the reason of my love* (when his marriage with Juliet is made public)

70   *tender* regard

71   *... be satisfied.* A wonderful moment of suspense (though it is difficult to be certain, from the words, exactly what is intended to happen on the stage). Tybalt does not reply to Romeo's pacifying remarks. Is he calmed by being called *good Capulet* and so forth, showing by his contemptuous expression that he agrees with Mercutio's words about Romeo's *calm, dishonourable, vile submission*? He says nothing until he is insulted by Mercutio: *Tybalt, you ratcatcher, will you walk?*, and then only replies with unusual mildness: *What wouldst thou have with me?* He had already once rejected Mercutio's challenge (*Well, peace be with you, sir*) in line 55. It is Mercutio who, by his second insolent challenge, brings on the disaster.

72   *submission* (four syllables)

73   *Alla stoccata.* Mercutio continues (from II.4.19–26) his jeers at Tybalt's manner of duelling with the rapier by thus nicknaming him (*stoccata* thrust). He is also contrasting Tybalt's direct insults with Romeo's evasive politeness. He had already mockingly expressed his doubts whether Romeo was a match for Tybalt at the duel (II.4.16–17).

        carries it away 'gets away with it'

74   *ratcatcher* (because he is the *King of Cats* (line 76). Compare II.4.19, where Mercutio calls him the *Prince of Cats*. A few lines later (lines 76–8) Mercutio mocks at his alleged *nine lives*.)

        walk withdraw in order to fight a duel

77–8   *as you shall use me hereafter* according to your subsequent behaviour to me

78   *dry-beat* cudgel (without drawing blood)

79   *pluck ... by the ears* (contemptuous phrasing); *ears* presumably means 'hilt'.

        pilcher scabbard (probably; 'pilch' means 'leather coat')

83   *passado*. Compare the *immortal passado* at II.4.25.

88   (stage direction) *Tybalt under Romeo's arm thrusts Mercutio*. This appears in Q1 only. It is a transference of Mercutio's words at line 103: *I was hurt under your arm*.

89   *Away, Tybalt!* This is printed as if it were a stage direction in Q2, meaning 'Exit Tybalt'.

91   *A plague a'both houses!* A dying man's curse, thrice repeated (lines 99, 106, 108) and certain to be fulfilled. Q2 omits *your* the first time Mercutio curses; probably correctly, as he is there almost talking to himself, rather than addressing others.

        sped dispatched

92   *and hath nothing* is not wounded

93   *a scratch, a scratch* (made by the *King of Cats*)

94   *villain*. The word is used for a person of lowly station in life, not necessarily in an insulting sense (as lines 60, 63 above).

        surgeon physician

98   *a grave man*. Mercutio jests to the end; he puns about his burial, describing himself as becoming (out of character) serious-minded.

100   *Zounds*. See note on line 48 above.

100-101 *a cat, to scratch a man*. See note on line 93 above.

102   *book of arithmetic* text-book with diagrams of the movements. See notes on II.4.19-26, III.1.73.

105   *Help me into some house, Benvolio*. Mercutio does not deign to answer Romeo's feeble *I thought all for the best*, and turns for support to Benvolio. Romeo is left on stage alone.

109-15 *This gentleman, the Prince's near ally ... softened valour's steel!* Romeo is given more serious lines than he has spoken hitherto.

109   *ally* relative. Mercutio's relationship to the Prince is emphasized (III.1.145, 189; V.3.295).

112   *Tybalt's slander*. See lines 60 and 65-6 above.

113   *cousin* kinsman. The word was used to indicate a vague

kinship, like that of Romeo now that he was married to Juliet.

115   *temper* state of mind, with a pun on the hardening of steel by 'tempering'

117   *aspired* soared up to

118   *scorn the earth* (alluding to his bold and magnanimous character)

119   *depend* impend. (Today's ill fortune threatens the days to come with similar misery.) The rhymed couplet seems to indicate the moment of the turning of Fortune's wheel.

122   *Alive.* This is the reading of Q1. Q2 has *He gan*, which does not make sense; but a plausible emendation is *Again*, spelt *Agen*, misread in the manuscript as *'A gan* and printed *He gan*.

123–9   *Away to heaven respective lenity,* | *And fire-eyed fury* ... *go with him.* Romeo now becomes a 'revenge hero', of a type found often in Elizabethan plays, and he uses the typical language, which is in striking contrast with his mild responses to Tybalt's insults earlier (lines 61–4, 67–71). Romeo now mentions these insults and avenges them (*Now, Tybalt, take the 'villain' back again* | *That late thou gavest me*, lines 125–6).

123   *respective lenity* (gentleness which respects the Prince's edict about street-fighting, or takes into consideration that Tybalt is Juliet's blood-kinsman)

124   *conduct* guide. It is no longer Providence (I.4.112–13) that directs his sail. He dispatches mercy to heaven and invokes a *fire-eyed fury* from hell.

125   *'villain'.* See line 60 above.

130   *boy.* Compare line 65 above.

        consort. Compare line 44 above.

131   *This* his sword

        (stage direction) *They fight. Tybalt falls.* Presumably the fight between Romeo and Tybalt, unlike that between Mercutio and Tybalt, is brief. Benvolio later says *to't they go like lightning* (line 172).

231

134   *amazed* dazed

135   *Hence, be gone, away!* The remainder of the scene
        (apart from Benvolio's narrative to the Prince) is mostly
        written in rhymed couplets, which differentiate it from
        the excited exchanges that have gone before.

136   *I am fortune's fool!* I am like a household fool for
        fortune to mock and amuse herself with. Only the
        audience (not Benvolio) understands Romeo's agonized
        dilemma here.

139–40 *Up, sir, go with me.* | *I charge thee in the Prince's name
        obey.* This is attributed to a *Citizen* in the original text,
        but he seems a person of authority, perhaps an *Officer*.

140   (stage direction) *Enter Prince, Montague, Capulet, their
        wives, and all.* This is the second symmetrical assembly
        of the Prince, the two families, and the citizens. It is
        curious that neither Capulet nor Lady Montague speaks
        in this scene. Lady Capulet is given the passionate out-
        bursts on behalf of her nephew Tybalt, so that her
        hatred of Romeo is to make Juliet's position more diffi-
        cult.

142   *discover* uncover, reveal

145   *thy kinsman.* Benvolio mentions this at once, to influence
        the Prince against Tybalt.

146–50 *Tybalt, my cousin! O my brother's child!...* Lady
        Capulet delivers her pleas over the dead body of Tybalt
        (on stage).

146–7   *O my brother's child!* | *O Prince! O cousin! Husband!
        O, the blood is spilled.* Probably *child, spilled* were a
        rhyme in Shakespeare's pronunciation.

152–75 *Tybalt, here slain, whom Romeo's hand did slay ... or let
        Benvolio die.* The excited syntax of this speech is
        noteworthy (the connecting relative pronouns, lines
        160, 167; *Romeo he . . .*, line 164; (he) *rushes*, line
        167).

153–6   *Romeo, that spoke him fair, bid him bethink ...* Ben-
        volio's account is a little exaggerated.

154   *nice* trifling

157   *take truce with the unruly spleen* come to terms with the
       outrageous ill-temper

161–3 *with one hand beats | Cold death aside and with the other
       sends | It back to Tybalt.* This probably indicates that
       Mercutio and Tybalt fought with two weapons, rapiers
       in their right hands and daggers in their left.

164   *Retorts it* turns it back

167   *rushes.* See note on lines 152–75.

168   *envious* full of enmity

170   *by and by* immediately

171   *but newly entertained revenge* only just admitted the
       idea of revenge into his thoughts

177   *Affection* partiality
       Affection makes him false. He speaks not true. Benvolio
       is, indeed, not quite accurate in his account. He ignores
       Mercutio's provocation to Tybalt and in particular
       (lines 158–9) conceals the fact that Mercutio was the
       deliberate challenger. Benvolio exalts the Prince's kins-
       man (*brave, bold,* and *stout* Mercutio, with his *martial
       scorn*). But Lady Capulet fails to make her point be-
       cause she goes on to make vague accusations about
       Some twenty of them.

183   *Who now the price of his dear blood doth owe?* Who is
       now to pay the penalty for shedding Mercutio's (prob-
       ably, rather than Tybalt's) blood?

185   *His fault concludes but what the law should end* (in killing
       Tybalt Romeo had anticipated the law, which would,
       in the end, have condemned Tybalt to death for killing
       Mercutio)

187   *exile* (accent on second syllable)

188   *I have an interest in* I am personally concerned in
       hate's. This is the reading of Q1. Q2 has *hearts*, which is
       difficult, but could be defended in the light of the
       Prince's words at I.1.85 (*purple fountains issuing from
       your veins*).

189   *My blood* the blood of someone related to me (that
       is, Mercutio)

190   *amerce* punish by a fine

193   *purchase out abuses* buy off the penalty for crimes

196   *Bear hence this body.* Shakespeare arranges that Mercutio goes off stage to die, but the body of Tybalt remains on stage until the end of the scene, a visual object of great importance emphasizing Romeo's disastrous act. There are now enough persons on stage to carry it off.

         attend our will come to be judged and respect my decision

197   *Mercy but murders, pardoning those that kill.* If the law is merciful to murderers, then it participates itself in the murders and causes more of them. The Prince is now taking a stronger line than he did in I.1.96–7; but he is not implementing the threat he there made, as he recognizes in V.3.294.

III.2.1–31   *Gallop apace, you fiery-footed steeds ... And may not wear them.* While Juliet speaks her own passionate marriage-hymn, the audience knows that her ecstatic happiness is about to be ruined by the news of the disastrous murder in the previous scene.

1   *fiery-footed steeds.* The horses which draw the chariot of the sun-god (Phoebus Apollo) from the east to their night's *lodging* below the western horizon. Compare *day's pathway made by Titan's wheels* II.2.191.

3   *Phaëton* (three syllables, with accent on the first vowel; the traditional pronunciation in English is 'fay-i-ton') His story is found in Ovid's *Metamorphoses* (where doubtless Shakespeare read it, either in the original Latin or in the verse-translation by Arthur Golding – who calls Phaeton a 'waggoner'). He was allowed to drive the sun-chariot of his father Apollo for one day, but let the horses get out of hand and drove the chariot too near the earth. In some respects Juliet's comparison is not appropriate, because it was Phaeton's incom-

petence rather than speed that was important in the story. It is possible that there is some irony in this. But Shakespeare often treats classical mythology in a casual or independent way.

6   *runaway's eyes*. The meaning is uncertain. The *runaway* may be: (a) the sun (the eyes of the sun will close when night falls); (b) Phaeton (who let the horses get out of hand); (c) (*runaways'*) the horses of Phaeton (whom Juliet imagines as driving the day forward); (d) Romeo (who may relax his vigilance in the Capulet house when he is enjoying Juliet's love); (e) (*runaways'*) officious observers of the actions of the lovers. After all, the word may be an error of transcription or printing.
     wink close (and, if *runaway* means the sun, cause darkness)

9   *if love be blind*. Cupid, according to the old mythology, was blind.

10   *civil* serious

12   *learn* teach
     lose a winning match. She surrenders herself, but she gains a lover.

13   *a pair of stainless maidenhoods*. The innocent inexperience of the lovers is often emphasized.

14   *Hood my unmanned blood, bating in my cheeks*. A falcon was said to be *unmanned* when it was untrained and unable to be quiet when held by its trainer; it then 'bates', that is, flutters its wings up and down excitedly. One method of training a young falcon in this condition was to cover its head with a hood, so that it grew accustomed to a man without nervousness. Juliet puns, of course, on *unmanned* as she is a virgin awaiting the coming of her husband; night will conceal her blushes. On Juliet's blushing see note on II.2.85–7 and compare II.5.70.

15   *strange* unfamiliar and so causing reserve

16   *Think true love acted simple modesty* regard the physical act of true love as straightforward chastity

17   *Come, night.* Probably she puns on 'knight' (her Romeo).

21   *when I shall die.* Many editors prefer the change made in the printing of Q4: *he* for *I.* Juliet's fancy is extravagant and we cannot feel sure that the slightly simpler *he* is more appropriate. She may be imagining, a little jealously, the destiny of Romeo after *her* death rather than *his.* On the other hand, it would be very like Shakespeare to let Juliet have a passing premonition of her belief in lines 40–60 below that Romeo is dead.

30   *impatient child.* The shift from the fantastic imagery of night and sun and sky to this domestic comparison is striking.

34   *cords* (the rope ladder which Romeo was to use to climb into her window that night)

37   *weraday* well-a-day, alas!

40   *envious* full of enmity
         Romeo can. She means (though Juliet does not understand her) that Romeo can be so full of enmity as to kill Tybalt.

45–51   *Say thou but 'Ay' . . . determine of my weal or woe.* Juliet's frenzied punning on 'I', 'eye', 'ay' (=yes), and the vowel, was formerly condemned as unnatural. It is, however, consistent with Shakespeare's dramatic practice of using un-comic puns in tragic situations; of allowing words to acquire a terrible ambiguity at moments of great emotion. For the Elizabethan *reader* the pun was visually a little closer, since 'ay' was customarily spelt as 'I'.

47   *cockatrice* the basilisk (a fabulous animal which was hatched by a serpent from a cock's egg and was able to kill by a glance of its eyes)

49   *those eyes shut* if the eyes of Romeo be shut. But *shut* is an emendation of *shot* in Q2, and some editors retain *eyes' shot,* giving the meaning: 'the glance of the Nurse which implies her saying "yes" '. This is rather strained.

51   *Brief sounds* (that is, 'ay' or 'no')
         determine of make a decision about

52   *I saw the wound. I saw it with mine eyes* ... The Nurse
has, in her distraction, heard only the sound of Juliet's
speech, but not taken in the meaning. She carries on
the *I* and the *eyes*.

53   *God save the mark!* As usual the Nurse, in spite of her
earthiness, apologizes for mentioning anything indeli-
cate. She presumably points to the place on her own
chest to show where Tybalt received his wound.

54   *corse* corpse

56   *swounded* (rhymes with 'sounded') swooned. Her gory
description has a strong effect on Juliet, who takes it to
refer to Romeo; it is an imaginative premonition of how
Juliet *will* see Romeo at V.3.161–7.

57   *break, my heart!* This phrase had a biblical background
which made it stronger than the modern sentimental
usage. Compare Psalm 34.18, 'The Lord is nigh them
of a broken heart.'

57–8 *poor bankrupt, break at once!* | *To prison, eyes.* As *break*
can mean 'be declared insolvent', perhaps Juliet is punning, linking *bankrupt* and *to prison*.

59   *Vile earth, to earth resign* yield up her body to the grave
('ashes to ashes, dust to dust')

61–3 *O Tybalt, Tybalt, the best friend I had!* ... Her exaggerated praise of the dead Tybalt is excellently in
character.

66   *dearest.* Some editors adopt *dear-loved* from Q1. But
the exaggeration of *dearest* and the slight paradox of the
following *dearer* seem right.

67   *dreadful trumpet, sound the General Doom!* See 1 Corinthians 15.52: 'at the last trump; for the trump shall
blow ...' (Bishops' Bible).

73   *hid with* hidden by
flowering face. In pictures the Serpent in Paradise was
sometimes represented as appearing to Eve with a
human face surrounded by flowers.

74   *dragon keep so fair a cave.* A dragon was supposed to
keep guard over treasure in a cave.

75   *tyrant* (because he is usurping qualities not his by right)
fiend angelical. Compare 2 Corinthians 11.14: 'Satan himself is transformed into an angel of light.'

76   *Wolvish-ravening lamb.* This is another scriptural phrase; compare Matthew 7.15: 'Beware of false prophets, which come to you in sheep's clothing, but inwardly they are ravening wolves.'

78   *Just* exactly (with a play on the *justly* that follows)

81–2   *the spirit of a fiend | In mortal paradise.* Juliet is thinking of the Serpent in Eden.

83–4   *Was ever book containing such vile matter | So fairly bound?* For the imagery of the book-binding compare Lady Capulet at I.3.82–95.

87   *naught* wicked

88   *aqua vitae* brandy or other strong spirits

90   *Blistered be thy tongue.* Juliet is sometimes given passionate language in addressing the Nurse. Compare *Ancient damnation!* at III.5.236.

98   *what tongue shall smooth thy name* who shall speak thy name kindly (but *smooth* also contrasts with *mangled* in the next line)

99   *three-hours wife* (another indication of time: it is now later in the afternoon and two hours since the Tybalt–Mercutio–Romeo quarrel)

101   *That villain cousin would have killed my husband.* Juliet begins shrewdly to understand the situation.

103   *tributary drops* tears paying a tribute

105   *that* whom

109   *fain* gladly

112–24 *banishèd.* Juliet repeats the word five times, with increasing agony.

117   *needly will be ranked with* will of necessity be accompanied by

119   *Thy father, or thy mother* (her own; she is, as it were, addressing herself)

120   *modern* ordinary. The deaths of her father and mother would be events that human experience leads us to

regard as usual; but the exile of Romeo at such a time is a grief totally unexpected.

121   *rearward* rearguard (behind, as it were, the main part of the navy or army causing destruction)

126   *No words can that woe sound.* She probably puns on *sound* as meaning 'give expression to' and 'plumb the depths of'.

130   *spent* expended

137   *death, not Romeo, take my maidenhead!* See notes on I.5.135, III.5.140, IV.5.35–9, and V.3.102–5.

139   *wot* know

I.3   The audience has been told by the Nurse (III.2.141) that Romeo is in hiding at Friar Laurence's cell. Having seen Juliet's reaction to the catastrophic misfortune of the killing of Tybalt and the exile of her husband, we now see Romeo's condition. In the midst of death and calamity the preparations are made by the Friar and the Nurse for the marriage to be consummated.

1   *fearful* full of fear (about the consequences of his having killed Tybalt). But the word is ambiguous because in Shakespeare *fearful* also means 'terrible': Romeo is a 'fatal' and so a frightening character.

2–3   *Affliction is enamoured of thy parts,* | *And thou art wedded to calamity.* The words of the Friar take the mind back to the end of II.6; it is misery, rather than Juliet, who has fallen in love with him and whom he has married.

2   *parts* personal qualities (as in III.5.182)

3   *wedded to calamity.* Romeo had described himself as 'fortune's fool' (III.1.136).

4, 8, 9   *Prince's doom* judgement decreed by the Prince

6   *familiar* (four syllables). The Friar says that Romeo's relation to sorrow is closer than an *acquaintance* (line 5).

9   *doomsday* the Day of Judgement (that is, death)

10   *vanished.* Presumably this means 'was breathed out and disappeared into air, so that it cannot be recalled'. But

the sense is strained and some editors have seen a printer's or transcriber's error here (for *issued* or *vantaged* or – as if quoting the Prince's word – '*banished*').

17   *without* outside

19   *Hence banishèd* banished from here. Romeo repeats the word *banished* many times, as Juliet has done (III.2. 112–24).

20   *world's exile* exile from the world
        exile (accent on the second syllable, as in lines 41 and 140; but in line 13 the accent is on the first syllable)

24   *deadly sin* ingratitude

25   *Thy fault our law calls death* our law demands death as a punishment for your crime

26   *rushed aside.* This presumably means 'forcefully overruled'. But the word is strained, and some editors suspect an error for *thrust* or *brushed* or *pushed*.

28   *dear mercy* unusual mercy which should be valued

29   *Heaven is here.* The emphasis falls on *here*.

32   *Live.* 'Every' may be followed by a plural verb in Elizabethan English.

33   *validity* value

34   *courtship* courtly behaviour. But Romeo puns on the other meaning of the word, 'wooing a lady'.

36   *the white wonder of dear Juliet's hand.* Romeo remembers her hands; compare I.5.51 and 93–102.

37   *immortal blessing* (carries on the idea of *heaven* in lines 29, 32)

38   *vestal* virgin (like the chastity of the Vestal Virgins in ancient Rome)

39   *Still blush, as thinking their own kisses sin.* In Romeo's extravagant language: her lips are red as if blushing at the way one of them touches the other and so 'kisses' it. At I.5.95 he had called his own lips *two blushing pilgrims.*

40–44   The text here follows Q2. But the repetitions of phrase and idea have led many editors to suppose that we have here an example of the accidental inclusion, by transcriber or printer, of a line cancelled by Shakespeare in his manuscript; they place line 41 after 44, and omit either 40 or 43. In these lines Romeo seems to echo Juliet's playing with *ay, eye,* and *I* in her lament at III.2.45–50; and his pun on *flies* and *fly* is as harsh.

45–6   *Hadst thou no poison mixed ... ne'er so mean.* The thoughts of the means of suicide seem to anticipate the tragic catastrophe; and they keep before the audience the Friar's skill with drugs (II.3.1–26).

46   *mean of death* means of procuring death. Romeo then puns on *mean* (base).

50   *confessor* (accent on first syllable)

53   *fond* foolish

58   *Yet 'banishèd'?* do you still keep saying 'banished'?

63   *when that wise men have no eyes* when a wise man like you cannot see what is so obvious. Romeo's retort is petulant, but the Friar continues calmly.

64   *dispute with thee of thy estate* have a philosophical discussion on the present state of your affairs with you

65   *Thou canst not speak of that thou dost not feel.* The Friar's vows of celibacy must have kept him ignorant of the passion of love.
     that that which

66–9   *Wert thou as young as I, Juliet thy love,* | *An hour but married, Tybalt murderèd,* | *Doting like me, and like me banishèd,* | *Then ...* Romeo's broken syntax is expressive. 'If you were as young as I am, if Juliet were your love, if you had been only an hour married and had murdered Tybalt, if you were as much in love as I am, and if you were banished as I am, then ...'

69   *tear thy hair* (as often in Shakespeare, the actor's 'business' is indicated within the speech)

71   *Taking the measure of an unmade grave.* He lies on the ground as if his outstretched body provides the measurement of the grave in which he is to be buried.

74   *Mist-like infold me from the search of eyes* (as happened to the heroes in epic poetry)

77   *By and by* immediately

78   *simpleness* stupidity (in not getting up and concealing himself, as the Friar had urged from line 72 onwards)

86-7   *O woeful sympathy ! | Piteous predicament !* Some editors transfer these words from the Nurse to the Friar, on the grounds that it would be out of character for the Nurse to use such long and learned words (in Shakespeare's time) as *sympathy* and *predicament*. To this it can be replied that exclamations of woe are unlike the Friar; and it is best to leave the text unchanged.

86   *woeful sympathy* agreement in woefulness

91   *an O* an exclamation of sorrow (presumably Romeo is groaning as he lies on the ground). The Nurse may be here (though it is hardly the moment for it) falling into her familiar trick of unwitting bawdry.

94   *old* hardened by experience

98   *concealed* (accent on first syllable and so jingling with *cancelled*) not yet acknowledged as his wife
       cancelled invalidated

101   *on Romeo cries* cries out against him

102-7   *As if that name . . . | Did murder her . . . | Doth my name lodge ?* This is a reminder of Juliet's words at II.2.38-42.

103   *Shot from the deadly level of a gun* (another example of the recurring gun-imagery)
       level line of aim

106   *anatomy* a human body for dissection

107   *sack* pillage (like a house in a sacked city)

108   *mansion.* Juliet had used this word of Romeo's body in III.2.26.
       (stage direction) *He offers to stab himself, and the Nurse snatches the dagger away.* The stage direction is from Q1 and seems to indicate the business in an early production. We might have expected the Friar, rather than the Nurse, to snatch the dagger away, but it may be that appropriately both the Nurse and the Friar, in their different ways, take steps to prevent Romeo's folly. His rash attempt at suicide here prepares us for

his later determination for suicide when he hears bad
news without the support and restraint of the two older
people.

113   *ill-beseeming* unnatural and inappropriate (because
apparently both man and woman)

114   *my holy order* (of St Francis)

115   *tempered* mixed so that the ingredients (the four
'humours' of Elizabethan physiology) are well balanced

116   *Wilt thou slay thyself?* Ironically, what the Friar upbraids him for seeming to want to do, Romeo actually
does, later on.

117   *And slay thy lady that in thy life lives* . . . The emphasis
falls on the second *thy*.

118   *damnèd* (because suicide is a mortal sin)

119   *Why railest thou on thy birth, the heaven, and earth?*
Romeo had not, in fact, done this. But it is interesting
to note that in Arthur Brooke's poem Romeo does rail
bitterly against Nature, the time and place of his birth,
and the stars. It seems that Shakespeare was here
remembering what he had read in Brooke, not what he
had written in his play.

120   *birth and heaven and earth.* His human origin in his
family, his immortal soul, his earthly body, all unite in
him; he could destroy them all by suicide.

122, 125, 130 *wit* intelligence, sense of reason

123   *Which* who

123–4 *usurer . . . usest . . . use.* He puns on *use* as meaning 'to
lend out at interest'

124   *true use* honourable handling of his wealth

126   *but a form of wax* only a waxwork figure (a different
meaning from the Nurse's *a man of wax* at I.3.77)

127   *Digressing* if it deviates

129   *Killing* if it kills
       vowed to cherish (in the recent marriage-ceremony)

131   *Misshapen in the conduct* going awry in the guidance

132–4 *Like powder in a skilless soldier's flask . . . thine own
defence.* For the imagery, see Introduction, pp. 31–2.

132   *powder* gunpowder
        flask horn for the gunpowder

134   *dismembered with thine own defence* blown to pieces by your own gunpowder, which should have been the means for your defending yourself (destroyed by your intellect which should have saved you)

136   *dead* 'worried to death', or wishing to be dead (as in line 71)

137, 138, 140 *There* (emphatic) in that respect

137, 138, 140 *happy* fortunate

137–8   *Tybalt would kill thee,* | *But thou slewest Tybalt.* The Friar reasons as did Juliet in III.2.100–107.

139   *The law* (as declared by the Prince at I.1.96–7)

143   *mishavèd* misbehaved (which is the form of the word found in Q1)

144   *pouts* poutest. In verbs ending in -t, the second person singular often has -ts, instead of -test, in Elizabethan English.
        fortune good fortune

146   *decreed* arranged beforehand (II.4.183–87, III.2.34–5 and 132–7)

148–9   *But look thou stay not till the Watch be set,* | *For then thou canst not pass to Mantua.* Romeo must leave Verona before nightfall, for then the city-gates would be closed and a guard posted. But see lines 167–8 below.

149   *Mantua.* This – already mentioned by the Nurse at I.3.29 – is in fact the nearest considerable town to Verona, twenty-odd miles away, as Shakespeare could have learned from books and travellers of his time. Shakespeare had already set a good deal of *The Two Gentlemen of Verona* in or near Mantua (IV.1; V.3 and 4), and it is mentioned in *The Taming of the Shrew* as a town not far from Padua. The name is sometimes three syllables, sometimes (III.5.88, IV.1.124) two.

151   *blaze* proclaim
        your friends the members of your two families

154   *lamentation* (five syllables)

163   *Here, sir, a ring.* Juliet sent the ring at III.2.142.

164   *Exit Nurse.* The Nurse's exit is not marked in Q2. It is
        put after line 166 in Q1. Some editors insert it after the
        Good night in line 166.

165   *comfort* happiness

166   *here stands all your state* your situation depends on this
        (what I am going to say now)

167   *the Watch be set.* The Friar's repetition from line 148
        emphasizes Romeo's danger.

168   *break of day.* At lines 148-9 the Friar wanted to get
        Romeo out of the city before nightfall, but now he gives
        him the alternative of staying with Juliet until just
        before break of day. The marriage would not, of course,
        have been valid unless consummated. The Friar's
        words look forward to the dawn-parting in III.5.

169   *your man* (Balthasar, who appears at V.1 and 3)

171   *good hap.* But it is the (mistaken) ill hap that Balthasar
        reports to Romeo at V.1.17-23.

173   *But that a joy past joy calls out on me* were it not that
        I am summoned away by the thought of the surpassing
        joy of going to Juliet

174   *It were a grief so brief to part* it would be a grief so
        hurriedly to part

II.4   We have not seen Juliet's wooer, the County Paris,
        since I.2; nor have we heard of him since in I.3.75-95
        Juliet was informed of his intended proposal. His
        arrival now, at the time of the deep distress and hastily
        snatched joy of the lovers, introduces a new and omi-
        nous element into the plot. We are given further in-
        sights into the character of father Capulet: his merely
        proverbial wisdom (*Well, we were born to die*, line 4;
        compare the Nurse at III.3.92) and his concern for
        appearances (lines 24-8) prepare us for his stubborn in-
        sistence in III.5, which hastens on the tragic catastrophe.

1   *fallen out* happened

2   *move* persuade by talking

5–7   *She'll not come down tonight … abed an hour ago.* Capulet gives a polite dismissal to his visitor, and the gentlemanly Paris understands and takes it.

6   *promise* assure

8   *These times of woe afford no times to woo.* Paris jingles his words quite like Romeo.

11   *Tonight she's mewed up to her heaviness.* Actually she is meanwhile with her bridegroom Romeo.
     mewed up (as a falcon in its cage)
     heaviness grief

12–32   *Sir Paris, I will make a desperate tender | Of my child's love …* The contrast between the marriage arranged by parents and the marriage now being consummated is striking. Capulet assumes that his daughter *will be ruled | In all respects* by him, and he is indignant at her disobedience and folly in III.5.141–96.

12   *desperate tender* bold offer

15   *Wife, go you to her ere you go to bed.* The time-scheme is a little vague, but dramatically effective. The hour is late (III.3.172, when Romeo leaves the Friar's cell; and III.4.5 and 34–5). It is a moment of tension when Capulet twice tells his wife to visit Juliet before going to bed (lines 15 and 31), because Romeo is already with her. Lady Capulet comes to Juliet at III.5.64, when Juliet wonders at her early call (III.5.66–7).

16   *son Paris.* Capulet clearly intends Paris to be his son-in-law.

17, 19   *Wednesday.* Eventually (IV.2.24) Capulet returns to this first idea for the marriage on Wednesday.

18   *Monday.* The emphasis on the days of the week and the fivefold repetition of *Thursday* makes the audience feel the urgency of the situation.
     my lord. See note on I.2.6.

19   *Ha, ha!* This represents a deliberative hum.

21   *She shall be married to this noble earl.* His *desperate tender* (line 12) has now become an order.

21   *earl* nobleman (indefinitely; Paris is usually a Count or County)

22   *Will you be ready?* It is not easy to decide whether he is now talking to Paris or to Lady Capulet. If to Paris, his tone has changed to one of banter. But it may be that in lines 20–28 the whole passage is addressed to Lady Capulet; and he then turns to Paris: *But what say you to Thursday?*

23   The *friend or two* become *half a dozen friends* by line 27, and this prepares us for IV.2.1–2, where his liking for hospitality has turned what was to be a private wedding into a large gathering.

25   *held him carelessly* had little esteem for him

32   *against* in time for

33   *Light to my chamber, ho!* (summoning a servant)

34   *Afore me* (a mild oath: As God is before me!)

35   *by and by* immediately (rather than the modern meaning 'a little later on'; compare III.1.170)

III.5   (stage direction) *Enter Romeo and Juliet aloft, at the window.* This derives from Q1 and seems to indicate that Romeo and Juliet appear on the upper stage to speak their farewells. Compare *He goes down* at line 42.

1   *It is not yet near day.* In III.2.1–31 Juliet had implored the sun to hurry across the sky so that night might come. Now she laments that the fiery-footed steeds of the sun do indeed gallop apace: *More light and light it grows* (line 35).

2–5   *It was the nightingale* ... Although it is, we have been told, mid-July, the birds still sing. (Nightingale song is very irregular after mid-June; skylark song continues till early July and may be heard occasionally in any month of the year.)

3   *fearful* full of apprehension

4   *she sings.* In Shakespeare's traditional bird-lore it is the female nightingale (not, as in reality, the male) that sings.

4   *pomegranate* (three syllables). This fruit-tree had been
     grown in England since the mid-sixteenth century; but
     it remained an exotic and so gives a touch of local
     colour here.

7   *envious* malicious

9   *Night's candles* the stars

11   *and live* if I am to live

13   *meteor*. Meteors were believed to be vapours drawn up
     out of the earth and ignited by the heat of the sun.

17   *ta'en* taken (usually pronounced to rhyme with 'lane')

18   *so* if

20   *reflex* reflection
     Cynthia the moon-goddess (Diana)
     brow forehead (but also the whole face). Romeo is
     willing to pretend that the eastern light is not the rising
     sun but the reflected light of the moon.

21   *Nor that is not*. Emphatic double negatives quite often
     occur in Shakespeare's grammar.

23   *care* concern

29   *sweet division*. The emphasis is on the adjective.
     division (four syllables) a trilling or run of notes

31   *Some say the lark and loathèd toad change eyes*. This
     piece of folk-lore is obscurely authenticated. Apparently
     the toad's remarkable eyes are contrasted with the lark's
     insignificant eyes.
     change exchange

32   *changed voices*. Then an ugly croaking like the toad's
     would be more appropriate than a joyful song like the
     lark's.

33   *arm from arm . . . doth us affray* startles us out of each
     other's arms

34   *hunt's-up* a hunting-song for daybreak

41   *life* (because Romeo is this to her)

42   (stage direction) *He goes down* (by means of the rope-
     ladder; presumably at some point during the next
     twenty-two lines Juliet pulls it up and conceals it)

43   *love-lord, aye husband-friend* both illicit lover and lawful

husband. Apparently *aye* (=ever; pronounced to rhyme with 'play') merely intensifies the meaning. But the reading *my*, from Q1, may be right.

44–7   *I must hear from thee every day in the hour . . . behold my Romeo*. Juliet speaks this not knowing (as the audience knows) of the intended marriage with Paris.

44–5   *every day in the hour, | For in a minute there are many days*. It will seem that in each minute there are many days of waiting – still more in each hour.

46   *count* method of counting time
    much in years (grown) much older

51–7   *O, thinkest thou we shall ever meet again? . . . thou lookest pale*. For these characteristic premonitions see Introduction, p. 20.

52   *I doubt it not*. Since 'ay' (yes) was spelt 'I', this could be read *Ay, doubt it not*.

54   *ill-divining* having premonitions of ill

59   *Dry sorrow drinks our blood*. It was commonly supposed that sighing exhausted the blood, so that sorrow made one pale.

64   (stage direction) *She goes down from the window. Enter Juliet's mother*. Presumably Juliet 'goes in' on the upper balcony, and she appears to meet her mother on the main stage.

65–7   *Who is't that calls? . . . procures her hither?* This is apparently an aside. Her question *Who is't that calls?* may seem odd (unless she calls out as a deliberate deception), for at line 39 the Nurse had told her *Your lady mother is coming to your chamber*. But as she speaks these three lines to herself Juliet is recovering from her distraction at Romeo's departure, and begins to feel anxiety about the reason for her mother's surprise visit.

66   *down* in bed. (Is she very late in going to bed, or is she up very early?)

67   *procures* brings

72   *Some* a certain amount of (in moderation)

73   *still* always

74   *feeling* deeply felt. Juliet begins a series of remarks with double-meanings; Lady Capulet supposes that her grief is for the death of Tybalt, but the audience knows it is for the separation from Romeo.

75-6   *So shall you feel the loss, but not the friend | Which you weep for.* If you do so, you will feel your loss; but your grief won't bring him to life so that you can feel *him*.

77   *friend.* For herself and the audience the *friend* means her lover; compare line 43 above.

83   *like he* as much as he

88-91   *I'll send to one in Mantua . . . keep Tybalt company.* The talk of *one in Mantua* who will give Romeo an *unaccustomed dram* prepares the audience for the catastrophe by which Romeo is given such a poison for himself so that he will *keep Tybalt company.*

89   *runagate* fugitive vagabond. Lady Capulet's words ignore the time-scheme of the play; for Romeo has only left for Mantua (on the Friar's advice at III.3.148-9) a few minutes before.

90   *Shall give* who shall give
       dram dose

93-102 *Indeed I never shall be satisfied | With Romeo till I behold him – dead . . . that hath slaughtered him!* Juliet continues to speak with double meanings, one of which is concealed from her mother. But her words, especially lines 93-4, have a further ironic meaning for the audience: the next time she will see Romeo he will be dead.

97   *temper* mix (but with the double meaning 'make more moderate')

101   *wreak* pay

102   *his body that* the body of him who

103   *means* (of mixing such a poison)

107   *careful* provident

109   *sorted out* arranged

110   *nor I looked not.* For this emphatic double negative, compare the note on line 21 above.

111   *in happy time!* how fortunate just now! (ironically)

114   *County.* See note on I.3.105.

119   *Ere he that should be husband comes to woo.* Paris is
       aware of his backwardness (III.4.8 and IV.1.7).

126   *When the sun sets the earth doth drizzle dew* . . . Capulet
       sees Juliet in tears.
       earth. Q4 reads *air* and this is adopted by some editors.
       But the *earth* of Q2 can be supported by sixteenth-
       century notions of meteorology.

126-7 *sun* . . . *sunset* . . . *son.* Capulet's puns are of the simplest.

127   *my brother's son.* In view of Lady Capulet's strongly
       personal words at III.1.146–50, presumably Tybalt is
       the son of Capulet's brother-in-law.

129   *conduit* a city-fountain with a spout of flowing water.
       Often they were in the form of a human figure; this
       gives a jocular effect to Capulet's description of Juliet.

130-37 *In one little body | Thou counterfeitest a bark* . . . *| Thy
       tempest-tossèd body.* Capulet's elaborate comparison of
       Juliet in tears to a ship in a storm prepares for Romeo's
       seasick weary bark (V.3.118).

136   *Without a sudden calm* unless there comes a sudden calm

139   *she will none* she will have none of it

140   *I would the fool were married to her grave!* Parental
       curses were considered ominous. Lady Capulet's wish
       will be fulfilled. Compare Capulet's bitterness in lines
       164–7 below, again ominous.

141   *take me with you* I don't understand you (with mounting
       anger)

145   *bride* bridegroom ('bride' could still be used for either
       sex in Shakespeare's time). Texts later than Q2 read
       bridegroom.

148   *meant love* meant to be love

149   *chopped logic* bandying argument to and fro

151   *Mistress* (three syllables, as in II.4.189)

153   *fettle* make ready

156-7 *Out, you green-sickness carrion! Out, you baggage! | You
       tallow-face!* These descriptions of Juliet give the audi-
       ence information about her appearance. The boy-actor

could hardly simulate *green-sickness* and *tallow-face*, but these words supplement the doleful face he could assume here.

157   *Fie, fie! What, are you mad?* Lady Capulet, who was petulant enough herself at line 140, is driven to protest at Capulet's fit of temper. Compare line 175. (An alternative suggestion – that she is addressing Juliet – seems less probable.)

164–6 *we scarce thought us blest | That God had lent us but this only child* . . . On Juliet as an only child, compare I.2.14–15, I.5.116–17, IV.5. 46–8.

168   *hilding!* the jade!

169   *rate* upbraid

171   *Smatter* prattle

172   *God-i-good-e'en* God give you good evening (impatiently)

175   *You are too hot.* Compare line 157.

176   *God's bread!* (the bread consecrated in the Communion Service)

177   *tide* season

181   *demesnes* estates

        trained. Q2 reads *liand*, which does not make sense. The reading of Q1, here adopted, is acceptable but some editors prefer emendations: *limbed* or *liened* (with noble 'liens' or connexions).

182   *parts* personal qualities (as in III.3.2)

184   *puling* whimpering

185   *mammet* doll, puppet

        in her fortune's tender when she is offered a good chance of marriage

188   *I'll pardon you!* (threateningly) I'll pardon you in another sense – I'll give you leave to go!

190   *I do not use to* it is not my habit to

196   *I'll not be forsworn* I shall not break my word (in fulfilling my threats to you and in promising you in marriage to Paris)

206–9 *My husband is on earth, my faith in heaven* | . . . *By leaving earth?* my husband Romeo is alive on earth and my marriage-vow to him is registered in heaven; therefore I cannot be released from my vow, unless my husband were to die

210–11 *that heaven should practise stratagems | Upon so soft a subject as myself!* Juliet had before attributed her misfortunes to the malice of Providence (*Can heaven be so envious?* III.2.40). But such self-pity is rare in Juliet.

210 *practise stratagems* dishonestly contrive traps

214 *all the world to nothing* the odds are a million to one

215 *challenge* claim possession of

222, 228 *Beshrew* cursed be

229 *Amen!* Juliet replies thus to the Nurse's imprecations (*beshrew* her heart and soul)

231 *Well, thou hast comforted me marvellous much.* Juliet has now acquired sufficient strength to be able to treat the Nurse ironically.

235 Q1 inserts the stage direction: *She looks after Nurse.*

237 *forsworn* false (to marriage-vows)

239 *above compare* as being beyond comparison

240 *many thousand times.* The time-scheme of the play scarcely allows for this unless extreme exaggeration is intended. Compare, similarly, II.4.199 (and note).

241 *bosom* (sweet thoughts)
twain separated

242–3 *to know his remedy. | If all else fail, myself have power to die.* Compare IV.1.52–67.

IV.1.2 *My father Capulet.* Paris is over-confident of his marrying Juliet, and anticipates the relationship, as did Capulet by speaking of his *son Paris'* love at III.4.16.

3 *nothing slow to slack his haste* show no reluctance which might cause him to reduce his haste

5 *Uneven* irregular

7 *have I little talked of love.* Compare III.4.8, and Juliet's words at III.5.118–19.

253

11   *marriage* (three syllables)

13   *too much minded by herself alone* too much brooded upon in her solitude

18–43   *Happily met, my lady and my wife! . . . this holy kiss.* This is the first time the audience has seen Paris and Juliet together, and she arrives to face him unexpectedly a few moments after the crisis with her father, mother, and nurse. Paris is amiably possessive (*my lady and my wife*) and Juliet manages to preserve a dignified bearing – cool, but indulging in a little courteous banter with the admirer who is unwittingly causing her such desperate distress.

31   *before their spite* before their malice in marring it

34   *to my face.* Here the phrase means both 'openly' and 'about my face'.

37   Juliet turns away from these rather flippant interchanges with Paris, after her final ambiguity (*it is not mine own –* because it is Romeo's), giving him a polite hint to go.

38   *evening mass.* This seems to have been an occasional practice in the sixteenth century; but presumably Shakespeare uses the word *mass* in a general sense for 'divine service'.

39   *pensive* sorrowful

41   *God shield I should disturb* God defend me from disturbing

47   *compass* range

48   *may prorogue* can postpone

52–67   *If in thy wisdom thou canst give no help . . . speak not of remedy.* She amplifies the statement she made in III.5.242–3.

54, 62 *knife.* It was not unusual for Elizabethan ladies to carry knives.

54   *presently* immediately

57   *label to another deed* codicil modifying another legal document

59   *this* (knife)
       both (hand and heart)

62–5 *this bloody knife | Shall play the umpire, arbitrating that | Which the commission of thy years and art | Could to no issue of true honour bring*. There are legal metaphors here: her dagger will act as a third party arbitrating (between herself and her miseries) where the usual judicial functionaries cannot satisfactorily decide.

65 *Could to no issue of true honour bring*. After this line the Friar is silent.

74 *chide away this shame* drive away this disgrace

75 *That copest with death himself to 'scape from it* (you) who are prepared to face death itself in order to escape from the shame of marrying Paris

76 *remedy*. This echoes *remedy* in line 67 above.

78 *any tower*. Q1 reads *yonder tower*, which is apparently a more effective reading.

79 *thievish ways* places made dangerous by thieves

81 *charnel house* a small building adjacent to a church where skulls and bones from graves were deposited. Human remains seem to have been dug up and put in a charnel house after they had been in the ground a number of years (compare Hamlet's conversation with the grave-digger). That Shakespeare disliked the practice is perhaps suggested by the inscription on his tombstone in Stratford-upon-Avon church.

81–5 *Or hide me nightly in a charnel house . . . dead man in his tomb*. This is a striking anticipation of what is to happen to her and a preparation for her soliloquy before drinking the potion (IV.3.30–59).

83 *reeky shanks* shinbones giving off foul-smelling vapour *chapless* without lower jaws

85 *tomb*. The word is omitted in Q2. The printer of Q4 in 1622 gave *shroud*. The printer of F put *grave*, repeated from the previous line. Either is possible; but it has been pointed out that it would be difficult to hide in the *shroud* already occupied by a dead man.

90 *Wednesday is tomorrow*. But owing to the bringing forward of the marriage to Paris by one day (IV.2.24)

Juliet has to take the potion the same evening (Tuesday).

94   *distilling* penetrating or infusing the body. The reading of Q1 *distillèd* is easier, looking back to the Friar's account of his herbs in II.3.1–26.

96   *humour* fluid

97   *native* natural
         surcease cease

100   *wanny.* See 'An Account of the Text', pp. 282–4.
         windows shutters (hence *eyes' windows* eyelids)

105   *two-and-forty hours.* This length of time does not seem to fit the time-scheme of the play precisely. But an exact figure is appropriate in the context theatrically.

110   *In thy best robes uncovered on the bier.* In Q2 the line printed after this is *Be borne to burial in thy kindred's grave.* This seems to be a line rewritten as lines 111–12 and accidentally not deleted from the manuscript.
         uncovered with face uncovered

113   *against thou shalt awake* in expectation of the time when you will awake

119   *toy* whim

122   *prosperous* successful

125   *help afford* provide help

IV.2.1–2   *So many guests invite as here are writ . . . twenty cunning cooks.* It is not, after all, to be a private wedding (as Capulet intended in III.4.23: *We'll keep no great ado – a friend or two*), and the family mourning has been forgotten. Capulet is hospitably inclined (I.2.20–37 and I.5.17–29).

2   *cunning* expert

3   *none ill* no bad ones

5   *try* test

6–7   *'tis an ill cook that cannot lick his own fingers.* A pro-verbial expression: only a bad cook would not want to taste the dishes he has prepared.

10   *We shall be much unfurnished* the household prepara-

tions and provisioning will not be completed. Nevertheless, Capulet promptly brings forward the marriage from Thursday to Wednesday, in spite of Lady Capulet's protest (*We shall be short in our provision*, line 38).

14   *harlotry* hussy

15   *shrift* confession

16   *How now, my headstrong!* . . . Capulet now quite good-humouredly mocks his daughter.

17–22   *Where I have learned me to repent . . . ever ruled by you.* Juliet follows the Friar's instructions at IV.1.89 (*Go home, be merry, give consent | To marry Paris*). But she slightly overacts the part. Her ready compliance prompts Capulet to bring the marriage forward a day, a fatal mischance. Lady Capulet demurs (*No, not till Thursday. There is time enough*); but while fate hangs in the balance, Capulet overrides her. His impetuosity, like Romeo's, hastens the catastrophe.

19   *behests* commands

20   *to fall prostrate.* Juliet here kneels, as is plain from Capulet's *Stand up* at line 28, and from the stage-direction in Q₁. *She kneels down* (compare III.5.150: *I beseech you on my knees*).

24   *knot* (of marriage)
       tomorrow morning Wednesday

26   *becomèd* befitting

32   *bound* indebted

33   *closet* private room

34   *sort* choose

38   *provision* (four syllables)

39   *'Tis now near night.* The day has been dramatically shortened.

40   *warrant* assure

44   *They are all forth.* The servants are all out of the house, so that there is no reply to his *What, ho!*

IV.3   Juliet, now that the marriage-day has been brought forward from Thursday to Wednesday, must take the
poison twenty-four hours before the Friar had planned
(IV.1.89–117).

1–5   *Ay, those attires are best . . . cross and full of sin*. With
courageous guile Juliet now addresses the *Ancient damnation* of III.5.236 as her *gentle Nurse*, like the *good Nurse*
and *sweet Nurse* of II.5.28 and 54.

2   *leave me to myself tonight*. The Friar had instructed her
to remain on her own at IV.1.91–2.

3–5   *For I have need of many orisons . . . full of sin*. This is
one of many religious pretences of Juliet.

3   *orisons* prayers

5   *cross* perverse

7–8   *We have culled such necessaries | As are behoveful for
our state tomorrow*. Presumably Juliet speaks with a
double meaning: her mother thinks she is talking about
her clothes, but Juliet's mind is on the vial of poison
and on her dagger.

7   *culled* picked out

8   *behoveful* appropriately needed
state public ceremony (of marriage)

12   *business* (three syllables)

15   *a faint cold fear* a fear causing faintness and chill
thrills shivers

23   *This shall forbid it* (the knife she had shown to the Friar
at IV.1.54)

29   *still been tried* always been proved by experience to be
. . . *tried a holy man*. After this, some editors add the
line: *I will not entertain so bad a thought*, which derives
from Q1.

30–54   *How if, when I am laid into the tomb . . . dash out my
desperate brains?* Juliet's imaginings are an expansion of
what she herself had already described with horror in
IV.1.81–6.

30–32   *How if . . . | I wake before the time that Romeo | Come . . .*
The Friar had promised that he and Romeo would

258

come to *watch thy waking* (IV.1.116), but the altering of the time-plan prompts her fear, repeated in
line 46.

36, 45   *like* likely

37   *conceit* fantasy

39   *receptacle* (accent on first syllable or third syllable)

42   *green in earth* freshly placed in the earth

43   *festering* (of a dead body) corrupting

47   *mandrakes.* The mandrake (sometimes known by its
Italian name *mandragola* or *mandragora*) was a famous
plant in medicine (as an opiate) and in superstition.
Its forked root sometimes gives it a resemblance to the
lower part of a man's body. It was supposed to utter
a shriek as it came out of the ground and to drive mad
anyone who uprooted it; it was therefore customary to
tie it to a dog by a piece of string in order to pull it out
of the ground.

48   *That* so that

49   *wake.* This is an emendation (in Q4) of *walk* in Q3. But
walk could be defended on the grounds that Juliet has
already spoken of waking (lines 31, 46) and now imagines herself moving about in the vault.

53   *rage* madness

    great kinsman's bone. The *kinsman* is great (as in 'great
grandfather'), not the bone.

55–7   *O look! Methinks I see* ... She imagines she sees
Tybalt's ghost in some way attacking the intruding
Romeo as he comes to fetch her from the tomb.

57   *Stay* stop

58–9   *Romeo, Romeo, Romeo.* | *Here's drink. I drink to thee.* An
alternative line *Romeo, I come. This do I drink to thee*
derives from Q1. Although it makes a smooth line and
has been accepted by stage tradition, it cannot be said to
have authority, because Q1 has a garbled version of
Juliet's soliloquy. It can be argued that the Q2 version
(here printed) is theatrically more appropriate: Juliet
is becoming hysterical, and this is better expressed

by her repetition of Romeo's name and the ghastly
jest of *Here's drink* than by the ambiguous *Romeo, I
come.*

IV.4   (stage direction) *with herbs* (from Q1)

2   *pastry* the part of the kitchen-quarters where the 'paste'
           (dough or pastry) was made
           (stage direction) *Enter Capulet*. Presumably he comes
           back from seeing Paris (IV.2.44–5).

4   *curfew* (used not only for an evening bell)

5   *baked meats* pies
           Angelica. This is probably intended to be the name of
           the Nurse, for she is definitely associated with the
           pastry in line 2 above and with the *pantry* in I.3.103,
           and it is she who replies to the present remark with her
           banter at lines 6–8. It is possible, however, that Capulet
           is addressing his wife or some servant. Angelica does
           not seem to have been used as a Christian name in
           Shakespeare's time; later it appears in Molière (Angé-
           lique) and in English Restoration comedies. If Capulet is
           addressing the Nurse, the effect is comic, for Angelica
           was the pagan princess of exquisite beauty and heartless
           coquetry who came to sow dissension among the
           Christian princes in Ariosto's *Orlando Furioso*.

6–8   *Go, you cot-quean . . . this night's watching*. The Nurse
           speaks with unexpected familiarity or indeed imperti-
           nence to the master of the house. But she is a privileged
           retainer, of many years' service (as we gather from I.3).
           Compare her interference at III.5.168–73.

6   *cot-quean* a man who meddles with a woman's house-
           hold matters

8   *watching* keeping awake; similarly, *watched* (line 9) and
           watching (line 12); but Lady Capulet's *watch you from* in
           line 12 means 'observe you closely' so that you don't
           have a chance of 'doing that sort of thing'.

9–10   *I have watched ere now | All night . . .* He hints at the amorous exploits of his youth (like Justice Shallow in *2 Henry IV*, III.2.206–32). Compare his words at I.5.22–5.

11–12   *Ay, you have been a mouse-hunt . . . from such watching now.* Lady Capulet comments sharply or contemptuously; or perhaps (since everyone is in a good mood) merely jocularly; *in your time* is a characteristic reference to her husband's age.

11   *mouse-hunt* pursuer of women; 'mouse' was used as an amorous word for a young woman. 'Mouse-hunt' was also a name for a weasel.

13   *A jealous hood* a jealous woman (as we say 'a bad hat' or 'a big wig'). Some editors prefer to spell it *jealous-hood* (as if it were a word formed like 'womanhood'), meaning 'jealousy'.

16   *drier logs.* See I.5.29, note.

18   *I have a head, sir, that will find out logs* my wooden head has a natural affinity for logs

20   *Mass!* By the mass!
      whoreson fellow (literally, bastard)

21   *loggerhead* 'fat head', blockhead. Capulet enjoys his pun on *logs* (lines 16, 18).
      Good Father! Later editions, perhaps correctly, amend to *Good faith!*, the familiar oath.

22   *straight* immediately

V.5.1   *Fast* (asleep)

4   *pennyworths* (two syllables: penn'orths) small quantities (of sleep)

5–7   *Sleep for a week . . . rest but little.* The Nurse makes the same lewd jokes about Juliet's coming experiences with Paris as she did about those with Romeo (II.5.75–6).

6   *set up his rest* ventured his whole stake (at cards), firmly resolved (with bawdy double-meaning)

7–8   *God forgive me! | Marry, and amen.* As usual she apologizes for her naughty jests. There are probably further jests in *take you in your bed* (line 10) and *fright you up* (line 11).

12   *and down again* and then lain down on your bed again

15   *weraday* well-a-day, alas!

16   *aqua vitae* brandy or other strong spirits (the Nurse's characteristic first appeal: compare III.2.88: *Give me some aqua vitae*)

25–7   *she's cold,* | *Her blood is settled . . . long been separated.* These are the signs of apparent death described by the Friar in IV.1.95–103.

26   *settled* congealed

28–9   *Death lies on her like an untimely frost* | *Upon the sweetest flower of all the field.* Shakespeare gives Capulet an appropriate solemnly trite image.

28   *untimely* out of season (like a frost in spring)

31–2   *Death . . . will not let me speak.* In fact, Capulet is very voluble on the subject. The concern with himself, indicated by his *me . . . my . . . me*, is one of the many little devices by means of which Shakespeare detaches the audience from the grief of the deceived parents. Compare Lady Capulet at line 48 below.

32   (stage direction) *Enter Friar Laurence and the County Paris.* The entry of the Musicians is not marked in Q2 and some editors follow Q4 in bringing them on here. But Q1 puts their entry after line 95 and this may represent stage practice, at any rate at an early date.

35–9   *the night before thy wedding day* | *Hath death lain with thy wife . . .* Capulet's elaborate imagining of death as his daughter's lover links with Juliet's words at I.5.135 and III.2.137 and with Lady Capulet's curse at III.5.140, and prepares for Romeo's fantasy, later, about death as amorous of Juliet and as keeping her as his paramour (V.3.102–5).

37   *deflowerèd* (four syllables)

38   *Death is my heir.* Juliet was his heiress-daughter. See line 46 below.

40   *living* means of living: that is, property (carrying on the idea of *heir* in line 38 and *leave* in line 40).

41   *long*. This is the Q1 reading. It has scarcely been for very long that he has been looking forward to this day, but the time-scheme is occasionally ignored for theatrical effect (compare note on II.4.199). Q2 reads *love* (as vocative, addressing the body of Juliet); it is awkward, but possibly correct.

43–64   *Accursed, unhappy, wretched, hateful day! . . . my joys are buried!* These exaggerated and stylized expressions of family lamentation are perhaps almost ridiculous. But the audience knows that Juliet is not dead and that the grief is unjustified. Shakespeare here avoids forestalling the true tragic passion that follows at the end of the play.

45   *in lasting labour* in the unceasing toil

46   *But one, poor one, one poor and loving child.* Compare I.2.14–15, I.5.117, and III.5.164–7.

48   *catched* snatched

55–61   *Beguiled, divorcèd, wrongèd, spited, slain! . . . murder our solemnity?* Both Paris and Capulet are thinking of the effects of Juliet's death on themselves.

56   *detestable* (accent on first syllable)

60   *Uncomfortable* discomforting, depriving us of our consolation

61   *To murder, murder our solemnity* spoil the festivity. Even in his grief, Capulet remembers that the marriage party to which he had been looking forward is spoilt.

65   *Confusion* being confounded by a blow of fate. But *confusions* in line 66 means their disorderly behaviour in lamentation.

69   *Your part* her mortal body begotten by you her parents

70   *his part* her immortal soul

71   *promotion* (four syllables) advancement to the marriage state either in itself or by her alliance with Paris

72   *your heaven* your idea of bliss (as distinct from God's idea)

73   *is* (emphasized)

76   *she is well* (the characteristic phrase for the dead)

77–8   *She's not well married that lives married long, | But she's best married that dies married young.* The Friar's views on marriage here seem to go beyond the usual limits of the pious 'contempt of life'. Probably Shakespeare is deliberately giving him nervous, exaggerated words, out of character, and pointing the dramatic irony. Contrast his advice to Romeo at II.6.14–15.

79   *your rosemary.* They are carrying rosemary for the wedding and are now to use it for the funeral (see stage direction after line 95). The Nurse had associated rosemary and Romeo at II.4.202.

80–81 *and, as the custom is, | In all her best array bear her to church.* The Friar encourages them to do what he had expected (IV.1.109–12), to fall in with his plan for extricating Juliet.

82   *fond* weak and foolish (but there is a hint of the other meaning of *fond*, too affectionate)

83   *nature's tears are reason's merriment* common sense makes a mockery of our grief, natural though it is (because Juliet is now happy in heaven). In *Twelfth Night* (I.5.64–78) Feste had been given leave to prove Olivia a fool:

FESTE Good madonna, why mournest thou?
OLIVIA Good fool, for my brother's death.
FESTE I think his soul is in hell, madonna.
OLIVIA I know his soul is in heaven, fool.
FESTE The more fool, madonna, to mourn for your brother's soul being in heaven. Take away the fool, gentlemen.

85   *Turn* (imperative)
      office function
86   *instruments* (musical)
87   *wedding cheer* the festive banquet
88   *sullen* mournful
90   *change them* change themselves (imperative)

91–3　*Sir, go you in; and, madam, go with him;* | *... unto her grave.* The Friar begins to take control, and hastens the funeral, to fit in with his own plans for Juliet's escape.

94–5　*The heavens do lour upon you for some ill.* | *Move them no more by crossing their high will* (a trite conclusion to his funeral sermon, which, in the circumstances, can only be regarded as somewhat hypocritical)

94　*lour* (rhymes with 'sour') look angrily
　　for some ill on account of some sin

95　*Move them* move them to anger
　　(stage direction) *Enter Musicians.* For their point of entry see note on IV.5.32 above. The number of musicians and the allocation of their speeches is not clear from Q2. One of them is a Fiddler (see note on line 99 below) and from line 106 onwards the speech-prefixes show them as 'Minstrels'. The Fiddler speaks lines 99 and 102, and probably lines 133–4, as this speaker is addressed as 'Hugh Rebeck'; so a producer of the play could conveniently give him the other speeches of the Second Musician (lines 120–21 and 143–4). This would leave line 136 for a tongue-tied Third Musician (the singer).

96　*Faith, we may put up our pipes and be gone ... and stay*
to end
of scene　*dinner.* The farcical conclusion to this scene helps to keep well before our consciousness that Juliet is not really dead, and we move with greater apprehension into the tragic misunderstanding of the next scene.

96, 97　*put up our pipes* 'pack up'. The use of this common phrase does not imply that the musicians are pipers: they are apparently strings, if we are to judge by their names (Catling, Rebeck, Soundpost). See notes on IV.5.129, 132, 135.

99　*Ay, by my troth ...* This is attributed to *Fid.* (presumably for *Fiddler*, as in line 102) in Q2, and this points to a jest in *the case may be amended*: his instrument case is worn and needs repairing; thus he can

265

quibble on the Nurse's *pitiful case* (state of affairs) in line 98.

99 (stage direction) *Exit Nurse*. This is the last we see of the Nurse. She can have no role in the tragic climax of the fifth Act.

100 In Q2 line 99 is followed by the stage direction *Exit*
to end *omnes* and the fiddler's jest *the case may be amended*
of scene sounds like an exit line. But the Musicians clearly remain on stage until the end of the scene. Moreover, *Exit omnes* is followed by the surprising stage direction *Enter Will Kemp*, which preserves the name of the principal comic actor in Shakespeare's company, who took the part of Peter. All this points to the lines 100–144 as being an addition, providing an extra comic scene to take off the edge of lamentation for Juliet's supposed death.

100 '*Heart's ease*'. This was a popular song of the time. The music is preserved in John Playford's *The English Dancing Master* (1651) and is reprinted in E. W. Naylor, *Shakespeare and Music* (second edition, 1928) and in William Chappell, *Popular Music of the Olden Time* (reprinted 1965). The words of the song are lost.

103–4 '*My heart is full*'. The tune has not certainly been identified. In 1622 Q4 quotes the title of the song as 'My heart is full of woe'; this is a line in *A Pleasant New Ballad of Two Lovers*, which may be old but is not known to have been printed until some time after the play.

104 *merry dump*. A dump is a sorrowful song or dance.

110 *give it you soundly* pay you out thoroughly (with a pun on *soundly*, as they are musicians)

112 *gleek* jeer

112–13 *give you* nickname you

113 *minstrel* (a somewhat derogatory name for musicians, as Mercutio had revealed at III.1.45: *dost thou make us minstrels?*)

114–15 *serving-creature* (more contemptuous than 'serving-man')

117   *carry no crotchets* endure none of your caprices (with a pun on the musical sense of *crotchets*: quarter notes)
      I'll re you, I'll fa you. Peter uses the names of the second and fourth notes on the musical scale as insulting verbs, probably punning on 'ray', 'beray' (befoul), and 'fay' (clear away filth).

118, 119 *note* (punning on the musical sense: set to music)

119   *you note us* (with emphasis on *you* and *us*)

121   *put out* display (probably, rather than 'extinguish')

122   *dry-beat* cudgel (without drawing blood), as in III.1.78.

125–7, *When griping griefs the heart doth wound* . . . This is the
140–41 beginning of a poem in praise of music, printed in *The Paradise of Dainty Devices* (1576) and there attributed to Richard Edwards (1523–66), a poet and playwright of the generation before Shakespeare. A contemporary setting has been preserved. The words in Shakespeare's text show small differences from those printed in 1576 ('Where griping grief . . . There music with . . . Is wont with speed to give redress').

129   *Simon Catling.* A catling is a catgut lute-string. Presumably Peter is inventing surnames for the musicians.

132, 135 *Pretty.* This is the Q1 reading. Q2 reads *Prates* (he prattles), which may be correct.

132   *Hugh Rebeck.* A rebeck (pronounced *ree-beck*) was a kind of three-stringed fiddle.

135   *James Soundpost.* The soundpost is the interior peg which supports the belly of a bass viol.

137   *I cry you mercy!* I beg your pardon

137–8 *You are the singer. I will say for you* (emphasis on *for*). The Third Musician (although called Soundpost) is a singer, and so not much of a speaker.

139   *for sounding* as payment for their making music and for jingling (in their purses)

143   *Jack* low fellow (compare II.4.149 and III.1.11)

144   *stay* wait for

V.1   The place now changes to Mantua (see note on III.3.149), where Romeo had gone immediately after leaving Juliet on Tuesday morning (III.3.148–54, 169; III.5.15, 88–9; IV.1.117). Romeo has not appeared in the fourth Act. An absence of the principal performer during approximately the third quarter of the play is usual in Shakespeare. It gives the actor a chance of a rest, which is especially needed if he is to give a good display of swordsmanship in the fifth Act.

1–9   *If I may trust the flattering truth of sleep . . . revived and was an emperor.* For the premonition see Introduction, p. 21.

1   *flattering truth of sleep.* We are often inclined to accept premonitory dreams as truthful because they flatter us.

3   *My bosom's lord . . . in his throne* Cupid in my heart, or (perhaps) my heart in my body

10   *love itself possessed* love enjoyed in reality

11   *love's shadows* dreams of love

    (stage direction) *booted.* It indicates that he has just come from riding.

12   *Balthasar* (accent on third syllable, like Italian Baldassare)

13   *Dost thou not bring me letters from the Friar?* We learn from the next scene that the Friar's letter (which he had promised the audience he would send to Romeo at IV.1.113–14) has miscarried. Balthasar has reached Mantua with his (false) bad news first.

18   *Capel's monument.* Capulet may be abbreviated to Capel (III.1.2) and is usually so abbreviated when applied to the monument (burial vault); see V.3.127.

21   *presently* immediately

23   *did leave it for my office* left me the duty of bringing you news (as arranged by the Friar, III.3.169–71)

24   *e'en.* Q2 has *in*, which probably represents a spelling of *e'en*. Q1 and later editions have *even*.

    I defy you, stars! Q2 reads *I deny you stars* and Q1 *I defy my stars.* Although *deny* has been defended by some editors and is found in the more authoritative text, it can hardly be doubted that *defy* gives the required meaning. Romeo is not making a denial of astrological influence, but stands in defiance of his ill-luck, in a posture which immediately makes his servant plead: ... *have patience.* | *Your looks are pale and wild.* ...

25   *ink and paper* (for the letter mentioned at V.3.23–4, 275, 278, 286–90)

27   *patience* (three syllables)

28–9   *import* | *Some misadventure* convey some (coming) tragic accident

31   *Hast thou no letters to me from the Friar?* The question is repeated from line 13 above.

38   *noted* noticed

39   *overwhelming* beetling, overhanging

40   *Culling of simples* selecting the ingredients of herbal medicines

42–4   *And in his needy shop a tortoise hung,* | *An alligator stuffed, and other skins* | *Of ill-shaped fishes....* Surviving pictures of apothecaries' shops show that tortoise shells, stuffed alligators, and fishes were among the usual furniture.

45   *beggarly account* wretched collection

46   *bladders.* These were used for holding liquids.

47   *cakes of roses* rose petals compressed into tight packs (used as perfume)

51   *Whose sale is present death* for the sale of which, immediate death is the penalty. English law in Shakespeare's time did not, it seems, include this penalty, though it was usual on the Continent.

52   *caitiff wretch* wretched creature
     would who would

53   *forerun my need* anticipate my necessity. He puns on *need* and *needy* (next line).

59   *there is* here are
     forty ducats. The ducat was a gold coin, slightly larger

than a sixpence (or a dime). Romeo shows him the
money in his hand – temptingly, for it is a considerable
sum.

63–5　*And that the trunk may be discharged of breath . . . the
fatal cannon's womb.* For the imagery, compare II.6.10
and III.3.132 (Introduction, pp. 31–2).

64　*powder* gunpowder (to which Shakespeare elsewhere
compares the poison aconite: *2 Henry IV*, IV.4.48)

66　*mortal* deadly

66–7　*Mantua's law | Is death . . .* Romeo had himself said
this in lines 50–51.

67　*any he that utters them* any person who makes them
available

70　*starveth* produce the effects of hunger

71　*Contempt* (by the world)

74　*this* the money Romeo offers

77　*Put this in any liquid thing you will.* But apparently
Romeo eventually drinks it off neat (V.3.119–20).
this a vial of poison

78–9　*if you had the strength | Of twenty men it would dispatch
you straight.* The Apothecary's claim is borne out by
Romeo at V.3.119–20.

85　*cordial* medicine (originally, for the heart)

V.2　In the previous scene (lines 13 and 31) Romeo had
twice specifically asked Balthasar whether he had a
letter from Friar Laurence. Now is explained the unlucky chance whereby the expected letter did not reach
him.

1　*brother* friar

5–12　*Going to find a bare-foot brother out . . . there was stayed.*
The confused syntax of Friar John's story suggests his
anxiety.

5　*bare-foot brother* Franciscan

6　*associate* accompany. It was usual for members of the
religious orders to travel in pairs.

8   *searchers of the town* 'health officers', who were ap-
      pointed to view dead bodies and report causes of death

11   *Sealed up the doors.* This was the common practice in
      London during the plague, to enforce quarantine.

12   *stayed* stopped

16   *infection* (four syllables)

17   *Unhappy fortune!* See Introduction, pp. 18–23.
      brotherhood Franciscan order

18   *nice* trivial
      charge weighty matters

19   *dear import* serious importance

21   *crow* crowbar

25   *beshrew me much* reprove me severely

26   *accidents* happenings

V.3   (stage direction) *sweet water* perfumed water (see line 14
      below)

1–9   *Give me thy torch, boy. Hence, and stand aloof. . . .* There
      seems to be no adequate cause for Paris's anxiety, but
      this speech helps to create the atmosphere of suspense.

3   *yew trees, churchyard* (lines 5 and 11) and *graves* (line 6)
      help to establish the scene
      lay thee all along lie flat on the ground

6   *Being loose* because the soil is loose

10   *stand* stay

11   *adventure* take the risk

12–17 *Sweet flower, with flowers . . .* Paris's little rhymed poem
      and flowers to express his sorrow for Juliet are in
      striking contrast with Romeo's despair and poison.

12   *Sweet flower* (Juliet)
      bridal bed. Lady Capulet had said at III.5.140: *I would
      the fool were married to her grave!*

13   *canopy* covering (of her bed of death)

14   *sweet water.* See note on stage direction above.

15   *wanting* lacking

16   *obsequies* funeral rites

16   *keep* observe regularly

30–32   *But chiefly to take thence from her dead finger ... In dear employment*. This is merely Romeo's pretence, to deceive his servant about his real intention, which is suicide.

32   *dear* personally important

33   *jealous* suspicious

36   *hungry churchyard* (because death has a ravenous appetite; compare lines 45–8 below)

41–2   *Take thou that. | Live, and be prosperous*. Again, as with the Mantuan apothecary, Romeo thinks of the welfare of others.

41   *that* money (perhaps his purse)

43   *For all this same* all the same, in spite of all this

44   *doubt* suspect

45   *detestable* (accent on first syllable)
        womb belly (rather than the female organ)

46   *dearest morsel* (Juliet)

48   *in despite* defiantly
        more food his own body

52   *villainous shame* (such as stealing parts of bodies for purposes of witchcraft)

53, 56, 69 *apprehend* arrest

59   *Good gentle youth*. Romeo does not recognize Paris until line 75, after he has killed him.

60   *these gone* (Juliet, Tybalt, and others, buried in the tomb)

65   *armed against myself* (because he brings the poison for suicide)

67   *bid* (past tense)

68   *conjuration* warning entreaty. Q2 reads *commiration* and Q1 *conjurations*. An interesting conjecture is *commination*, meaning 'threatenings'.

75   *Mercutio's*. The only mention of Mercutio after his death-scene in III.1.

80   *him talk of Juliet* (emphasis on *him*, Paris). See line 73 above.

82   *sour misfortune*. See Introduction, pp. 17–24.

83   *triumphant* glorious

84   *lantern* (in an architectural sense) a superstructure with openings giving light

86   *feasting presence* festival presence-chamber

87   *Death* the dead body of Paris
     a dead man (himself – by anticipation)

89   *keepers* nurses or gaolers

90, 91   *lightning*. Juliet had spoken of their love as a lightning (II.2.119–20). Perhaps the *lightning* in line 90 is a pun on the 'lightening of the spirits'.

92–6   *Death, that hath sucked the honey . . . is not advancèd there.* Seeing Juliet's lifelike appearance in (supposed) death Romeo almost stumbles upon the truth; and again at lines 101–2. This adds a feeling of suspense, almost a ray of hope, to the agony with which we listen to Romeo's suicide-speech.

101   *cousin* (Tybalt)

102   *Why art thou yet so fair?* See note on lines 92–6.

102–5   *Shall I believe | That unsubstantial death is amorous . . .* See note at IV.5.35–9 on death as Juliet's lover.

102–3   Before *Shall I believe*, Q2 has a superfluous *I shall believe*. This is probably one of Shakespeare's 'false starts', accidentally not deleted in his manuscript. Compare I.2.15, IV.1.110, and V.3.106–10 (just below).

105   *to be his paramour?* This is a curious hint of the classical legend of Proserpina, who was abducted by Pluto (or Dis) and taken to Hades to be his consort.

106–10   In Q2 these lines are printed as follows:
     (a) For feare of that I still will staie with thee,
     (b) And neuer from this pallat of dym night.
     (c) Depart againe, come lye thou in my arme,
     (d) Heer's to thy health, where ere thou tumblest in.
     (e) O true Appothecarie!
     (f) Thy drugs are quicke. Thus with a kisse I die.
     (g) Depart againe, here, here, will I remaine,
     (h) With wormes that are thy Chamber-maides: O here
     (i) Will I set vp my euerlasting rest:

273

It seems that Shakespeare, having written lines (c) to (f), cancelled them and started again at (g). But the lines were imperfectly deleted in his manuscript, and so *both* versions came to be printed. He transferred parts of (d), (e), and (f) to lines 119–20 in the text.

107   *palace*. Q2 has *pallat* which might represent *pallet* bed. Although *pallet of dim night* is a strained phrase, it could be right. The change to *palace* was made in the printing of Q 3.

110   *set up my everlasting rest* make my resolve to remain here for ever (with a pun on *rest*, as in IV.5.6)

111   *inauspicious stars*. See Introduction, pp. 19–22.

115   *A dateless bargain* an everlasting agreement (one without a terminable date)
        engrossing monopolizing

116–18 *Come, bitter conduct, come, unsavoury guide . . . thy sea-sick weary bark*. For the ship–guide–pilot imagery, see Introduction, pp. 22–3.

116   *bitter conduct . . . unsavoury guide* (the vial of poison)
        conduct conductor

117   *Thou desperate pilot* (himself; or perhaps his own soul)

118   *bark* his body

119   *Here's to my love!* Compare Juliet's *I drink to thee* at IV.3.59. Presumably the Apothecary's poison had been handed to Romeo in a bottle, corresponding to the *vial* (IV.1.93 and IV.3.20) given by the Friar to Juliet. But at V.3.161 below Juliet finds *A cup, closed in my true love's hand*. This may indicate some stage-business by which Romeo pours the poison from a vial into a beaker and so drinks a toast to his love. It is not easy to drink with stage-dignity from a small bottle.

119–20 *O true Apothecary! | Thy drugs are quick*. The Apothecary had claimed a speedy effect for his poison in V.1.77–9.

120   *Thy drugs are quick. Thus with a kiss I die*. From the frequency of verbal quibbles in the play, even at the

most serious moments, we should expect that the other
meaning of *quick* ('alive') would be brought to mind
by its opposite idea in Romeo's *die* (which could itself
also mean 'to experience the sexual pleasure'). Probably such paradoxes are irrelevant here.

121 *speed* protector

122 *stumbled at graves*. This refers to the superstition about
stumbling when taking a decisive step.

125 *vainly* uselessly

136 *unthrifty* unlucky

137-9 *As I did sleep under this yew tree here ... my master
slew him*. Balthasar appears to be prevaricating. He has
seen the death of Paris at Romeo's hands, but pretends
it was a dream.

142 *masterless* abandoned by their owners

145 *unkind* (accent on first syllable) unnatural

148 *comfortable* bringing fortitude and consolation

151-7 *I hear some noise. Lady, come from that nest ... sisterhood of holy nuns*. The Friar's words as he faces the real
disaster are strikingly different from his formal speech
after the supposed death of Juliet (IV.5.65-83). His
humbled admission that *A greater power than we can
contradict | Hath thwarted our intents* (lines 153-4) re-
lates ironically to his hypocritical couplet at IV.5.94-5.

161-70 *What's here? A cup, closed in my true love's hand? ...
and let me die*. Juliet has a short dying speech, in contrast to Romeo's long one. Probably Shakespeare could
not altogether trust his boy-actor to maintain the tension
for long. (In his plays only Cleopatra, among the
women, is allowed to take her time dying. Cordelia is
carried on stage already dead.)

161 *cup*. See note on V.3.119.

162 *timeless* untimely

163 *O churl!* (addressing Romeo)

166 *restorative* (the kiss she gives him)

169 *happy* opportunely found

170 *rust*. Some editors prefer the reading *rest*, which comes

from Q1. But *rust* has better authority and is more vivid.

173   *attach* arrest

176   *two days*. The Friar had spoken of forty-two hours at IV.i.105.

179–80   *ground ... ground*. He puns on the meanings 'earth' and 'reason'.

179   *woes* woeful creatures (the three dead bodies)

181   *circumstance* detailed surrounding facts

187   (stage direction) This is the third symmetrical assembly of the two families and the Prince, this time over the dead bodies of their heirs. Compare I.i.80 and III.i.140.

194   *your ears*. Some editors emended to *our*. This gives an easier meaning, but *your* makes sense.

203   *mista'en* gone away
        his house its sheath

204   *Montague* Romeo

207   *my old age*. On Lady Capulet's age see note on I.3.73–4.

209   *down* dead on the ground

210   *my wife is dead tonight!* Lady Montague is a small part: she only speaks three lines in the play. Presumably it was doubled with a part required in this last Act (perhaps the Page) and so Shakespeare makes a virtue out of the necessity and gives an extra touch of pathos by killing her off. Q1 even adds: *And young Benvolio is deceasèd, too.* But who would notice the absence of Benvolio, Montague's nephew, at this moment? It is possible that Q1 here preserves a line subsequently deleted by Shakespeare as an unnecessary explanation, even though the actor of Benvolio was required for another part in this last scene.

211   *exile* (accent on second syllable)

214   *O thou untaught!* He chides his son, with affectionate pity, for his ill manners.

216   *mouth of outrage* utterances of passionate grief

219   *general of your woes* leader in lamentation

220   *even to death* even though sorrow were to kill me

221   *let mischance be slave to patience* let our patience control our misfortunes
        patience (three syllables)

222   *suspicion* (four syllables)

223   *the greatest, able to do least* the most liable to be suspected, although actually the weakest

225   *make against me* weigh to my discredit, implicate me

226   *impeach and purge* accuse and exonerate

229–69 *I will be brief, for my short date of breath . . . severest law.* This long narrative by the Friar is often omitted in modern productions as being unnecessary. But it is needed if there is to be a strong emphasis on the reconciliation of the two families. See Introduction, pp. 35–7. It is noticeable that the one thing the Friar omits in his narrative is his motive of reconciling the families (see II.3.87–8).

229   *date of breath* period of life allowed

233   *stolen* secret

234   *doomsday* day of death

236   *For whom, and not for Tybalt, Juliet pined.* Compare Paris's belief at lines 50–51 above.

237   *You* (the Capulets)
        siege of grief assailing grief

247   *as* on

248   *borrowed* temporarily taken, since she was not dead

253   *prefixèd* prearranged

255   *closely* secretly

260   *She wakes* (a vivid present tense)

261   *patience* (three syllables)

266   *privy* accessory in the secret

268   *his* its

270   *still* always

273   *in post* post haste

275   *letter.* See lines 23–4 above.
        early early in the morning (see line 23 above)

280   *made your master* was your master doing

284   *by and by* at once

289   *therewithal* with the poison

293   *your joys* (their children, Juliet and Romeo)
       with love by means of their love

294   *winking at* 'turning a blind eye to'

295   *a brace of kinsmen* (Mercutio and Paris)

297   *This is my daughter's jointure.* The hand of Montague he is holding (that is, reconciliation) is the only marriage-settlement which, as the father of Juliet, he expects from the bridegroom's father.

299   *raise her statue.* He does not necessarily mean an upright statue. See line 303 below. Q2 reads *raie* (array), which some editors have defended. The change to *raise* was made, apparently independently, in Q4 and in F.

301   *at such rate be set* be put at such a high value

303   *As rich shall Romeo's by his lady's lie.* Shakespeare is thinking of the recumbent effigies of man and wife on Renaissance tombs (like those of the Cloptons in Stratford-upon-Avon church).

AN ACCOUNT OF THE TEXT

When John Heminge and Henry Condell presented the first collected edition of Shakespeare's plays in 1623 they said in their prefatory address 'To the great variety of readers' that 'It had been a thing, we confess, worthy to have been wished that the Author himself had lived to have set forth and overseen his own writings . . .'. Every editor of Shakespeare, and every reader and producer who cares about the words that Shakespeare used, must echo this wish. For, of all the world's great authors since the invention of printing, Shakespeare is the most unlucky in the way his works have come down to us.

The plays were printed without his supervision and without anything of what would be regarded by a modern author or printer as proof-correction. Yet it would seem that Shakespeare himself set his printers high standards of accuracy. We can judge this from the first editions of his poems *Venus and Adonis* and *The Rape of Lucrece* (1593 and 1594). These were issued by a fellow Stratfordian, Richard Field, who, like Shakespeare, had come to London to make his name. They were distinctly *literary* works; they were graced by dedications to Shakespeare's young patron, the Earl of Southampton; and they were accorded due care by the printer. Scarcely a misprint sullies their pages.

With the plays the situation is quite different. Until Ben Jonson issued his *Works* in 1616, a stage-play in English does not seem to have been regarded as a literary work. One or two dramatists may have given the printing of their plays a little cursory attention. But most of them left printing entirely to the printer, and in many cases they seem to have had no say at all in the publication of their plays; for it was usual for a play to belong, not to its author, but to the theatre-company which performed it. Many of Shakespeare's plays were issued in his own lifetime in what, from their size, are termed 'quarto' editions.

Some of these plays were printed from good, reliable copy, obtained honestly from the theatrical companies. Some were printed from bad copy, surreptitiously acquired from disloyal actors in the plays, who had memorized their own parts and tried to remember the speeches of the other characters. In none of the quartos is the quality of printing high; for play-books were merely 'popular' literature.

These quartos – and even the collected edition, issued some seven years after Shakespeare's death, in the larger, folio, size (hence the term, the first Folio) – contain hundreds of observable printing errors that no intelligent reader, and certainly not the author, would have passed in proof. Furthermore, where plays were issued in quartos and in the Folio, they often show remarkable differences in content. *Hamlet*, indeed, is available to us in a thoroughly bad quarto, a good quarto, and a good, but often differing, Folio version. To make matters even worse, it is probable that Shakespeare himself, like some modern writers, was responsible for different versions existing concurrently. (T. S. Eliot has 'Northolt' in the English version of *The Family Reunion* but 'airport' in the American version.) Sometimes a cancelled version of a line or two, or a 'false start' imperfectly deleted, accidentally gets printed from Shakespeare's manuscript (or a transcription of it), as well as the lines Shakespeare wrote in substitution; so we are confused by having awkward repetitions of words and ideas (see notes on I.2.15, IV.1.110, V.3.102–3 and 106–10 in *Romeo and Juliet*).

Although some changes were made in proof and some in the course of printing, an Elizabethan printer of plays did not stop his presses working in order to read proofs; pages were printed in 'incorrect' versions until proofs had been read and the 'corrections' were made. Unfortunately, these 'corrections' lack authorial support. The proof-reader *may* have consulted his manuscript copy; but often it is evident he was only concerned to smooth out nonsense and to make the page look tidy typographically.

Many of the differences between the Folio and preceding texts, and many of the words and passages for which no alternative version exists, are clearly corrupt. Often the correction is obvious (as *theu* may need to be changed to *then*). But far too frequently we cannot be sure exactly what form the correction should take. Many of the awkward readings may be defended by an appeal to topical allusions, different verbal and grammatical practices, and the linguistic fantasies so beloved of Elizabethan and Jacobean writers. Furthermore, professional scribes, keepers of prompt-books in the theatre, compositors, and proof-readers have often so much smoothed out lines that puzzled them that we cannot now be sure that passages seemingly sound are, in reality, what Shakespeare wrote. We do not know how accurately printers could set Shakespeare's manuscript. But we *do* know that they were capable of introducing dozens of alterations into what they reset from a printed book; some are errors due to mere carelessness, some are deliberate falsifications. What is so disconcerting is to realize that, had we not a copy of such an earlier version, we should not have been able to detect these errors and changes. So, there must be hundreds of printers' errors and alterations in Shakespeare's plays which we cannot discover because the false word or words make a kind of sense, though not the sense the author intended.

The situation is familiar to anyone who has a typist working from handwritten drafts. Most of her errors can be put into categories. There are mechanical ones; inversions (*mna* for *man*) and errors due to the proximity of keys (*hot* for *jot*). There are certain recurring errors which derive from difficulties in the handwriting: a similarity in the forming of *n/r/u* in a particular handwriting may lead to errors of the kind *land/lard/laud*. Normally, the sense helps the typist to choose the right alternative. But especially inconvenient, and easily missed, is the error made when an intelligent typist produces a word which makes good sense in the sentence but is not the word intended.

Just so, a compositor may, inadvertently, reverse letters. He may, like a typist striking an adjacent key, select a piece of type from a box adjacent to the correct one, or pick up a piece that has fallen into the wrong box. Some letters, too, are easily confused in Elizabethan handwriting: the way of writing *e* and *d* could be very similar and thus a word like *turn* (regularly spelt with an *e* at the end) could appear in the past tense, *turnd*, instead of the present, *turne* (and both are 'normal' Elizabethan spellings). Usually a compositor (like a modern typist) would 'make sense' of what was put before him, but it may not be the sense required and the results may be absurd or feeble or obscure: in any case, destructive of Shakespeare's meaning. Conditions for the Elizabethan printer were much worse than for a modern printer or typist. Writing and spelling were highly idiosyncratic, equipment less regular, hours much longer, and heating and lighting not up to modern standards. Though we regret the poor quality of the texts of Shakespeare's plays, and their variability, we do well to bear in mind the conditions under which they were produced. Indeed, it is by a knowledge of these conditions that we may be helped to restore a lost reading, or make an intelligent supposition.

Thus the preparation of the text of a play by Shakespeare may require a great deal of informed and carefully controlled guessing. Decisions often have to be made on a delicate balance of probabilities, and the balance may be so fine that a decision will have to be reached without much confidence. An editor may be helped by a knowledge of Elizabethan handwriting, theatre documents, printing-house practices, and the language (especially the idiomatic usage) of Shakespeare's time. In many instances, literary taste ultimately has to decide; and what one editor or reader finds admirable another may think intolerable or absurd.

To take an example: *Romeo and Juliet* IV.1.98–101 in the Quarto of 1599 reads as follows (the Friar is describing to Juliet what will happen after she has taken the potion):

98   No warmth, no breast shall testifie thou liuest,
99   The roses in thy lips and cheekes shall fade:
100   Too many ashes, thy eyes windowes fall:
101   Like death when he shuts vp the day of life.

We can begin by amending the punctuation to accord with modern logical indications: the second half of line 100 goes with line 101; so we can remove the colon. Lines 98 and 99 are independent sentences and so we can perhaps put a heavier stop than a comma between them. We can confidently amend *breast* (line 98) as being a misprint for *breath*. In line 100 *Too many ashes* cannot be right: the words are ungrammatical and meaningless in this position. We can remove the colon at the end of line 99, and for *Too* read *To* (this is only a spelling change). Presumably *many* is an error for some other adjective. A knowledge of Elizabethan handwriting suggests that a compositor (or a scribe writing a 'fair copy' of Shakespeare's play from his manuscript) might have misread *many* for *wany* (that is, *wanny*); or he might have set up *many*, thinking he saw *manie* (for *y* and *ie* could both be used in this fashion). But the *manie* he thought he saw could as easily have been *wanie* or (because of the possibility of confusing *e* and *d*) even *waned*. Thus an editor relying on evidence of confusion caused by similarities in handwriting might choose *wanny* or *waned*, believing not only that this word was appropriate to the sense but that his argument showed how such an error had arisen – even though we do not know exactly what the handwriting of the manuscript looked like. (We get no help from the 'Bad Quarto' of 1597 here, for the four lines are represented by only one line, corrupted: 'No signe of breath shall testifie thou liust.')

But there is another fact to consider. When *Romeo and Juliet* was printed for the fourth time (in 1622), we find that the phrase has been replaced by *paly ashes*. Where has *paly* come from? We cannot assume it has Shakespeare's approval. It may be without any authority. But we observe that the person who made the change has at least been reading the text carefully and noticed something was wrong (though, alas! there were many new errors introduced elsewhere into this reprinting). The correction makes good sense; but is it merely a guess on the part of the printer, of no more or less value than yours or mine? In answering that question we have to bear in mind two things. First, whoever made the change spoke the idiom of the time of Shakespeare and might be in a better position to judge the appropriateness of an epithet than we are. Secondly, *Romeo and*

Juliet was a very popular play on the stage and the change to *paly* might have been made by someone who had heard what Friar Laurence said – and it can hardly have been the nonsensical *Too many ashes*. We cannot know what phrase he used. But it is possible that the sudden appearance of *paly* here reflects stage practice, and that stage tradition preserved Shakespeare's word or, at least, a word used in a production by Shakespeare's company. In seeing *wanny* behind the erroneous *many* we may be relying too much on the clue of handwriting; *many* may be due to the picking up of the wrong sort of type being followed by unintelligent 'correcting' – or even to absentminded substitution.

A study of all the instances where Shakespeare uses the words *ashes*, *wan(n)y*, *wane(d)*, *pale*, *paly* does not seem to help us much in determining literary probabilities here. On balance, a modern editor will probably choose, but without much confidence, to print *wanny*. And so in our text the passage appears as:

> No warmth, no breath, shall testify thou livest.
> The roses in thy lips and cheeks shall fade
> To wanny ashes, thy eyes' windows fall
> Like death when he shuts up the day of life.

A version of Shakespeare's play of *Romeo and Juliet* was first published in 1597. (We refer to this as Q1.) The title-page describes it as 'An excellent conceited tragedy of Romeo and Juliet, as it hath been often, with great applause, played publicly by the right honourable the Lord of Hunsdon his servants.' Like similar 'pirated' texts – editions printed without the permission of the author or the acting company – it is a detestable text, probably a reconstruction of the play from the imperfect memories of one or two of the actors. It is short (2232 lines, in comparison with the 3003 lines of the present edition), for it has been heavily cut. It is confused, often ungrammatical; much of the poetry has gone or been spoilt by the corrupting of the lines. The following is an average specimen, in modernized spelling, of this text (Juliet's soliloquy before taking the sleeping-potion, IV.3.14–59, is reduced from forty-six lines to eighteen):

Farewell; God knows when we shall meet again.
Ah, I do take a fearful thing in hand.
What if this potion should not work at all?
Must I of force be married to the county?
This shall forbid it. Knife, lie thou there.
What if the friar should give me this drink
To poison me, for fear I should disclose
Our former marriage? Ah, I wrong him much.
He is a holy and religious man.
I will not entertain so bad a thought.
What if I should be stifled in the tomb?
Awake an hour before the appointed time?
Ah, then I fear I shall be lunatic,
And, playing with my dead forefathers' bones,
Dash out my frantic brains. Methinks I see
My cousin Tybalt, weltering in his blood,
Seeking for Romeo. Stay, Tybalt, stay!
Romeo, I come! This do I drink to thee.

Two years later (1599) another version of the play appeared (issued by a different and more respectable printer), described on the title page as: 'The most excellent and lamentable tragedy of Romeo and Juliet, newly corrected, augmented, and amended, as it hath been sundry times publicly acted by the right honourable the Lord Chamberlain his servants.' (This text we call Q2.) It is essentially the play we know. Much of it was set up from Shakespeare's manuscript or (at least) from a transcription fairly close to Shakespeare's manuscript. The 1599 printing (Q2) is, by comparison with Q1, a good text. Yet we soon discover, from a careful study of it, that in this play, as in most of Shakespeare's plays, we are dealing with a work of art that has not been finally 'polished', not prepared for the press by the tidying up of details and petty inconsistencies. This, the only authoritative text we have, has been subjected by scholars to careful analysis, and the disquieting situation (in all probability) is this:

1. The beginning of the play, up to about I.2.52, seems to have been set up by the printer from a fair copy of Shakespeare's manuscript;

2. From I.2.53 to about I.3.35 was printed directly from the imperfect and corrupted form of the play which had been issued two years before (Q1);

3. I.3.36 to III.4 was from the fair copy again;

4. From III.5 onwards the printer seems to have been working from Shakespeare's 'foul papers': that is, from his rough working manuscript which had not been copied out fair.

The heterogeneous nature of the printer's copy is reflected in many ways: for example, in the differing names given to some of the speakers. Juliet's mother is variously 'Lady of the House', 'Old Lady', 'Lady', 'Wife', and 'Mother'. A modern editor has to tidy this up and use 'Lady Capulet' throughout.

The 1599 text of the play (Q2) was reprinted in 1609 (Q3) and again (though the title-page was undated) in 1622 (Q4) and in 1637 (Q5). The text in the Folio edition of 1623 (F) derives from Q3. Later Folios appeared in 1632 (F2), 1663–4 (F3), and 1685 (F4). The reprints after Q2 contain many alterations and corrections, though these cannot be assumed to have any authority. They also contain many new errors.

The main problem of the text of *Romeo and Juliet* depends on the nature of the 'Bad Quarto' of 1597 (Q1). It would be convenient if we could reject the whole thing as a garbled version of the play, and depend entirely on the authoritative Q2. Unfortunately no editor can do this, for three reasons:

1. Q2 itself is corrupt in many places and in some fifty of these instances the reading in Q1 has the appearance of being the correct (or at least a probable or reasonable) one. A list of the readings from Q1 accepted in this edition is given in section 1 of the Collations below (p. 287).

2. The printer of Q2, though apparently fairly conscientious, unquestionably had a copy of Q1 beside him and used it. As already mentioned above, he used a leaf of it for one long passage of his text (I.2.53 to I.3.35), perhaps because a piece was missing from the manuscript copy he had been given. There is, moreover, evidence that he consulted the Bad Quarto at various other places in the play where the Bad Quarto text seemed fairly accurate and where therefore it was possible – and

much quicker and easier – to work from printed rather than manuscript copy.

3. Whatever the circumstances of the compilation of the text of the 'Bad Quarto' may have been, it clearly derives from a *performance* of the play. The reporters remember and record a good deal of what was seen on the stage. The stage directions are, in fact, remarkably full and interesting, and they help us to visualize an early performance (though we cannot be sure that it was a performance by Shakespeare's own company, the Lord Chamberlain's Men). A list of these stage directions is given in section 4 of the Collations (p. 294). Several of them have been taken over into the present text, where they add something to the stage business not explicit in the words of the characters.

COLLATIONS

The following lists are *selective*. They include the more important and interesting variants. Minor changes which are not disputed, small variations in word-order, obvious misprints, and grammatical corrections not affecting the sense are not usually included here.

1

The following readings in the present text of *Romeo and Juliet* derive from Q1, and not from Q2. The reading (which generally represents the Q1 form in, of course, modernized spelling) is followed by the Q2 form, unmodernized.

I.i. 177 create] created
     179 well-seeming] welseeing (Q1: best seeming)
     192 lovers'] louing (Q1: a louers)
     202 Bid a sick man in sadness make] A sicke man in sadnesse makes

I.2. 29 female] fennell
68 *Rosaline and Liuia*] Rosaline, Liuia
76 thee] you
I.3. 67, 68 honour] houre
100 make it fly] make flie
I.4. 7–8 Nor no without-book prologue, faintly spoke |
After the prompter, for our entrance.] *omitted in*
Q2
39 done] dum
42 Of] Or
45 like lamps] lights lights
69 maid] man
72 O'er] On
90 elf-locks] Elklocks
113 sail] sute
I.5. 95 ready stand] did readie stand
142 What's this, what's this] Whats tis? whats tis
(Q1: Whats this? whats that?)
II.1. 6 MERCUTIO] *continued to* BENVOLIO *in* Q2
10 Pronounce but 'love' and 'dove'] prouaunt, but
loue and day
13 trim] true
II.2. 41 nor any other part] *omitted in* Q2
99 'haviour] behauior
101 more cunning] coying
162 mine] *omitted in* Q2
II.3. 18 sometime's] sometime
II.4. 19 I can tell you] *omitted in* Q2
28 fantasticoes] phantacies
112 for himself] himself
III.1. 2 Capels are abroad] Capels abroad
122 Alive] He gan
124 fire-eyed] fier end
166 agile] aged
188 hate's] hearts
192 I will] It will
III.2. 56 swounded] sounded

288

III.2. 72 NURSE] *continued to* JULIET *in* Q2
    73 JULIET] NURSE
III.3. 15 Hence] Here
    53 Thou] Then
    117 lives] lies (Q1: too, that liues in thee; Q2: that in thy life lies)
    144 upon] vp (Q1: frownst vpon; Q2: puts vp)
III.5. 181 trained] liand
IV.1. 7 talked] talke
    45 cure] care
IV.5. 41 long] loue
    81 In all] And in
    126 And doleful dumps the mind oppress,] *omitted in* Q2
132, 135 Pretty] Prates
V.1. 24 defy] denie
    76 pay] pray
V.3.3, 137 yew] young, yong
    68 conjuration] commiration (Q1: coniurations)

2

The following readings in the present text of *Romeo and Juliet* are emendations of the words found in Q2 (which are placed afterwards, in the original spelling except that the 'long s' [ʃ] has been replaced by 's', with where appropriate the forms found in other early texts). A few of these alterations were made in the printing of Q3 (1609), Q4 (1622), or the Folios F (1623), F2 (1632), F3 (1663–4). Most of the other emendations were made by the eighteenth-century editors; a few are gratefully attributed to recent editors (see 'Further Reading').

I.1. 72 CITIZENS] *Offi.*
    153 sun] same
    197 left] lost
I.2. 32 Which, on more] Which one more

I.4. 47   our five wits] our fine wits

57   atomies] Q 3; ottamie Q2; Atomi Q1

59–61   Her chariot . . . coachmakers] *placed after line 69 in* Q2

I.5. 18   a bout] about

II.1. 38   open-arse and thou] J. S. Farmer and W. E. Henley, *Slang and its Analogues* (1903), vol. I, p. 68, and J. Dover Wilson; open, or thou Q2; open *Etcætera*, thou Q1

II.2. 167   nyas] J. Dover Wilson, 1955; Neece Q2; Madame Q1; Deere Q 4; sweete F2

III.1. 89   A FOLLOWER Away, Tybalt!] W. W. Greg; *Away Tybalt. (as stage direction)*

184   MONTAGUE] Q 4; *Capu.*

III.2.   9   By] Q 4; And by

49   shut] shot

76   Dove-feathered raven] Rauenous douefeatherd rauē

79   damnèd] Q 4; dimme

III.3. 144   pouts] Q 4; puts

IV.1. 85   tomb] *omitted in* Q2; shroud Q 4; graue F

100   To wanny] Too many Q2; Too paly Q 4

110   Q2 *adds a superfluous, probably rewritten, line:* Be borne to buriall in thy kindreds graue. *See Commentary.*

IV.3. 49   wake] Q 4; walke

IV.5. 65   cure] care

82   fond] F2; some

122   Then have at you with my wit] *attributed to Second Musician in* Q2

V.3. 102   Q2 *adds superfluous words:* I will beleeue. *See Commentary.*

107   palace] Q 3; pallat

108   Q2 *adds four superfluous, probably rewritten, lines. See Commentary.*

299   raise] Q 4; raie

3

The following are some of the more interesting and important variant readings and proposed emendations *not* accepted in the present text of *Romeo and Juliet*. Many of these rejected readings will be found in older editions (especially nineteenth-century ones).

The reading of this edition (which derives from Q2 unless otherwise stated) is given first, followed by the rejected variants. If a source of the variant is not given, the reading is an emendation by an editor (most of such emendations are of the eighteenth century).

I.1.	21	civil] cruell Q 4
	62	washing] swashing Q 4
	120	drive] drave Q 3
	127	Which then most sought where most might not be found] That most are busied when th'are most alone Q1
	190	made] raisde Q1
	211	uncharmed] vnharmd Q1
I.2.	65	Utruvio] Vitruvio F3
I.3.	66	dispositions] disposition F
	99	endart] engage Q1
I.4.	1	ROMEO] BENVOLIO
	3	BENVOLIO] MERCUTIO
	45	like lamps] Q1 ; light lights, light lamps, like lights
	53	Q1 *adds*: BENVOLIO Queene Mab whats she?
	57	atomies] Q 3 Atomi Q1
	58	Over] A thwart Q1
	81	he dreams] dreames he Q 1
	91	untangled] entangled F3
	103	side] face Q1
I.5.	41	Q1 *adds*: Good youths, I faith. Oh youth's a iolly thing.
	45	It seems she] Her Beauty F2

I.5. 94   sin] fine

132   here] there Q1

II.1. 13   Abraham Cupid] Adam Cupid

II.2. 31   lazy, puffing] lasie pacing Q1; lazy-passing

44   word] name Q1

69   stop] let Q1

84   should] would Q1

107   vow] sweare Q1

152   strife] sute (=suit) Q4

163   'My Romeo!'] my Romeos name Q1

167   What o'clock] At what a clocke Q1

168   By the hour] At the houre Q1

180   silken thread plucks] silke thred puls Q1

188–91   *attributed to* ROMEO] *attributed to* FRIAR *as opening lines of* II.3 *in* Q1; *printed twice in* Q2

192   Friar's close cell] fathers Cell Q1; sire's close cell

II.3. 1   *see under* II.2.188–91 *above*

19   weak flower] small flower Q1

22   stays] slaies Q1

36   with] by Q1

81   chide me not. Her I love] chide not, she whom I loue Q1

II.4. 14   run] shot Q1

22   He rests his minim rests] rests me his minum rest Q1

33   pardon-me's] pardonnez-moi's, perdona-mi's

60   Sure wit] Well said Q1

105   fairer face] fairer of the two Q1

142   Q1 *adds* Marry farewell. *at beginning of Nurse's speech*

160, 161   bid . . . bid] bad . . . bad Q1

211   Before] Peter, take my fanne, and goe before Q1

II.6. 34   sum of half my wealth] half my sum of wealth

III.1. 59   love] hate Q1

91   a'both houses] a both your houses

113   cousin] kinsman Q1

122   Alive] again

III.1. 147   O Prince! O cousin! Husband!] cousin *omitted*

III.2. 15   grow] grown

   21   when I shall die] when hee shall die Q 4

   66   dearest] deare loude Q1

III.3. 10   vanished] issued *or* 'banished'

   53   hear me a little speak] heare me but speake a word Q1

 86–7   O woeful sympathy! | Piteous predicament!] *attributed to Friar, not Nurse*

III.5. 43   love–lord, aye husband–friend] my Lord, my Loue, my Frend Q1

   55   so low] below Q1

  126   earth] Ayre Q 4

  145   bride] Bridegroome Q 3

  181   trained] Q1; allied Q 3; lien'd

IV.1. 78   any] yonder Q1

   81   hide] shut Q1

   94   distilling] distilled Q1

IV.3. 29   Q1 *adds* I will not entertaine so bad a thought

 58–9   Romeo, Romeo, Romeo. | Here's drink. I drink to thee] Romeo I come, this doe I drinke to thee Q1

IV.4. 21   Good Father!] good faith! Q 4; God Father!

IV.5. 36   There she lies] see there sho lies Fa

 103–4   'My heart is full'] my hart is full of woe Q 4

V.1. 15   How doth my lady Juliet?] How fares my Juliet? Q1

V.3. 68   conjuration] Q1 (coniurations); commination

  136   unthrifty] vnluckie Q 3

  170   rust] Rest Q1

  194   your ears] our ears

  209   now early] more early Q1

  210   Q1 *adds* And yong *Benuolio* is deceased too

4

The following are the more interesting of the stage-directions in Q1, probably indicating impressions drawn from a contemporary performance of the play. (The line references are to the present edition.)

I.1.	0	Enter 2 Seruing-men of the Capolets.
	31	Enter two Seruingmen of the Mountagues.
	58–81	They draw, to them enters Tybalt, they fight, to them the Prince, old Mountague, and his wife, old Capulet and his wife, and other Citizens and part them.
I.4.	0	Enter Maskers with Romeo and a Page.
I.5.	16	Enter old Capulet with the Ladies.
	122	They whisper in his eare.
II.4.	98	Enter Nurse and her man.
	130	He walkes by them, and sings.
	151	She turnes to Peter her man.
II.6.	15	Enter Iuliet somewhat fast, and embraceth Romeo.
III.1.	88	Tibalt vnder Romeos arme thrusts Mercutio, in and flyes.
	131	Fight, Tibalt falles.
III.2.	31	Enter Nurse wringing her hands, with the ladder of cordes in her lap.
III.3.	71	Nurse knockes.
	78	Shee knockes againe.
	91	He rises.
	108	He offers to stab himselfe, and Nurse snatches the dagger away.
	162	Nurse offers to goe in and turnes againe.
III.4.	11	Paris offers to goe in, and Capolet calles him againe.
III.5.	0	Enter Romeo and Iuliet at the window.
	36	Enter Nurse hastely.
	42	He goeth downe.

III.5. 64   She goeth downe from the window.

159   She kneeles downe.

235   She lookes after Nurse.

IV.2. 22   She kneeles downe.

IV.3. 59   She fals vpon her bed within the Curtaines.

IV.4. 0   Enter Nurse with hearbs, Mother.

13   Enter Seruingman with Logs & Coales.

IV.5. 42   All at once cry out and wring their hands.

95   They all but the Nurse goe foorth, casting Rosemary on her and shutting the Curtens.

V.1. 11   Enter Balthasar his man booted.

V.3. 0   Enter Countie Paris and his Page with flowers and sweete water.

12   Paris strewes the Tomb with flowers.

21   Enter Romeo and Balthasar, with a torch, a mattocke, and a crow of yron.

48   Romeo opens the tombe.

70   They fight.

120   Enter Fryer with a Lanthorne.

139   Fryer stoops and lookes on the blood and weapons.

147   Iuliet rises.

170   She stabs herselfe and falles.

181   Enter one with Romeos Man.

183   Enter one with the Fryer.

187   Enter Prince with others.

READ MORE IN PENGUIN

In every corner of the world, on every subject under the sun, Penguin represents quality and variety – the very best in publishing today.

For complete information about books available from Penguin – including Puffins, Penguin Classics and Arkana – and how to order them, write to us at the appropriate address below. Please note that for copyright reasons the selection of books varies from country to country.

In the United Kingdom: Please write to *Dept. EP, Penguin Books Ltd, Bath Road, Harmondsworth, West Drayton, Middlesex UB7 0DA*

In the United States: Please write to *Consumer Sales, Penguin Putnam Inc., P.O. Box 12289 Dept. B, Newark, New Jersey 07101-5289.* VISA and MasterCard holders call 1-800-788-6262 to order Penguin titles

In Canada: Please write to *Penguin Books Canada Ltd, 10 Alcorn Avenue, Suite 300, Toronto, Ontario M4V 3B2*

In Australia: Please write to *Penguin Books Australia Ltd, P.O. Box 257, Ringwood, Victoria 3134*

In New Zealand: Please write to *Penguin Books (NZ) Ltd, Private Bag 102902, North Shore Mail Centre, Auckland 10*

In India: Please write to *Penguin Books India Pvt Ltd, 11 Community Centre, Panchsheel Park, New Delhi 110017*

In the Netherlands: Please write to *Penguin Books Netherlands bv, Postbus 3507, NL-1001 AH Amsterdam*

In Germany: Please write to *Penguin Books Deutschland GmbH, Metzlerstrasse 26, 60594 Frankfurt am Main*

In Spain: Please write to *Penguin Books S. A., Bravo Murillo 19, 1° B, 28015 Madrid*

In Italy: Please write to *Penguin Italia s.r.l., Via Benedetto Croce 2, 20094 Corsico, Milano*

In France: Please write to *Penguin France, Le Carré Wilson, 62 rue Benjamin Baillaud, 31500 Toulouse*

In Japan: Please write to *Penguin Books Japan Ltd, Kaneko Building, 2-3-25 Koraku, Bunkyo-Ku, Tokyo 112*

In South Africa: Please write to *Penguin Books South Africa (Pty) Ltd, Private Bag X14, Parkview, 2122 Johannesburg*

ROYAL SHAKESPEARE COMPANY

The Royal Shakespeare Company today is probably one of the best-known theatre companies in the world, playing regularly to audiences of more than a million people a year. The RSC has three theatres in Stratford-upon-Avon, the Royal Shakespeare Theatre, the Swan Theatre and The Other Place, and two theatres in London's Barbican Centre, the Barbican Theatre and The Pit. The Company also has an annual season in Newcastle upon Tyne and regularly undertakes tours throughout the UK and overseas.

Find out more about the RSC and its current repertoire by joining the Company's mailing list. Not only will you receive advance information of all the Company's activities, but also priority booking, special ticket offers, copies of the RSC Magazine and special offers on RSC publications and merchandise.

If you would like to receive details of the Company's work and an application form for the mailing list please write to:

RSC Membership Office
Royal Shakespeare Theatre
FREEPOST
Stratford-upon-Avon
CV37 6BR

or telephone: 01789 205301

READ MORE IN PENGUIN

POETRY LIBRARY

Arnold	Selected by Kenneth Allott
Blake	Selected by W. H. Stevenson
Browning	Selected by Daniel Karlin
Burns	Selected by Angus Calder and William Donnelly
Byron	Selected by A. S. B. Glover
Clare	Selected by Geoffrey Summerfield
Coleridge	Selected by Richard Holmes
Donne	Selected by John Hayward
Dryden	Selected by Douglas Grant
Hardy	Selected by David Wright
Herbert	Selected by W. H. Auden
Jonson	Selected by George Parfitt
Keats	Selected by John Barnard
Kipling	Selected by James Cochrane
Lawrence	Selected by Keith Sagar
Milton	Selected by Laurence D. Lerner
Pope	Selected by Douglas Grant
Rubáiyát of Omar Khayyám	Translated by Edward FitzGerald
Shelley	Selected by Isabel Quigley
Tennyson	Selected by W. E. Williams
Wordsworth	Selected by Nicholas Roe
Yeats	Selected by Timothy Webb

READ MORE IN PENGUIN

A SELECTION OF PLAYS

Edward Albee	**Who's Afraid of Virginia Woolf?**
Alan Ayckbourn	**Joking Apart and Other Plays**
James Baldwin	**The Amen Corner**
Dermot Bolger	**A Dublin Quartet**
Bertolt Brecht	**Parables for the Theatre**
Anton Chekhov	**Plays (The Cherry Orchard/Three Sisters/ Ivanov/The Seagull/Uncle Vanya)**
Michael Hastings	**Tom and Viv**
	Unfinished Business and Other Plays
Henrik Ibsen	**A Doll's House/League of Youth/Lady from the Sea**
Eugène Ionesco	**Rhinoceros/The Chairs/The Lesson**
Ben Jonson	**Three Comedies (Volpone/The Alchemist/ Bartholomew Fair)**
D. H. Lawrence	**Three Plays (The Collier's Friday Night/ The Daughter-in-Law/The Widowing of Mrs Holroyd)**
Arthur Miller	**Death of a Salesman**
Peter Shaffer	**The Royal Hunt of the Sun**
Bernard Shaw	**Plays Pleasant**
	Pygmalion
	John Bull's Other Island
Sophocles	**Three Theban Plays (Oedipus the King/ Antigone/Oedipus at Colonus)**
Keith Waterhouse	**Jeffrey Bernard is Unwell and Other Plays**
Arnold Wesker	**Plays, Volumes 1-7**
Oscar Wilde	**The Importance of Being Earnest and Other Plays**
Thornton Wilder	**Our Town/The Skin of Our Teeth/The Matchmaker**
Tennessee Williams	**Cat on a Hot Tin Roof/The Milk Train Doesn't Stop Here Anymore/The Night of the Iguana**

READ MORE IN PENGUIN

CRITICAL STUDIES

Described by *The Times Educational Supplement* as 'admirable' and 'superb', Penguin Critical Studies is a specially developed series of critical essays on the major works of literature for use by students in universities, colleges and schools.

Titles published or in preparation include:

The Poetry of William Blake
Dickens' Major Novels
Doctor Faustus
Emma and Persuasion
Great Expectations
The Great Gatsby
Heart of Darkness
The Poetry of Gerard
   Manley Hopkins
Joseph Andrews
Jude the Obscure
The Poetry of Keats
Mansfield Park
The Mayor of Casterbridge
The Metaphysical Poets
Middlemarch
The Mill on the Floss

Milton: The English Poems
The Portrait of a Lady
A Portrait of the Artist as a
   Young Man
The Return of the Native
Rosencrantz and Guildenstern
   are Dead
Sense and Sensibility
The Poetry of Shelley
Sons and Lovers
Tennyson
Tess of the D'Urbervilles
To the Lighthouse
The Waste Land
Wordsworth
Wuthering Heights
The Poetry of W. B. Yeats

READ MORE IN PENGUIN

CRITICAL STUDIES

Described by *The Times Educational Supplement* as 'admirable' and 'superb', Penguin Critical Studies is a specially developed series of critical essays on the major works of literature for use by students in universities, colleges and schools.

Titles published or in preparation include:

SHAKESPEARE

Antony and Cleopatra
As You Like It
Coriolanus
Henry IV Part 2
Hamlet
Julius Caesar
King Lear
The Merchant of Venice
A Midsummer Night's Dream
Much Ado About Nothing
Othello
Richard II
Richard III
Romeo and Juliet
Shakespeare – Text into Performance
Shakespeare's History Plays
The Tempest
Troilus and Cressida
Twelfth Night
The Winter's Tale

CHAUCER

Chaucer
The Pardoner's Tale
The Prologue to The Canterbury Tales

READ MORE IN PENGUIN

THE NEW PENGUIN SHAKESPEARE

All's Well That Ends Well	Barbara Everett
Antony and Cleopatra	Emrys Jones
As You Like It	H. J. Oliver
The Comedy of Errors	Stanley Wells
Coriolanus	G. R. Hibbard
Hamlet	T. J. B. Spencer
Henry IV, Part 1	P. H. Davison
Henry IV, Part 2	P. H. Davison
Henry V	A. R. Humphreys
Henry VI, Parts 1–3	Norman Sanders
(three volumes)	
Henry VIII	A. R. Humphreys
Julius Caesar	Norman Sanders
King John	R. L. Smallwood
King Lear	G. K. Hunter
Love's Labour's Lost	John Kerrigan
Macbeth	G. K. Hunter
Measure for Measure	J. M. Nosworthy
The Merchant of Venice	W. Moelwyn Merchant
The Merry Wives of Windsor	G. R. Hibbard
A Midsummer Night's Dream	Stanley Wells
Much Ado About Nothing	R. A. Foakes
The Narrative Poems	Maurice Evans
Othello	Kenneth Muir
Pericles	Philip Edwards
Richard II	Stanley Wells
Richard III	E. A. J. Honigmann
Romeo and Juliet	T. J. B. Spencer
The Sonnets *and* A Lover's Complaint	John Kerrigan
The Taming of the Shrew	G. R. Hibbard
The Tempest	Anne Barton
Timon of Athens	G. R. Hibbard
Troilus and Cressida	R. A. Foakes
Twelfth Night	M. M. Mahood
The Two Gentlemen of Verona	Norman Sanders
The Two Noble Kinsmen	N. W. Bawcutt
The Winter's Tale	Ernest Schanzer